The Way of Beauty

Liturgy, Education, and Inspiration
for Family, School, and College

David Clayton

The Way of Beauty

Liturgy, Education, and Inspiration
for Family, School, and College

 Angelico Press

For information, address:
Angelico Press
4709 Briar Knoll Dr.
Kettering, OH 45429
angelicopress.com
www.thewayofbeauty.org

978-1-62138-141-9

Color versions of all the paintings
referred to in the book can be found at
www.angelicopress.com/clayton-way-of-beauty/

Cover design: Michael Schrauzer

The school is a privileged place in which,
through a living encounter with a cultural inheritance,
integral formation occurs.[1]

1. *The Catholic School* (The Sacred Congregation for Catholic Education).

CONTENTS

PART FOUR *Afterword and Appendices*

PART ONE

The Connection Between Liturgy, the Culture, and Education

Introduction

The Way of Beauty and the New Evangelization

Man's standards are conditioned by those of Earth, the standard of Earth by those of Heaven, the standard of Heaven by that of the Way [Tao] *and the standard of the Way is that of its own intrinsic nature.*
Lao Tzu, from *Tao Te Ching*, XXV (6th century BC)

I am the Way.
Jesus Christ (John 14:6)

IN ITS DOCUMENTS about education, the Church tells us that central to the purpose of Christian education is the formation of the person to be one who is capable of ordering the whole of human culture. This book explains how an education can form the student to apprehend beauty and engender creativity, so that every single one of us can contribute to the creation of a culture of beauty and evangelization of the wider culture.

This formation has at its heart a participation in the sacred liturgy. From this stem all the other essential parts, such as the creation of schools and colleges as educational *communities*; and the content of the curriculum taught.

Because I am an artist, I illustrate the general principles articulated through their application in visual art and an art education. This does not limit their value to those who wish to be artists, however. As I explain, a traditional art education can be incorporated into every Catholic's general education as part of the student's formation in beauty. This is why, for example, we include a chapter explaining the stylistic elements in Christian artistic traditions.

It would be a mistake for the reader to conclude that I am saying that an education in beauty is the only part of an education that is important. I focus in this book primarily on the themes that I do because they are the ones that I feel are currently most neglected. This is why, for example, I spend so much time discussing the study of symbolic number and proportion. However, I have done my best to position the study of these specific items relative to all others within the context of a general Catholic education. For it is important that its position within the whole corpus is understood as much as the material itself if it is to be valuable.

The Way of Beauty and the New Evangelization

I am a painter, and this book is the product of several years of research that began in response to the question, how can I be an artist in service of the Church? I anticipate that what it contains will be of interest to artists who are asking themselves the same question now.

However, to the degree that it will be of interest to any it will be of interest also, I believe, to those with a much broader interest: that of the re-establishment of a culture of beauty in the West. Many of the general principles that I articulate can be applied easily to any other field of human endeavor that might be executed gracefully; or for which the product of that work could be beautiful. In other words, just about any human activity. This is the Way of Beauty—a joyful path to God by which our work shines with the light of Christ and draws people in so that they might share in it. This is precisely what popes from Paul VI onwards have been calling for since the Second Vatican Council, most prominently John Paul II and Benedict XVI. At the time of this writing, early in the papacy of Francis, we see that he too has already spoken forcefully about the importance of beauty.

The beauty of Catholic culture can speak to all, of course, but it is especially needed in trying to open the hearts of those of the "post-Christian" society in the West. These are people who are not Christian, but whose parents or grandparents were. The task here is more than simply making the information available to them: it is to impart to them the belief that the Church offers them a joyful life that is better than what they have now. This is the aim of the so-called New Evangelization, and every single one of us who does believe is called to be an ambassador of the Church who can reach out to these people, through the example we provide of the joy of living.

We must all be formed in grace and love, so that our lives radiate with the light of Christ as part of his mystical body, the Church. This is the light that the apostles saw on Mount Tabor during the Transfiguration. We are unlikely to strike people with radiating light precisely in the way that Christ is seen by the Apostles (though it is possible). It is more likely that some aspect of what we do and the way we do it will strike those around us as graceful and beautiful.

Although I talk a lot about paintings and painters, this book is as much about the formation of these everyday evangelists as it is about forming painters.

I hope that it might help any who consider the study of our culture and the principles of beauty to be an important part of general education, so that through it might lead in turn to the formation of many more.

Culture, High and Wide

Some may be surprised that I imagine that a book that began with a question about painting might have such a broad appeal, and ask why this is. One reason is that I found in the course of my investigation that I had first to consider many of the general principles in order to understand their particular application in painting. As it turned out, therefore, even if I wished to focus only on painting, I could not do so properly unless I considered also the place of painting in the broader culture and what it is, in turn, that makes the broader culture a Catholic culture.

To illustrate: in order to understand gothic painting, as an example of a Catholic tradition in sacred art, I found that it was necessary also to investigate the nature of the connection between all sacred art and the public worship of the Church, her liturgy; otherwise, I would never know how any particular image, whatever style it might be—Gothic, baroque, Celtic and so on—could support our worship.

It is the aggregate of all graceful activity and beautiful things that result from that activity in any society that is the basis of a beautiful culture.[1] I had therefore to look at the wider culture and try to assess what formed it in order to understand what formed non-sacred painting. In the context of painting, therefore, I had to look at the connection between religious art (that which has an explicitly religious purpose) and mundane art (which does not). Because works of art are by definition created by people, this boiled down to trying to work out what it was that forms a person so that they can create beautiful things.

As my own research progressed I gradually came to the conclusion that there is a profound connection between all culture and our worship: that our participation in the sacred liturgy is the most powerful force in shaping and forming both the culture of faith and contemporary culture. The interrelationships between the three are as follows: contemporary culture is derived from and points to the culture of faith, which in turn is nourished by and directs us to the act of worship.

---

1. In talking of culture, I am thinking here of both the culture of faith and the wider culture that exists outside the church building, what Pope Benedict XVI refers to with the phrase "contemporary culture."

This book sets out and details the general connection between liturgy and culture. I discuss the importance of beauty in culture and how our participation in the liturgy forms us powerfully in our ability to apprehend beauty. Then I look at how the liturgy forms our attitudes to all the fundamental things in life—our worldview—and how this is manifested in both the culture of faith and the contemporary culture so that the forms of the culture of faith and the contemporary culture are closely related to each other. Because I am a painter and painting is the field of high culture about which I know most, many of the examples I use to illustrate general features of the culture are paintings.

In this regard I draw very strongly on the words of Pope Benedict. According to him there are three traditions of figurative art that are appropriate for the liturgy: the iconographic, the Gothic, and the baroque of the 17th century "at its best." Those who wish to know more about what characterizes these traditions can look to the latter part of this book in which there is a chapter that describes briefly the essential elements and refers those who wish to go to greater depth to authoritative texts.

For the Christian, the highest art is that which supports the highest purpose: the worship of God in the sacred liturgy.[2] So with art, and indeed all human activity, the mundane is derived from and points to that which goes on "in the temple" (i.e., that which is sacred). Benedict XVI, following Pius X, distinguishes between liturgical forms of art and music and religious art and music in general and then explains how preserving this distinction actually allows the liturgical forms to be the source from which the other religious forms and ultimately all art and music are derived. Following Pius X and then subsequently applying the same principle to the situation today, Benedict says:

> A clear distinction was made between liturgical music and religious music in general, just as visual art in the liturgy has to conform to different standards from those employed in religious art in general. Art in the liturgy has a very specific responsibility, and precisely as such does it serve as a wellspring of culture, which in the final analysis owes its existence to cult.[3]

This argument can be used in regard to all aspects of the culture: art, literature, music, architecture. The liturgical forms set the standard for the written word, art, music, architecture of the culture as a whole.

2. Cf. *Sacrosanctum Concilium*, 10: "The liturgy is the *summit* toward which the activity of the Church is directed."

3. Pope Benedict XVI, *The Spirit of the Liturgy* (San Francisco: Ignatius Press, 2000), p. 147.

Considering the past, we can see this demonstrated for example in the baroque period of the 17th century. The art forms that began with the work of Caravaggio in Rome in the early part of the century and which were developed to support the worship of God in the Tridentine liturgy became the standard for all sacred art in the Church, and then the basis for the mundane forms such as portrait, landscape, and still life. This was not restricted in its impact to painting or to the Catholic world. All the Protestants of Western Europe took the forms of baroque culture—sculpture, music, architecture, and so on—as their own.

Why, one might ask, did they do this? The short answer is: beauty. Those who saw this culture found its beauty compelling and wanted it for themselves.

Just as the Council of Trent laid the foundation for cultural renewal in service of the Church in its time, so the Second Vatican Council, in the words of John Paul II (written in his *Letter to Artists* in 1999), "laid the foundation for a renewed relationship between Church and culture" today. It falls onto us to decide whether or not we wish to build on those foundations through our actions. If we follow its guidance, we can contribute to the rebuilding the bridge that can span the divide that now exists between the culture of faith and the secular culture, a gap that appeared after the Enlightenment.

Once standards of beauty have been set in our liturgical forms, then a vision of human existence and its ultimate meaning have been established for all to see. We who worship will be transformed by this divine beauty and will take it out into the world, sharing in the Light of the transfigured Christ as we go about our daily activities, drawing people to Him. Society at large, and especially those who otherwise would never enter a church, will tend to measure itself against these standards and draw inspiration from this vision. Beauty is its own argument now just as it was in the baroque.

We must all be the agents, in the sense of creators if not actually the artists with paintbrush in hand, of the culture of beauty that drives the New Evangelization. When people see this beauty in our work, it will be natural to every person to respond to it by giving praise to the Creator. Some may resist this natural impulse, for they possess as well free will and are more inclined to follow prejudices that tell them otherwise; and some will not have sufficient faith or understanding of this impulse within them to know that it is directed towards God. But with God's grace these people can respond so that they move closer to that point when they leave prejudice behind, understand, and believe. They will be receptive to the Word.

We live in an age in which information, including the Gospel, is widely available to just about anyone who wants to get hold of it. How do we attract the attention of those who need God and don't know that this is what they desire more than anything? This is the special value of beauty. Pope Benedict spoke of this when he described the *via pulchritudinis*—the Way of Beauty—as the "most compelling" route that leads us to love God. Today this is an almost untapped power that could fuel the New Evangelization, in which the grace and beauty of all that we do will draw people towards not only our work, but also to us, curious to know of its source. What they are sensing is the love that underlies what we do. This, it seems to me, is the great message of Pope Francis to each of us. It requires each of us to look to ourselves first, and in cooperation with grace and through an active participation in the liturgy allow ourselves to be transformed in love.

In focusing strongly on the past traditions of the Church, there is no suggestion that I am looking for a future that is an unthinking replication of the past. Rather, I hope that this analysis might lead us to a re-application of the same principles, but in a way that is appropriate to our age. To this end, my intention is to demonstrate how the form of these past traditions reflects the worldview of the artist as much as its content. Each figurative tradition of the Church, for example, conveys a particular aspect of the understanding of the human person simply by the way that he is painted. Each seeks to portray man as body and soul. It is the controlled deviations from a rigid adherence to physical appearances that communicate to us, at an intuitive level, the invisible truths that are so necessary for the understanding of what a person is. In other words, it's not just *what* the artist paints, but *how* he paints it, that is important.

It is also possible to communicate something that is false through form. Most (but not all) modern forms of art, for example, communicate through form the errors of modern philosophy. It can happen through ignorance as much as through intent, and it is to avoid an unintentionally negative impact that a Christian artist must be grounded in the traditions of his faith.

Geometric Art, Symbolic Number, and the Quadrivium

For the ancients the beauty of the cosmos could be described numerically. This is a tradition that goes back to Pythagoras in the ancient Greek world of the 6th century BC, described by Plato in the *Timaeus*; it was incorporated into the Christian tradition by figures such as St. Augustine and Boethius about 1,000 years later. This numerical description of beauty gave rise to a tradition of an abstract, non-figurative Christian art form of geometric patterns, became the basis for design of the proportions of anything from a building to a spoon, and for order-ing in principle any aspect of daily living. It is through the writing of Pope Benedict XVI, who draws on the writing of Church Fathers such as Pseudo-Dionysius the Areopagite and Maximus the Confessor, that I became aware of how the numerical description of the beauty of the cosmos and the culture is connected also to the rhythms and patterns of the liturgy.[4] These ideas were vigorously rejected by Enlightenment thinkers of the 18th century, and so influential was this rejection that it affected even contemporary Catholic thinkers. The result is that by the early 20th century, the tradition had just about disappeared altogether.

My own attention was drawn to these ancient ideas by my consider-ation of two aspects of visual art. The first was in looking for some prin-ciples of design when seeking to order figurative paintings. Was I, as an artist, at complete liberty to pick whatever external shape I chose? Could I pick a circle, a square, a rectangle or something bound by a Gothic arch arbitrarily, or were there principles that governed this choice? Also, I wondered, could I place the prominent figures anywhere within it, or was there a set of geometric principles that I could draw on to help me make good choices in the compositional design of a paint-ing? I had seen, for example, complex analyses in which all sorts of lines and shapes were drawn over paintings of the French baroque artist Poussin, for example, which claimed to reveal his design principles. Was there any basis in this?

Something else that led me to find out about this was noticing on a trip to Assisi that the interiors of the Gothic Franciscan churches were richly adorned with complex geometric-patterned art. I was curious to know more about it, but initially struggled to get information. The guide books and art history books that I bought talked at length about the beautiful frescoes in the Gothic style of figurative art, but never mentioned the geometric art. As I delved further, I discovered that it wasn't only in Assisi that one could find this geometric art. In fact it was a centuries old Christian tradition of East and West. Was this just deco-ration that was the product of the unguided imagination of the artisan, I wondered, or was there careful thought and design going into its cre-ation?

In seeking to answer these questions, I discovered a whole field of mathematics that I had never been aware of before (even though at uni-versity I had studied natural science and so had had a good mathemati-cal education) and had application in all human activity. The same

---

4. Cf. Pope Benedict XVI, *The Spirit of the Liturgy*. See the chapter entitled "The Art of the Spheres."

numerical patterns underlying the artistic creativity of Poussin or the Franciscan artists, I found, were present in the proportions of the building, and had governed the proportions of architectural design from the ancient Greeks in the West right through to the early 20th century. The same mathematical system reflected the beauty of music, and the beauty of the cosmos, even the beauty of the pattern of interrelationships of similar sorts of numbers, say, squares or cubes within the abstract world of mathematics considered in isolation. It had even been used to articulate the moral order, and in the interpretation of scripture; it even governed the rhythms and patterns of our worship in Sacred Liturgy. Ultimately, this led to the consideration of the beauty of God: this mathematical pattern of interrelationships was understood historically as an unfolding of the exemplar of relationship in simple perfection, that which exists between the persons of the Trinity.

This complex system of harmonious proportion had its application in many aspects of daily life. For example, in the 12th century the same system of symmetry and harmony that governed the proportions of the buildings in which a community is housed and the design of the decoration and the art that hangs inside it might regulate also even the ebb and flow of daily living—that is, the regular pattern of prayer, work, rest and recreation of a community (secular or religious). In order to illustrate how this might be done in the future, I describe later in this book how such an institution of the past, the medieval university, was organized in this way (using the example of Oxford).

The beauty of number was not only manifested in harmonious combinations. A single number might have a symbolic meaning that would give it importance as well. We are used to the idea today of numbers being used to communicate *quantity*—that is, to answer the questions *how much?* or *how many?* This is unchanged from the past. However, we are not so used today to the idea that number can convey a *quality*. So the number four could count objects, in that sense is always greater than three and less than five. It could also convey a meaning through a symbolism. This would most commonly come from the Bible: for example, three representing the Trinity and four representing the "four winds" that emanate from the four corners of the world. When we consider number as a sign of quantity, four is always greater than three. However, when we consider number as a sign of the quality of something through its symbolism, we would say that three is communicating something greater than four. These numbers could be represented visually as geometric shapes, the triangle and the square respectively. The combination of these shapes was carefully worked out to create beautiful and complex geometric patterns that might be read as well as enjoyed for their beauty.

This qualitative aspect of number, and the harmonious relationships that can exist between numbers, together constitute a little-known bridge that connects the beauty of God to sacred liturgy and sacred scripture, to the cosmos and potentially to all human activity. It can be seen in traditional Western culture if you know how to look for it. It was taught to the people of the time as part of a classical education—a liberal arts education, in a grouping of four subjects called the quadrivium, or four ways—arithmetic, geometry, music/harmonious proportion, and astronomy (the remaining three subjects—rhetoric, logic, grammar—are called the trivium). It was also taught in the study of scripture. The scripture commentaries of Augustine, for example, are permeated with references to them.

Although most people today are unaware of the idea of symbolic number and harmonious proportions, when presented with the beauty that it reflects, they respond. Millions of people visit Oxford every year (just under 10 million last year according to the Oxford city website). When they come as tourists, they do not head on the whole for the modern housing estates or industrial buildings on the outskirts of the city. Rather, they go to older center of the town. The beauty of these buildings is crucial in selling the city in the tourist brochures that attracted them in the first place. These tourists very likely do not know why they find these buildings beautiful, but they know that they do.

The architects of the past who created the beautiful buildings that all those tourists flock to would not see any conflict between the beauty of a building and its utility. Firstly, it would also be assumed that the most beautiful building would be the most efficient in fulfilling its other purposes. Also, they would consider its beauty to be part of its utility; for all the work of man ought to influence those who see it to consider heavenly things. Just as the beauty of the cosmos directs our praise to God, so, it would be argued, we should strive to make the work of man do the same by making it as beautiful as possible.

The way in which these considerations of symbolic number and harmonious proportion generated from different source might come into play in daily work can be illustrated by the example which follows, which is the opening section of a Memorandum written in the 16th century by a Franciscan friar, Francesco Giorgi, regarding the proposed design of a church in Venice, S. Francesco della Vigna. Giorgi was commissioned by the Doge of Venice to write a Memorandum on the validity of the proportions of design of the church, submitted by the original architect. He wrote as follows:

April 1, 1535. In order to build the fabric of the church with those fitting and very harmonious proportions which one can do without altering anything that has been done, I should proceed in the following manner. I should like the width of the nave to be nine paces which is the square of three, the first and divine number. The length of the nave, which will be twenty-seven will have a have a triple proportion, which makes a diapason and a diapente. And this is the mysterious harmony that when Plato in the *Timaeus* wished to describe the wonderful consonance of the parts and fabric of the world, he took this as the first foundation of his description.[5]

So, for Giorgi the number three is the starting point because it symbolizes the Trinity. Then, in his analysis, this highly symbolic number is put in beautiful relation with other numbers through the operation of squaring the number twice, giving 9 and then 27. These numbers have been generated, in the manner of Plato, simply by consideration of operations within the abstract world of mathematics; and they are considered to be in good relation to each other, as a square number is to a cube. Finally, however, he remarks that this mathematical operation manifests beauty when applied to material things and so, it is assumed, is appropriate for the church. As confirmation he reports that the same ratios he has generated mathematically correspond to fundamental musical harmonies: in this case the octave (diapason), the perfect fifth (the diapente) and the "triple proportion" which is a combination of the first two.

To explain: it is the ancient Greek philosopher Pythagoras who, by tradition, discovered that tones can be measured in space. If two strings were made to vibrate in similar conditions and musical consonance resulted, it was found that whole numbers governed the lengths of the string. The fundamental musical harmonies are, according to the Pythagoreans, the octave, the fifth and the fourth. Put simply, the octave is the interval between the first note and the eighth note in a scale; the perfect fifth is that which is produced between the first and fifth note in the scale and, as one might expect, the fourth is the corresponding interval between the first and the fourth notes in a scale. If we were to play these notes on a stringed instrument, the octave would be produced by two strings of relative length 1:2, a fifth by the ratio 2:3 and a fourth by a ratio of 3:4. The Pythagoreans liked the fact that there is an arithmetic symmetry to this: for it means that the first four numbers, 1,

5. Francesco Giorgi, *Memorandum for S. Francesco della Vigna*, tr. Gianantonio Moschini; taken from Rudolph Wittkower, *Architectural Principles in the Age of Humanism* (New York, St. Martin's Press, 1988), Appendix I.

2, 3, 4, contain the secret of musical harmony, and the sum of these numbers is 10, which they believed to be a special number in the governing of the order of the universe. When the two intervals of an octave and a fifth are combined musically the result is a ratio of 1:3, which is the same numerically as 9:27 that Giorgi used in his church. It is the proportion in Giorgi's design and what he is referring to as a "diapason and a diapente."

The fact that this was not an unusual approach and that the use of these numbers was not limited to the profession of architecture at this time is demonstrated by looking at the people who assessed Giorgi's report. On reception of the Memorandum the Doge consulted a committee of three experts who had to approve it before he would implement it, which they did. The three were a philosopher (a humanist called Sansovino), a famous architect called Serlio, and an artist, who was no less than Titian.

If we could create a culture that conformed to this pattern of beauty today, one that participates in the beauty of God, it would direct the hearts of men to Him just as Christian culture had in the past. I do not think that what I envisage is overly optimistic. We still have all the essential ingredients that would have made it possible 500 years ago: God, man, and the materials with which to work. As to how quickly this will happen, that I cannot answer. It will depend upon when God chooses to inspire his artists, and on their capacity to cooperate when he does so. It is only the latter that we can hope to influence.

1

Sacred Liturgy and Beauty

*Sing from and to the spirit, sing in a way worthy of
and appropriate to the spirit, disciplined and pure.*[1]
Pope Benedict XVI, paraphrase of Psalm 47(46):7

O NE SUNDAY MORNING in 1990, I stumbled into a Catholic
church in London called the Brompton Oratory during Solemn
Mass. I had recently decided that I would experiment with the
idea of being a Christian (that is a story for another time) and a friend
had suggested that I try out this church. He gave directions and told me
very little else—I didn't even know it was Catholic—although I do
remember he said to me quite forcefully at least twice, "Make sure you
go at eleven o'clock!"

I arrived slightly late, and so by the time I entered and left the noise
and traffic outside it was a couple of minutes past eleven and the service
was well underway.

I can remember my impressions very clearly even today. It felt as
though I had left one world and entered another. There was a peace in
this new world that I had not known before. This was not the sort of
peace which was the *absence* of something, but rather a dynamic, active
peace; a sort that overcomes internal distraction and descends upon
you.

First, as I was coming in, I noticed the choir singing and smelt the
incense. I came through the threshold and saw the main body of the
church. It was full of people, all still with silent intent, their backs to me
and facing toward the altar. I stood at the back for a few minutes and
looked and listened and experienced what was happening.

The beauty of the music (it was Palestrina), especially in this setting

1. Benedict XVI, *A New Song for the Lord* (New York: Crossroad, 1996), p. 124.

13

of lavishly painted and framed paintings and magnificent architecture, was breathtaking. There were shafts of sunlight entering the church and I could smell the incense and see it floating upwards. As I listened to the music, I remember the thought crossing my mind that this must be what angels in heaven sound like. This angelic host comprised deep and powerful male voices as well as pure female voices. I could not see the choir (who were in a gallery halfway down the church) and I couldn't tell what direction the sound came from—it seemed to be part of the atmosphere, like the incense and the sunlight. As I cast my eye around the church looking for signs of a choir loft and the source of these angelic voices, I looked upwards and the first thing that caught my eye was an image on the ceiling. It was an angel in flight. It was as though the designers of the church had anticipated what I was thinking. At this point I started to realize that I was being subjected to a carefully arranged process whereby all my senses were being assailed, harnessed, and redirected. I could not help but be drawn in. I did not even want to resist. But to what end, I wondered?

The Mass was in Latin (in the new order, the "*novus ordo,*" for those who know about these things) but I had no idea of this at the time. I just knew that I couldn't understand the words. The three priests, one central and two flanking, each in ornately embroidered vestments, and the acolytes in white cotton had their backs to me and were facing towards the east (*ad orientem*) towards the giant altar. All the congregation faced east too, bowing, kneeling, standing and sitting together; and the priests seemed to be directing a common focus beyond themselves towards something mysterious. While I could not tell precisely what it was, they acted in unison, and so their body language spoke to me of their faith. They believed that what they were doing was of profound importance, I could tell. The mystery as to what that was in some way cleared, but in others intensified, when the priest held the white host aloft. I did not really know what I was seeing, but, nevertheless, my instincts told me powerfully that this was the focus of everything that had preceded it.

The beauty of the integrated whole of this spectacle was speaking to me. Each constituent part was beautiful when considered in isolation, but was made more beautiful through its harmonious relationship with every other aspect, the art, the architecture, and so on. It spoke of Christ.

At that point I was only vaguely aware of what this was telling me, but I knew at a deep unspoken level, however dimly, that I was grasping a profound truth communicated to me by music, art, architecture, and body language.

I could not have articulated a theological treatise as a result of my experience, but it did transmit to me strongly a sense that there was something good and true contained within the liturgy and it made me want to know more and understand what I had seen. This began the process of my reception into the Church, which was completed in 1993.

⊕

As I began to experience the Mass in different places, I realized that not all Catholic churches offered the beautiful experience that I had seen at the Brompton Oratory. Why was this?, I wondered. I could understand that not all churches had the resources to pay for a choir or beautiful art. But there was something more than this going on. What drove the point home to me was seeing the installation, in another church, of a painting of the crucifixion.

The newly installed painting had been deliberately chosen and had cost a lot of money. It was a large painting on a wooden panel that hung from the ceiling. The content was, as far as I knew, all as it ought to be. Christ was on shown on the cross and the figures of St. John and Our Lady were at the foot of the cross. It was the style that caused me difficulty. It was in a crudely painted 20th-century style, with distorted ugly figures and exaggerated, bright, clashing colors; you might call it expressionist. As I looked at it and remembered my Brompton Oratory experience, it occurred to me that if I had stumbled into this church on that Sunday morning, the art would not have had the same effect on me. The ugliness I saw here distracted me from my participation in the liturgy, rather than aiding it. Any art connoisseur might not have agreed with my assessment, and turned his nose up at the paintings in the Brompton Oratory, dismissing them as fairly ordinary late Victorian neo-Baroque art. But that is to miss the point. In the context of the liturgy they were good enough to the job very well. They were far more suited to the purpose of supporting and directing my worship than the ugly, distorted 20th-century crucifix I was looking at now, I thought.

As I reflected further, I wondered if I was the only one who felt so negative about it. I assumed that those who commissioned and installed it felt the opposite. As we left the church, I asked the people with me what they thought about it. Most of those I talked to felt the same, although some of them I had to push a bit to get them to say what they really thought. When they did it was usually with a qualification such as "well, I don't really know about art, but. . . ."

I wondered if there was anyone I could look to for an authoritative judgment. Was this purely a matter of opinion, in which case he who holds the wallet holds the power; or was there some objective standard that could guide me? My initial research wasn't so good. There was very little prescribed in canon law that I could see. There didn't seem to be any definitive Church document that would help me to decide whether or not this painting was good or bad for the liturgy.

I did some research and found some useful information in the writings of the Popes from Pius XII onward. Each emphasized tradition as a principle of authority. Each asserted that there were artistic traditions which manifested the timeless principles of goodness, beauty, and truth. These works of the past should be respected and could be relied upon to guide me today, they said. While we should never stifle the creation of new forms, all that is new should be seen in the light of principles that unite all sacred art traditions.

So this told me what I had to do next. I had to learn about the Church's traditions in liturgical art. But where to start? I could find very little to provide me with the greater detail I now required (this was in the mid-late 1990s) and in the end I temporarily abandoned the academic research and started to learn icon painting from an Eastern Orthodox painter who was prepared to teach me. His name was Aidan Hart.

Then in 1999 I read Pope John Paul II's *Letter to Artists*. This reinvigorated my research. In this he spoke to me directly, it seemed, with his call for artists to contribute to a *"new epiphany of beauty"* in the spirit of the Second Vatican Council. He talked about the nature of beauty itself, defining it in this context as "the visible form of the good." This made it plain to me that good painting is always beautiful painting. So, even when portraying evil and suffering, which artists sometimes do, it must be infused with the Light, the hope that transcends all and which overcomes. John Paul II included a summary of the artistic styles in the West since the ancient Greeks.

Shortly afterwards I found further written inspiration: it was a small book that came to my notice when one of the Fathers of the Brompton Oratory suggested that I read it. It was the *Spirit of the Liturgy*, by the then Cardinal Ratzinger, who was to become Pope Benedict XVI. As the title suggests, this book is about the sacred liturgy of the Church, but what excited me was his discussion of the forms of art and music appropriate to it and his description of the connection between this and contemporary culture.

Both were informative and inspiring, but of the two John Paul II's *Letter* was the more inspiring, and had its greatest impact on me in stressing the importance of beauty; while Ratzinger's book was the most clear and informative, and opened my eyes to the importance of the liturgy to all that we do. As time went on, this little book steadily became more useful, and is still the one I look to most regularly for guidance. It revealed to me the connection between the liturgy and a culture of beauty in a way that I had never understood before.

Is Beauty Really So Powerful?

Some may doubt the effectiveness of beauty to act on the souls of men, but this is to underestimate its power. It is worth noting that John Paul II did not appeal to society as a whole, or even to Catholic communities, to educate themselves and develop good taste in art; nor did he appeal to educators to transform the tastes of young people and so change the general taste of a future society so that it would appreciate and demand good art (not that each is undesirable; far from it). He addressed artists, because it is the creators of beautiful work who will make the first move in effecting this epiphany.

The Holy Father's assumption is that people do not need to be educated or cultured to be affected by beauty. It touches the hearts of all. The clear implication of this is that the problem of the day lies not in a lack of education of those who are meant to recognize beauty, but in those who ought to create it. They are unable to make anything that is beautiful enough to have the desired effect.

In the same way, in stressing the importance of beauty, Pope Benedict after John Paul II chose to address *artists*, as did Paul VI before him. Each is echoing what the Fathers of the Second Vatican Council articulated. It is those who participate in the creative process who must change first. It is the artists whom we must address.

At the end of his *Letter* John Paul II makes this point. In writing about the Second Vatican Council he says: "At the end of the Council, the Fathers addressed a greeting and an appeal to artists. This world—they said—in which we live needs beauty in order not to sink into despair. In this profound respect for beauty, the Constitution of the Sacred Liturgy *Sacrosanctum Concilium* recalled the historic friendliness of the Church towards art and, referring more specifically to sacred art, the 'summit' of religious art, did not hesitate to consider artists as having a 'noble ministry' when their works reflect in some way the infinite beauty of God and raise people's minds to him. Thanks to the help of artists 'the knowledge of God can be better revealed and the preaching of the Gospel can become clearer to the human mind.'"

It is worth reiterating what was said in the introduction to this book. We are not talking here of an unthinking step back into the past. Certainly we must look to the styles of the past and understand the timeless principles from which they are derived, but every generation must reapply these principles in order to speak to people today. This is the mark of a living tradition. The success of the Baroque was that it incorporated the timeless principles of beauty, truth, and goodness, but presented them in such a way that the ordinary people of its time could respond to them. It was the popular culture of its day. Today's artists must do the same. The art of Vatican II, I suggest, when it emerges, will be something that seems at once both traditional and fresh.

As an artist, I regularly used to complain that the culture doesn't support art, or that most people have "plebeian tastes" and don't appreciate good work (by which I meant my art, of course!); or that the Church doesn't train its priests to be good patrons. All of this may be true and relevant to some degree; but complaining about it never got me anywhere. The point I had missed was the very one that the popes were making: that if the art is sufficiently beautiful it will connect with people. The hard truth I had to accept is that the problem lay in the quality of my work. Rather than expecting society to change until it demands what I am already producing, I was forced to conclude that my success depends more on creating beautiful forms that appeal to people as they are now. In short, I had to become a better artist.

What is Beauty?

What does the famous and mysterious phrase of Dostoyevsky, "Beauty will save the world" (quoted by John Paul II in his *Letter*), mean? Does this mean that the beauty that is in the world will save it? Or must we look for a beauty from beyond the world? The answer is a bit of both. The beauty that is in the world comes from beyond it. It directs us to where it comes from. The Christian religion, especially, is all about this saving beauty.

Beauty, like truth and goodness, is an objective quality. It is a quality in a thing that directs us to God. It calls us to first to itself and then beyond, with an invitation to go to Him. If we heed that call, we respond with love to that beauty and open ourselves up to it and to its ultimate source, the inspiration of the artist, God. When we do this, it elevates the spirit and provides consolation to the soul. Beauty is the quality in a painting through which the artist can "bear witness to the Light."

Beauty appeals to what is good in us (as ugliness appeals to what is disordered). The great power of the beauty of both the cosmos, which is the work of the Creator, and of man-made culture is that it awakens in us a desire for God, the ultimate Beauty that each reflects and which directs us along the path to him. Quoting Pope Benedict XVI:

The *via pulchritudinis*, the way of beauty, is a privileged and fascinating way to approach the Mystery of God. What is beauty, which writers, poets, musicians, and artists contemplate and translate into their language, if not the reflection of the splendor of the Eternal Word made flesh? St. Augustine states: "Ask the beauty of the earth, ask the beauty of the sea, ask the beauty of the ample and diffused air. Ask the beauty of heaven, ask the order of the stars, ask the sun, which with its splendor brightens the day; ask the moon, which with its clarity moderates the darkness of night. Ask the beasts that move in the water, that walk on the earth, that fly in the air: souls that hide, bodies that show themselves; the visible that lets itself be guided, the invisible that guides. Ask them! All will answer you: Look at us, we are beautiful! Their beauty makes them known. This mutable beauty, who has created it if not Immutable Beauty?"[2]

When we apprehend the beauty of something, we apprehend at an intuitive level that it is ordered; and we recognize that it is good. We may not be able to describe in any detail in the way that modern science does what that order is, but we know that it is ordered and good, and we delight in it. And that delight is a personal reaction—we take delight in it because it is good for us.

St. Thomas Aquinas wrote of this when he said *pulchra enim dicuntur quae visa placent*[3]—"things that give pleasure when they are perceived ('seen') are called beautiful." The perception he is describing is a perception with the senses. The term "pleasure" here does not have the contemporary meaning, but refers to our natural and properly ordered inclinations (affections or appetites) and is not limited to our emotions. When what we see causes delight, awe, and wonder, we call it beautiful. This is a personal reaction. For something may be very good for me, in which case it will cause delight when seen by me; but not so good for you, in which case you will be less delighted with the same object. This does not contravene the idea of objective beauty—we are perceiving what is true about the object, but it is true that some things are not equally good for all people. The sound of a babbling brook is always beautiful, but to the man dying of thirst searching for water it is more beautiful than any symphony.

There are other reasons for this apparent subjectivity of beauty. Due to our impurity, everybody's ability to see beauty is impaired in some way. Sin clouds the vision by impairing our sense of what is good for us.

2. Pope Benedict XVI, General Audience, Nov. 18, 2009.
3. St. Thomas Aquinas, *Summa Theologica*, I, 39, 8. Note this is not to be confused with Maritain's definition: *id quod visum placet*, "that which when seen pleases."

So our personal prejudices, our misplaced understanding of what is good for us, can make us blind to the beauty of an object. This is why an in-your-face statement of Christianity can be rejected but a culture that rests on an assumed faith rather than stating it explicitly can be effective. Once we open ourselves to this beauty, it transforms us by degrees, revealing to us in such a way that we can accept, perhaps dramatically or perhaps just incrementally, what is truly good for us. This leads, in turn, to the acceptance of explicit statements of the Faith.

For all that there are differences in perception, there is much consensus too. There are things that are universally good—that is, good for all of us; or in any one object, some aspects of it can be universally good. When this is so, that thing, or those aspects of it, will appear beautiful to all people. Consider, for example, how, while we may disagree by degrees on some aspects of it, as a general rule, everyone looks at the natural world and finds it beautiful. Delight, awe, and wonder in the face of nature is universal. It is this universal beauty that we seek especially for all human culture, and liturgical art and music especially, for we want as far as possible to include all and exclude no one.

Cosmos: Order

The word *cosmos* in ancient Greek meant both *order* and *ornament*—beauty. Few would contest that the cosmos (i.e., the whole of Creation) is beautiful and ordered. As we will discover later on in this book, this order can be described numerically in such a way that it takes into account the human response to it, and this becomes the basis of the traditional understanding of harmony and proportion.

Man has the choice of making any aspect of his work, not just those things that we would normally call art, participate in this same order. He can add to and even enhance the saving beauty of the world through his work. The beauty of creation saves us because it is directed towards *us*, mankind, so that we might open our hearts to God, in an initial response of love to God's loving activity directed towards us. This is why beauty is so important. Without being moved in love, we cannot accept the Word in faith and we cannot truly know anything. For all the cogent arguments and clear explanations of the truth, without a response in love there is no acceptance, no convincing.

No one is purely loving or, indeed, purely self-centered, and so no one is ever likely to be completely consistent in his or her reaction to beauty. Without a pure, visible standard available to us, which we could use to measure beauty objectively, it is difficult to know who is right and who is wrong. This difficulty is what gives rise to the currently fashionable, though false, idea that beauty is a subjective quality. Certainly, to know something as beautiful is a fragile kind of knowing, for it requires heart and mind, will and intellect, to be in harmony. But just as in the case of truth and goodness, we can be educated to improve our perception of beauty, which can then be directed towards the creative process.

All That Exists is Beautiful. . . . So What is Ugliness?

I have said that beauty is a property of being, which means that everything that exists possesses some beauty. If this the case, though, and we say that everything is beautiful, it raises the question, what is ugliness? In fact ugliness is not an attribute in itself, but rather a privation of beauty. A privation means a scarcity, so that there is less of something than there ought to be. Accordingly, when we call an object ugly, what we are in fact describing is something that is still beautiful, by virtue of its existence, but not as beautiful as it ought to be.

A comedy sketch on television comes to mind in this regard. The comedians Morecambe and Wise, who were household names in Britain when I was a boy, had the international conductor André Previn as a guest on their show. Everything was set up so that the symphony orchestra conducted by Mr. Previn should support Eric Morecambe, who was to perform a famous piano concerto (this was unexpected because everyone was pretty sure that he couldn't play the piano). In fact, things started surprisingly well, and after a flamboyant orchestral opening André Previn turned dramatically and decisively, pointing his baton at Eric Morecambe as a signal for him to begin a piano solo. All eyes were on the pianist, who noticed late that he was supposed to be playing, and when he did, hurriedly put his hands to the keyboard and started playing. And what he played was nothing like what it was supposed to be. Firstly, it was in a honky-tonk barroom style, and although very broadly recognizable as the theme, it was interspersed with clashing discordant notes. "Stop! Stop! Stop! What are you doing?" exclaimed Previn. "That's no good. You're playing all the wrong notes." Eric Morecambe stopped and without saying anything stood up slowly and walked over to the conductor. Then he grabbed hold of the front of the conductor's lapels and menacingly pulled him forward, pushing his nose into his face. Slowly and purposefully, with a hint of menace, Morecambe said: "You're wrong. I am playing all the *right* notes . . . but not necessarily in the right order." Well, it was funny in 1971 when I saw it as a young boy . . . but the point of telling this story is this: for this piano concerto, even with all the rights notes employed, the privation of one aspect of its perfection—having the notes in the right order—the result was ugliness!

When we see something that strikes us as ugly because we recognize this privation, it might be because the object itself has been distorted or damaged in some way; or it might be that our perception of it is flawed. If the senses are not fully developed or damaged then this will restrict our ability to see beauty. Even if our senses were perfect (which nobody's ever are), the way that the mind processes and responds to the information coming to it from the senses might be lacking or distorted. The Fall has introduced such a distortion into each of us. Our capacity to love has been reduced by impurity, and so with it our full ability to know.

If it is our capacity to love that is the difficulty, then if we grow in love, so will we in our ability to apprehend beauty. It is consideration of what might form us as better lovers that brings us to a connection between beauty and the liturgy.

The Liturgy is the Seat of Love and Beauty

There are different ways of coming to know something. The first is as step-by-step analysis in which different parts or properties of the object under consideration are considered separately; this often involves a process of rational deduction to confirm proposed hypotheses. This analytical approach is valid and useful. However, there is another form of knowing that arises by consideration of the whole and its setting, which can be considered by degrees as an ever-widening horizon, and which gives rise to an appreciation of its beauty and a sense of awe and wonder. Pope Benedict XVI calls this the "heart's encounter with beauty."[4]

The two are not set against each other; rather, they are complementary. No matter how analytical we become, if at some point the consideration of the whole is again made, it will provide a synthesis; and to the degree that our analyses are true and our synthesis is complete, this will lead to a greater sense of wonder at the beauty of the whole. Scientists, for example, will often talk with wonder about the world they are examining. That wonder arises at the moment of synthesis, when some newly found piece of information is put into its context, the wider horizon; and that wonder is the greater for the detailed scientific analysis that preceded the synthesis.

This encounter with the whole, in which we respond intuitively when we see its beauty, is a higher form of knowledge, Benedict tells us: "Beauty is knowledge, indeed a higher form of knowing, because it strikes man with the truth in all its greatness."[5]

In his third discourse on the university, Blessed John Henry Newman talks of this relationship between analytical and synthetic thinking; that

---

4. Benedict XVI, *On the Way to Jesus Christ* (San Francisco: Ignatius Press, 2005), p. 34.

5. Ibid., p. 35.

is, viewing the parts as analyzed and seeing them in relation to each other in the whole. He says:

> All that exists, as contemplated by the human mind, forms one large system or complex fact, and this of course resolves itself into an indefinite number of particular facts, which, as being portions of a whole, have countless relations of every kind, one towards another. Knowledge is the apprehension of these facts, whether in themselves, or in their mutual positions and bearings. And, as all taken together form one integral subject for contemplation, so there are no natural or real limits between part and part; one is ever running into another; all, as viewed by the mind, are combined together, and possess a correlative character one with another, from the internal mysteries of the Divine Essence down to our own sensations and consciousness, from the most solemn appointments of the Lord of all down to what may be called the accident of the hour, from the most glorious seraph down to the vilest and most noxious of reptiles.[6]

He explains that this to-and-fro of analysis and synthesis is necessary and natural for the human mind, for we cannot see that whole "complex fact" in one glance. Ultimately, we seek to complete this knowledge by contemplation of God himself:

> Summing up, Gentlemen, what I have said, I lay it down that all knowledge forms one whole, because its subject-matter is one; for the universe in its length and breadth is so intimately knit together, that we cannot separate off portion from portion, and operation from operation, except by a mental abstraction; and then again, as to its Creator, though He of course in His own Being is infinitely separate from it, and Theology has its departments towards which human knowledge has no relations, yet He has so implicated Himself with it, and taken it into His very bosom, by His presence in it, His providence over it, His impressions upon it, and His influences through it, that we cannot truly or fully contemplate it without in some main aspects contemplating Him.[7]

It is a traditional education in beauty, such as a working artist might receive (but which in fact all people could benefit from) that develops our powers of synthesis and our ability to recognize the beauty of things as a whole. In the four mathematical disciplines of the liberal arts, the *quadrivium* ("four ways") of arithmetic, geometry, harmony, and astronomy, students learn (if taught properly) about the beautiful pat-

6. J.H. Newman, *The Idea of a University*, Discourse 3.
7. Ibid.

tern of relationships that exists within the abstracted world of mathematics and then learn that it is present also in the beauty of musical harmony and the cosmos. As their education proceeds into philosophy and theology, they recognize the same patterns in the abstract, and so their intellects have been formed so that they more readily grasp the underlying truths. For example, when considering a description of the moral order, or the rhythms and patterns of our worship in the Mass and the Liturgy of the Hours, we can see how each contains these patterns too and all point to the Word, the Logos, in whom, as Pope Benedict XVI puts it, "the archetypes of the world's order are contained."[8]

In the final sentence of the quotation of Newman above, we get a clue as to how the act of synthesis and our first encounter with the beauty of the world is important for another reason. We become aware, albeit dimly, of what we previously did not know, for the pattern, beautiful as it is, is nevertheless somehow incomplete. That awareness is so dim that one might even say that we can go no further than to say that we are now aware of how incomplete our knowledge is. It has awakened our sense of the One to whom that beauty is directing us. The beauty around us inspires us to want to know and give praise to the One who made it. Because the object of beauty cannot fulfill this desire, it creates also a profound sense of lack, one that is so profound that it has been likened to a wound. To quote Benedict again: "Beauty wounds, but that is precisely how it awakens man to his ultimate destiny." That destiny, as Newman puts it, is "contemplating Him"—union with God.

The pain of this wound is sharp because the knowledge of God that it gives us is incomplete, coming as it does via a partial, flawed, and second-hand account; and so it does not satisfy. The world is fallen and imperfect and so its beauty, though still great, is not a full participation in the beauty of the Creator. No matter how beautiful the sunset, it does not put the seeker in full contact with the reality to which it points. Even though the beauty of the sunset participates in the beauty of Christ and it points to Him and speaks of Him, it is not Him and so lacks something crucial. Certainly, the knowledge that it gives is genuine, and this is how it creates a longing for Him. But, if this knowledge is based upon the beauty of a sunset and nothing else, it may be so generalized and vague that we do not know what it is that we are longing for. Furthermore, the knowledge of the means by which we might attain the good by which we will be satiated is likely to be similarly vague.

The culture of man, if it participates in this cosmic beauty, will point

8. Pope Benedict XVI, *The Spirit of the Liturgy* (San Francisco: Ignatius Press, 2000), p. 76.

to Christ, too, and create that longing for Him in those who behold it. In fact, because creation is fallen, by God's grace the culture of man can even surpass the beauty of the natural world, and it can speak more explicitly of the One to whom it points (though it needn't and shouldn't *always* mention Him directly). Nevertheless, it is still imperfect to a degree and still in some measure a second-hand account. No matter how beautiful the art or music or how precise the prose, how powerfully poetic or lyrical the words may be that describe Him, they still speak *of* Him. They do not put us in touch with the reality itself.

We can think of any friend whom we have come to know to illustrate the point: we might have read all their words, read biographies, seen film of them, and heard recordings; but we cannot know that person until we meet him. Sometimes the descriptions about him can be so vivid that we might say that it feels "as though" we know him, but not until we interact directly—that is, have a personal contact—do we say that we *know* him without qualification.

Benedict XVI, discussing the 14th-century Byzantine theologian Nicholas Cabasilas, put it as follows: "He distinguishes between two kinds of knowledge: one is knowing through instruction, which remains second-hand and does not put the knower in contact with reality itself. The second kind of knowledge, in contrast, is knowing through personal experience, through contact with things themselves."[9]

It is a longing not just to know, but also to *be* something greater than we are and to have our natures raised up so that we partake of the divine nature[10] in union with God. We want to step into the supernatural. Quoting Nicholas Cabasilas directly, Pope Emeritus Benedict XVI put it thus: "When men have a longing so great that it surpasses human nature and eagerly desire and are able to accomplish things beyond human thought, it is the Bridegroom himself who has wounded them. Into their eyes he has sent a ray of his beauty. The size of the wound is evidence of the arrow, and the longing points to the one who has shot the arrow."[11]

A profound personal contact with God is made when we pray with an icon or pray the psalms. This is at its most profound when we come into His presence in the Eucharist and praise Him directly. Therefore, it is to this encounter in the sacred liturgy of the Church that all of creation

---

9. Benedict XVI, *On the Way to Jesus Christ* (San Francisco: Ignatius Press, 2005), p. 35.

10. Cf. 2 Peter 1:3–4.

11. Benedict XVI, *On the Way to Jesus Christ*, p. 35. Quoting Nicholas Cabasilas, *Life in Christ*, Bk. II, 15.

and all other human activity points, although many do not realize it. The liturgy, the Mass and the Liturgy of the Hours, is the place where hearts meet in Christ. By the worship of God, in the sacred liturgy (and by God's grace), we now *pray* the psalms which previously we just read, and something profound happens: these words become *ours*, the articulation of our own direct dialogue with God. All that we previously understood is now lived, and it becomes known in a new way. We are now participating in something that transcends mere literature, art, music, architecture: there is a profound and higher synthesis of all these, centered on the Word. This is not a well-decorated concert hall housing a show, or an acted drama, but a more direct encounter. By the grace of God and to the degree that we cooperate, the Holy Spirit speaks the words for us that otherwise we could not, and God speaks these words to us so that we accept them in a way that otherwise we could not. The elevated *beauty* of this synthesis is greater than the sum of its parts and says something on our behalf that words alone cannot. This is an encounter with the living God, the worship of the Father, through the Son, in the Spirit.

Any who are touched by beauty but then resist its call and stop short of this are selling themselves short. Perhaps they content themselves with regard for the beauty of creation, refusing to see anything beyond it, as the neo-pagan does; or they are like the aesthete who thinks that the beauty of high culture is the end in itself. Each is like a person who inhales the aroma of steaming food but never actually sits down and eats the meal. This is also true of philosophy, or even the reflections of the theologian who ponders the inspired writing of the scripture. No matter how clear and how well-grasped the truth of what they portray, the object of their reflection is not fully known until it is known in love and we praise Him. Participating in the liturgy of the Church is the activity of loving God par excellence. As the psalmist says in Psalm 62(63), which is sung at Lauds on Sundays and Solemnities in the Liturgy of the Hours: "My soul shall be filled as with a banquet, my mouth shall praise you with joy."

That is not to underestimate the importance of theological reflection; it is still absolutely necessary, but, as Benedict once again tells us, "to despise, on that account, the impact produced by the heart's encounter with beauty, or to reject it as a true form of knowledge, would impoverish both faith and theology."[12]

This knowing in love is never *fully* realized until we reach full union

12. Benedict XVI, *On the Way to Jesus Christ* (San Francisco: Ignatius Press, 2005), p. 36.

with God, partaking of the divine nature, in heaven in the next life. This is the final end, the life of the world to come, to which all in this life points. But by degrees we can be transformed and deepen our experience and, therefore, our true knowledge of God in this life when we take that temporal step into the supernatural, into the heavenly realm, by an active and full participation in the sacred liturgy.

Beauty and Creativity

There is an additional aspect to beauty that has a profound impact on the culture: man is made to create beauty. For God, to think of something *is* to create it. For man, the creative faculty is exercised in the thought, but then the work of his hands must fashion the matter of the already-created world into a form that corresponds to his idea. This human act of creation, though a lesser act, is analogous to that of the divine mind. We desire to be like God, and we will be most fully human when we are most like Him, that is in union with God and partaking of the divine nature. Therefore, as Fr. Chris Renz says, "We become fully human not only in the presence of beauty but by 'living in beauty,' i.e., through our *creation* of beautiful things."[13] We are all called, therefore, to contribute in some way to the creation of beauty and thereby contribute to the re-establishment of a culture of beauty. This is an act of love for those who in turn will "see" this beauty. This is why an education in beauty must stimulate that creative faculty as well as develop the ability to apprehend it.

The call of the popes of the recent age is for the creation of beautiful things so that the culture of man can radiate with this wounding beauty and prepare those in whom this longing is created to hear the message that tells them the means by which they can be at rest; that is, through Christ and his Church.

Pope Francis, in his Apostolic Exhortation *Evangelii Gaudium*, tells us not only of the power of beauty in directing all to Christ, but also of the necessity to the evangelizers, that is, those who know him, of a formation in beauty so that their work can touch those who do not know him:

> Every expression of true beauty can thus be acknowledged as a path leading to an encounter with the Lord Jesus. This has nothing to do with fostering an aesthetic relativism which would downplay the inseparable bond between truth, goodness and beauty, but rather a renewed esteem for beauty as a means of touching the human heart

13. Private communication, 2014.

and enabling the truth and goodness of the Risen Christ to radiate within it. If, as Saint Augustine says, we love only that which is beautiful, the incarnate Son, as the revelation of infinite beauty, is supremely lovable and draws us to himself with bonds of love. So a formation in the *via pulchritudinis* ought to be part of our effort to pass on the faith.[14]

Pope Francis is telling us that a formation that opens our eyes to beauty also enhances our ability to work beautifully. That formation is an education in love of God and man.

It is the sacred liturgy that forms us in love and beauty. It will increase our capacity to love and our inclination to do so.

14. Pope Francis, *Evangelii Gaudium*, p. 167.

2

Sacred Liturgy and Culture
(or Cult and Culture)

At the heart of every culture lies the attitude man takes
to the greatest mystery: the mystery of God.
John Paul II, *Centesimus Annus*

C ULTURE IS THE INTEGRATED PATTERN of human behavior that
reflects the beliefs and values of any community. This can relate
to any identifiable group of people with a common bond, narrow or broad; it can be deeply held values or superficial interests, and
those values and interests can be good or bad. We could talk, for example, of British culture, American culture, 19th-century Western European culture, youth culture, pop culture, folk culture, pub culture,
soccer-hooligan culture, or drug culture, each with the positive or negative connotations we assign to them.

The discussion here incorporates the idea of culture in its widest,
deepest sense: I will say that culture is a reflection of—or incarnation
of—a society's core priorities, beliefs and values. All these lesser forms
of culture listed above are aspects of this wider culture. Those core priorities, beliefs, and values are those that relate to man's understanding
of God and of himself in relationship with God, and they touch everything that he does. I am interested specifically in Christian culture.

There are different aspects of a Christian culture. Some are obviously
connected to the practice of the Faith. This can be called the *culture of
faith*. It refers to the activity of worship, and includes also those works
of sacred art, music, architecture, and so on that we would normally
associate with an orthodox practice of the faith. The religious practices
(and associated art and music and so on) that are non-liturgical and
very often take place outside the church are also part of the culture of

faith (by this I am thinking of the devotions that constitute popular piety, such as the rosary). All such devotions and prayers are authentic to the degree that they are derived from and point to the highest form of prayer, liturgy. They may do this by incorporating a pattern of the liturgy in their structure. The rosary developed, for example, so that each Hail Mary represented one psalm, 150 in all. By praying the rosary a Christian is echoing the pattern of the liturgy of the hours, which prays all 150 Psalms in a cycle.

Aside from the culture of faith, there is another aspect of Christian culture, one that is associated with the everyday activities of life. One might term this, as Pope Benedict does, *contemporary culture*.

Every single action can be consistent with a Christian way of life. This includes all art, music, film, or architecture that is not directly associated with Christian worship, and may not appear explicitly Christian in any way. We can go further and include everyday activities of living that many do not normally associate with the word *culture*. These constitute all the personal interactions and, through the solidarity of different groups of people formed by networks of such interactions, the institutions that constitute society—the families, the neighborhoods, the political groups and social organizations, charities, and so on. To the degree that human interactions can be potentially loving or selfish they can be either consistent with or in opposition to a Christian worldview. All loving action radiates its message of goodness to us and when we apprehend it, impresses itself upon our souls as something driven by God's grace—we often use the word "graceful" to describe such actions—and the works that result from them are beautiful.

As already discussed, historically the culture of faith and the wider contemporary culture were connected in Christian society. When there is this full integration of the *culture of faith* and *contemporary culture*, each reinforces and reflects the other. The liturgy and the culture of faith preserve the faith of those who already possess it. However, this is not enough. It is particularly important that contemporary culture be a Catholic culture of beauty, too, because this may be the only aspect of Christian culture that non-Christians see. Contemporary culture speaks to those who don't go to church in a way that the culture of faith cannot. Contemporary culture, therefore, is at the forefront of our work of evangelization.

If we wish to transform society, therefore, we must focus first on what speaks to it most powerfully—contemporary culture. So before we can think on any grand scale of the evangelization of the people, we must achieve first the evangelization of contemporary culture so that every aspect of it should reflect Christian values, priorities, and beliefs. When it does, it will be beautiful, and through its beauty it will draw people to the faith.

As discussed earlier, when we live the Christian life of love its radiance is beauty. The impact of this will be to arouse the curiosity of those around us, for they will be attracted to it and they will start to ask questions. They will want what we have. To the degree that we are formed in beauty and love, we have prudence. This the wisdom that will enable us to respond. We will intuitively to know *how* to answer questions, as well as *what* to say.

The question, therefore, is how we achieve this inculturation. I have expressed in broad terms already what I think the answer is: a focus on the creation of liturgical forms of art, music and architecture that will be the standards of the wider culture; and even before that a piety that involves a life centered on the liturgy. This is a life with the Mass at its center, but, very importantly, also the praying of the Liturgy of the Hours.

I would add here two additional points that will serve these ends: that we reestablish the idea of tradition; and that we engender a humble attitude of faith that will leave those who are to be the creators of the new tradition willing and able to cooperate with inspiration when it comes. I will address these one by one and describe in more detail why I think they are important and how they are interconnected.

The Importance of Tradition in Culture

It is one thing to say that we must have a contemporary culture that reflects a culture of faith, but how can we establish that link? Part of the answer to this question is to recognize the importance of tradition. The word culture is derived from the Latin words *cultus*, which means field, and *cultura*, meaning tilling, husbandry. The derivation results from the understanding that the culture is something that is cultivated and grows organically. It develops, therefore, out of the culture of the preceding generation which in turn passes it on to the next. Those parts of culture that change and reflect a particular society and characterize its time and its place depend upon the capacity for inspiration, learning, and wisdom as well as the transmission of the culture to succeeding generations. Each successive generation builds on the foundation that is passed on to it. This is the principle of tradition—the passing on of the accumulated knowledge and positive experience of one generation to the next. For a culture to flourish, therefore, it must include within it the principle of tradition. Similarly, if you want to destroy a culture, an effective way to destroy it is to undermine the principle of tradition within it.

The Importance of Inspiration and Formation in Humility

However, tradition that relies on human effort alone is not enough. No one can pass on all he knows to someone else. Therefore, any culture that relies on this truncated version of tradition is doomed to failure, for the body of knowledge passed on would necessarily diminish with each successive generation, and something new and unconnected would rush in to fill the vacuum, ushering in change.[1]

In order to flourish, a culture must be re-created at each step. The diminished body of knowledge that is directly passed on is supplemented by something new that is consistent with the principles of the tradition. The wellspring of the creativity that will allow this to happen is inspiration from God.

Therefore, Christian culture is founded on both the transmission of the Faith and a humility that opens the person to the reception of inspiration, should God choose to give it, so that wisdom and creativity can give it life. No culture can be stable if it does not acknowledge this need for inspiration and constant creativity.

We must be clear as to what we mean by inspiration. Some can describe an idea as "inspired" when they mean original and good, but nevertheless still see it originating in the isolated "genius" of the individual. This is not true inspiration. Relying on individual genius, separated from any outside inspiration for the sort of creativity that can sustain a whole culture, is doomed to failure, for it is dipping into a well that runs dry very quickly. Only when inspiration is understood as something that is given to us from outside can it realistically be the nec-

---

1. This reliance on a distorted form of tradition is why, most dramatically, change is so strong a feature of modern culture. Using the example of art to illustrate: there has been a huge range of distinguishable art movements that have risen and fallen in the last hundred years. The principle of tradition that pervades modern art is so distorted that it has become inverted: one might say that we live in an age that lives by a principle of anti-tradition. It arose first from a desire to destroy the old order and since then has always sought to *differentiate* itself from what went on before. There is an inherent contradiction in this. The principle of anti-tradition is never applied to the principle itself. On the contrary, it is vehemently preserved and passed on from teacher to student within the art schools of our universities and colleges under the false banners of "diversity," "originality," "sincerity," and "self-expression." These are false because it cannot be truly diverse without some commonality that is rooted in universality—otherwise, it is not diversity, but difference; it cannot be truly original if does not look to the origin of all things; and it is not a sincere or true reflection of the self. But we should take heart from this: because this is not rooted in truth it is inherently unstable and cannot keep what is good out forever. At some point, the principle of anti-tradition itself will not be passed on, and the ethos of instability will itself become unstable. Let us hope that it is sooner rather than later.

essary, ever-present source of what is new and good. And only God is such a source of any inspiration that is good. Inspiration, then, is a prompting of the human spirit by the Spirit of God. While many who are anxious to reestablish Christian culture are quite likely to see the need for educating people today in the forms of our traditions, the absolute necessity of humble and inspired creativity is more often neglected. This is so, it seems—surprisingly—even for the small number of those orthodox Catholic schools and colleges that educate our children with the stated intention of forming them so as to become agents of the reestablishment of Christian culture.

Formation in faith and formation in humility are bound together; for a genuine faith is humble and cooperates with God's grace. We may teach the faith, but we are not *forming* the person in faith if we do not engender graceful living and creativity. The evidence is in the culture. If the wider culture is not a vibrant Christian culture, then we Christians must look anew at *ourselves* and ask how we are formed in our faith, for what we believe at the deepest level affects profoundly all that we do. John Paul II stated in *Centesimus Annus* that the basis of a culture is its attitude to God:

> At the heart of every culture lies the attitude man takes to the greatest mystery: the mystery of God. Different cultures are basically different ways of facing the question of the meaning of personal existence. When this question is eliminated, the culture and moral life of nations are corrupted. [2]

If we do not have a Christian culture that is sweeping away all others before it through the compelling power of beauty, then it is not truly a Christian culture.

At the heart of this is love. A genuine formation in faith is a formation in love. To love something is to know in a special way that surpasses all other knowledge. And when we truly love God then all that we do is beautiful. To know in this way engages the whole person, body and soul, in his desiring of something perhaps at first barely known, then grasping it intellectually, and finally responding in thought and action.

This is why at the root of every culture is a *cult,* meaning here a system of religious worship and ritual. And at the heart of the Christian culture is the sacred liturgy, in which we worship God the Father, through the Son, in the Spirit. This is the cult that nourishes and sustains Christian culture. God is the object to which all Christian culture points.

---

2. John Paul II, *Centesimus Annus*, 24.

Formation in Faith for the Renewal of Culture

The most powerful way in which we achieve this deep formation in faith is prayer, and in particular the prayer that is the public worship of the Church, the liturgy.

There is a saying of the Church Fathers which expresses this: it is often quoted as *lex orandi, lex credendi*—*rule of prayer, rule of faith*. In this context it means our worship—how we pray and what we pray—which most profoundly affects what we believe. The phrase "lex orandi, lex credendi" is a shortened version of something attributed to Prosper of Aquitain (c. 435-442), who stated: "Let us consider the sacraments of priestly prayers, which having been handed down by the apostles are celebrated uniformly throughout the whole world and in every catholic Church so that the law of praying might establish the law of believing [*ut legem credendi lex statuat supplicandi*]."[3]

Pope Benedict referred to the importance of this in his Apostolic Exhortation *Sacramentum Caritatis*, 34, in the section entitled *Lex orandi and lex credendi*:

> The Synod of Bishops reflected at length on the intrinsic relationship between eucharistic faith and eucharistic celebration, pointing out the connection between the *lex orandi* and the *lex credendi*, and stressing the primacy of the *liturgical action*. The Eucharist should be experienced as a mystery of faith, celebrated authentically and with a clear awareness that the *intellectus fidei* has a primordial relationship to the Church's liturgical action.

(The *intellectus fidei* is a Latin phrase meaning "the understanding of the faith.") I have seen some writers add a third law—*lex vivendi*—rule of living, which especially concerns the moral life as it is actually lived. There is a hierarchy here which is reflected in the order in which the terms appear: worship governs belief, which in turn governs praxis.

This is saying that the liturgy is inherently catechetical: it is the most powerful force that governs how we behave. This is articulated in the *Catechism*:

> The liturgy is the summit toward which the activity of the Church is directed; it is the font from which all her power flows. It is therefore the privileged place for catechizing the People of God. Catechesis is intrinsically linked with the whole of liturgical and sacramental activity, for it is in the sacraments, especially in the Eucharist, that Christ Jesus works in fullness for the transformation of men.[4]

3. Prosper of Aquitaine, *Patrologia Latina*, 51: 209–10.
4. *Catechism of the Catholic Church*, 1074.

Therefore, liturgy must be beautiful so that, as with all beauty, it will draw us in and then point us towards the source of all Beauty, God. It is not a "nice option" to bring beauty into the liturgy. It is a fundamental necessity, because it directs our worship to the heart of the liturgy, the Eucharist, so that the transformation will be more complete and its effect on us, including its catechizing effect, will be greatest.

This is not to say that the liturgy is the only influence on the culture, or that it is irresistible; but I would suggest that it is the most powerful single influence. For when we worship God, the whole person, body and soul, potentially at least, is engaged in a dynamic relationship with Him. We are opening ourselves up at the deepest level in an act of reception of God's love and of the giving of ourselves to Him.

So, when there are problems with society and culture, we look first to the liturgy: we can consider its content—*what* we pray; and we can consider the nature of our participation in it—*how* we pray. The modification of the content of the liturgy is a matter only for the few who have authority to consider such things. However, every single one of us can consider *how* we pray the liturgy. Is our participation full and active in the traditional understanding of these terms?

We are created to love God, and the liturgy is the activity of the love of God. All that the Church teaches is directed to this end (and as we have said all Christian culture therefore points to it, too). It is the dynamic of love between God and His saints and angels. This is union with God in heaven and it is what we are created for.

The liturgy is the primary source of grace in this life, by which we harmonize our work with God's will and in so doing are transformed by a life of love to be still greater lovers, fit to receive and return God's love. At its center is the Eucharist in the Mass. But to leave it at that is to neglect the full glory of what is being described here. The most commonly forgotten aspect of the liturgy is the Divine Office, also called the Liturgy of the Hours.[5]

The Divine Office (*Liturgy of the Hours*)

The liturgy of the hours is, in its essence, the marking of time by praying the psalms at regular periods throughout the day. It is what monks and nuns do in community and priests are bound to do in private or in community, depending on their particular vocation. In past times it was

---

5. Because this is a commonly neglected in the prayer lives of ordinary Catholics, the emphasis placed on it here is great. This should never be interpreted as raising its value above that of the Mass.

common practice for lay people in the Church, and she has urged them to resume it.

The Liturgy of the Hours is a form of worship that goes back to the early Church and is referred to in the Acts of the Apostles.[6] When we pray it, we pray it with Christ in a number of ways: first, we follow his example in history; second, as part of the formal worship of the Church, which is the mystical body of Christ, we pray in a special bond of communion with the Church as the person of Christ in the present; and third, again as part of the formal, public worship of the Church, we enter into the mystery of the Trinity. By being part of the body of Christ through the liturgy, we enter into the dynamic of love that exists between the Father and the Son in the Spirit. By our worship, we love the Father in a personal relationship through His Son in the Spirit. This is what we are made for, and it is the permanent and perpetual activity of love for the redeemed in heaven, compressed into a single moment that transcends all time. Through our participation in the earthly liturgy we step into the supernatural.

The Liturgy of the Hours is not an add-on to the Mass. Rather it is at once an overflowing of the Mass into the day, and a setting prepared to receive the Mass. In our prayer it is the means by which we take that eternal moment of the Mass out into our temporal lives beyond the Church. It acts to ventilate our lives with grace, allowing us all the more powerfully to sanctify our mundane activities.

In the Church's *General Instruction on the Liturgy of the Hours* there is a section headed **Consecration of Time**, which reads as follows:

> Christ taught us: "You must pray at all times and not lose heart" (Lk 18:1). The Church has been faithful in obeying this instruction; it never ceases to offer prayer and makes this exhortation its own: "Through him (Jesus) let us offer to God an unceasing sacrifice of praise" (Heb 15:15). The Church fulfills this precept not only by celebrating the Eucharist but in other ways also, especially through the liturgy of the hours. By ancient Christian tradition *what distinguishes the liturgy of the hours from other liturgical services is that it consecrates to God the whole cycle of the day and the night.*[7] The purpose of the liturgy of the hours is to sanctify the day and the whole range of human activity.[8]

If all times in the day and all human activity can be sanctified by praying the liturgy of the hours, as the Church tells us, then this is a wonderful gift. Through this prayer we can open ourselves up to God's inspiration

6. Cf. *General Instruction of the Liturgy of the Hours*, 1; and Acts 3:1.
7. The emphasis is mine.
8. Cf. Pope Benedict XVI, *Sacrosanctum Concilium*, 83–84.

and consolation in all we do, and to the degree that we cooperate with grace, all our activities will be good and beautiful; and will be infused with new ideas and creativity. And we will have joy. This then is the prayer that helps us directly to create a Christian culture in our everyday lives. It depends on the Mass for its true power, for it is an overflowing of the Mass into the day, and through it we are really empowered to carry out His work.

For those who wish to know more about praying the liturgy of the hours and really don't know where to start, the best introduction will come by doing it with someone who already knows how and can show you. Every priest or religious is bound to pray it, so you could ask a priest, a monk, or a nun. Otherwise, two books might be useful; the first is by Daria Sockey, and the second is by myself and Leila Lawler.[9]

All this is summarized in the words of the Church:

> Christ Jesus, high priest of the new and eternal covenant, taking human nature, introduced into this earthly exile that hymn which is sung throughout all ages in the halls of heaven. He joins the entire community of mankind to Himself, associating it with His own singing of this canticle of divine praise; for he continues His priestly work through the agency of His Church, which is ceaselessly engaged in praising the Lord and interceding for the salvation of the whole world. She does this, not only by celebrating the eucharist, but also in other ways, especially by praying the divine office. . . . Every liturgical celebration, as an activity of Christ the priest and of his body, which is the Church, is a sacred action of a preeminent kind. No other action of the Church equals its title to power or its degree of effectiveness.[10]

The Liturgy is the Prayer of Community

When any aspect of human society institutes the liturgy, including the liturgy of the hours, as part of its rhythm, it creates the possibility of the strongest communal bond within it. We bemoan the lack of community in modern society, but so rarely do we pray the prayer of community that might establish it. It does not even require every person to participate in the liturgy for it to be effective. If some members take it upon themselves to pray on behalf of their community, and the invitation is there for all to attend, community is established in grace. As mentioned already, this is true even if most never attend or even accept the pre-

---

9. David Clayton and Leila Lawler, *The Little Oratory, A Beginner's Guide to Prayer in the Family* (Manchester: Sophia Institute Press, 2014); Daria Sockey, *The Everyday Catholic's Guide to the Liturgy of the Hours* (Cincinnati: Servant Books, 2013).

10. *Sacrosanctum Concilium*, 83, 87.

mises upon which such prayer is based. We can create the community we seek around us if we want to. Wherever any group is bound together by some common goal, whether noble or apparently mundane—a family, a college, a business, a golf club—the sacrifice of praise by some on its behalf can create a community of people out of what was previously a collection of individuals. Every person will relate to each other differently as a result, very often despite themselves, for all are interconnected via a network of personal relationships to the one who prays.

When prayer is prayed as sacrifice centered on the Eucharist and the liturgy, great things will happen. This is a sacrifice in different ways: it is sacrifice by participation in the prayer of the mystical body of Christ, the Church. God's love for us is extraordinary in this regard; we participate in the sacrifice supernaturally, a sacrifice that Our Lord participated in, in person. He felt the pain and the anguish; we do not (usually), but we obtain all the benefits.

In a more mundane sense of the word, when we sacrifice our time and energy to make this an act for the world around us, beginning with those with whom we are in personal contact, we give on their behalf time and energy that could have been spent in other ways. This is the sacrifice of praise.

Consciously Choosing to Do What is Most Beautiful

From this foundation in prayer one envisages an inculturation based upon our personal interactions that permeates all that we do. To the degree that each loving action is seen by others, it conveys the beauty of God to those who see it. When considering how to behave we tend to consider first the moral implications in a negative way—that is, is what I am thinking about doing forbidden? In making the everyday decisions of life we are often faced with an array of choices that appear equivalent from this point of view. Does this mean, then, that each is equivalent when measured by the standard of the greatest good? I would say no— or not necessarily—and in considering which is higher we could be guided by reason. We can also use the principle of beauty to narrow the choice. Each person can choose what seems to be the most beautiful, and to do what he believes to be the most graceful and most gracious. These criteria will work their way through to permeate the culture even in activities that we don't normally associate with beauty. For example, when engaged in activities connected to caring for our fellow man, and when making a deliberated choice, it is usual to choose what appears the greatest good, but less common to think also of what might be the most beautiful. If we can think of doing what seems to offer the best practical result, and at the same time try to be conscious of taking those actions graciously, then the beauty of the act shines out. This is the light of love. St. Thérèse of Lisieux endeavored to make every little action loving in some way. This is an adaptation, the "little way of beauty" which is an additional facet to the way of love.

The interconnection of all activity in love in the culture is described by Pope Benedict XVI:

> The first and most fundamental way in which inculturation takes place is the unfolding of a Christian culture in all its different dimensions: a culture of cooperation, of social concern, of respect for the poor, of the overcoming of class differences, of care for the suffering and dying; a culture that educates mind and heart in proper cooperation; a political culture and a culture of law; a culture of dialogue, of reverence for life and so on. This kind of authentic inculturation of Christianity then creates culture in the stricter sense of the word, that is, it leads to artistic work that interprets the world anew in the light of God. In the religious sphere, culture manifests itself above all in the growth of authentic popular piety.[11]

This statement reflects the importance of a balanced prayer life that both nourishes and is nourished by a Christian culture in the broadest sense. It also introduces another important point. In my emphasizing the liturgy, one should not interpret this as a neglect of devotions such as the rosary. Rather, what we seek is an ordered balance of liturgical prayer and devotions that points to and radiates out of the Eucharist in the heart of the Mass.

All of this was put to me beautifully once by a priest in the following statement: "The Mass is a jewel in its setting, which is the liturgy of the hours. The liturgy as a whole is a jewel in its setting, which is the cosmos." Through its beauty the cosmos directs man's thoughts upwards, so to speak—the heavens point to Heaven—where the heavenly liturgy is glorifying God perpetually. We step supernaturally into the heavenly liturgy through participation in the Mass and the circle is completed. It is a positive-feedback cycle in which wonder and joy are reinforced at each turn.

The work of man, as reflected in the culture of faith and in the wider culture in cooperation with grace, participates in that same beauty that we see in the cosmos. It complements and completes the beauty of the cosmos and, just as the cosmos does, direct hearts and minds to heavenly things and ultimately to God.

---

11. Pope Benedict XVI, *Spirit of the Liturgy* (San Francisco: Ignatius, 2000), p. 201.

Man is made to love God. It is part of his nature. Man is *above all*, therefore, liturgical man; he cannot be fulfilled in life if he neglects this aspect of his nature. Any account of man and society that ignores his natural desire to worship God will be flawed. Through our worship of God in the liturgy we love Him and are transformed in love. By degrees we become like God and participate in his divine nature.

The Problems of Contemporary Culture

Why are we in the state we are in now? This is a complex question and the answer to it will have many parts, no doubt. Pope Benedict has pointed to problems with contemporary culture that began with the Enlightenment and which took hold in the late 18th and early 19th centuries in the West:

> The Enlightenment pushed faith into a kind of intellectual and even social ghetto. Contemporary culture turned away from the faith and trod another path, so that faith took flight in historicism, the copying of the past, or else attempted compromise or lost itself in resignation and cultural abstinence. The last of these led to a new iconoclasm, which has frequently been regarded as virtually mandated by the Second Vatican Council. The destruction of images, the first signs of which reach back to the 1920s, eliminated a lot of kitsch and unworthy art, but ultimately it left behind a void, the wretchedness of which we are now experiencing in a truly acute way. Where do we go from here? Today we are experiencing not just a crisis of sacred art, but a crisis of art in general of unprecedented proportions. The crisis of art for its part is a symptom of the crisis of man's very existence.... We might almost call it a blindness of the spirit.[12]

Many nowadays tend to see the Second Vatican Council and the 1960s in combination as the cause of the crisis of faith. This is not Pope Benedict's analysis. He says here very clearly that the problems began much earlier, and that by the 19th century, as a result of the influence that Enlightenment thinking had, the faith and therefore the culture of faith were separated from the wider culture. He describes three flawed responses to this:

First, "historicism," which is an extreme rejection of the modern cultural expressions that looks uncritically at the past without attempting to understand it fully. The attitude that typifies this is "past-good, present-bad," and it results in a blind copying of past forms. It is the resurrection of now-dead traditions in such a way that they can never have

---

12. Pope Benedict XVI, *Spirit of the Liturgy*, p. 130.

life, for it is profoundly suspicious of any innovation and so cuts out the possibility of having the properly directed innovation that is necessary in a living tradition.

The second is compromise with a secular contemporary culture. This can be illustrated by consideration of art and music in which the content—what is painted, or the words of a song for example—might be Christian, but its form is not (like the expressionist crucifixion that I described in the last chapter). The principles we are describing here apply as much to art[13] as they do to music (or any other aspect of culture), but are best illustrated here using the example of music.

So much pop or rock music is of a form that has developed specifically to reflect the culture of hedonism. This does not mean it cannot be adapted or modified in some situations so that it reflects something good; neither does it mean that it is all bad, for, after all, even this misdirected quest for sex and drugs is at root a search for something good. But it does mean that to ignore this aspect of the style of the music altogether and just change the words to those of Christian hymns runs grave risk of communicating something very bad regardless of how pious or holy the words of the song may be. Because worship of God is the activity in which we bare our souls most, it is where we are most vulnerable to adverse influence. I suggest that we should be more conservative and less inclined to take risks in choice of music in the liturgy than in the local dance hall. The music of our worship should be rooted in Christian tradition so that it naturally becomes the standard to which all else points. If we make the secular forms the standard by which the liturgical are measured, the hierarchy has been inverted and the result is disaster for both cultures—the culture of faith and contemporary culture.

In 1903, Pius X[14] criticized the tendency to adopt the then-popular operatic styles into liturgical music. It is an indication of how far we have fallen that opera seems like high culture to us today and the incorporation of operatic forms into the Mass would in many cases seem like a step up.

Today's equivalent of the problem that Pius X pointed to is Christian pop music. It is sad to see Christians trying to be cool in the eyes of the secular world and promoting music that is not even good pop music (otherwise it would sell much more than its non-Christian alternatives), and not good for the liturgy either.

---

13. See later chapter for a discussion on how this can be seen in Christian art.
14. Pius X, *Tra Le Sollecitudini*, 6.

The liturgical music of the Church for the last 40 years has been dominated by a style that is a pale version of a folksy pop music that was popular with hippies in about 1967 ... and then became unpopular again with most of them in about 1968. Unfortunately, those who held the power in the choir lofts of Catholic churches didn't move on with the rest of the pop world and everyone else has had to suffer this pale throwback to the Woodstock generation ever since. It is easy to imagine that many, without faith firm enough to see past it, found it unbearable and have left the Church. For me, this bad folksy music, which is neither traditional nor contemporary, tends to hide rather than illuminate the power of the liturgy.

The musical form that exemplifies the universal values that appeal to all people is Gregorian chant. Pius X tells us that only to the degree that music in the liturgy participates in this universality and beauty is it appropriate for the liturgy. Universality means that it appeals to something that is common to all human beings by virtue of its structure. Sacred polyphony (of the form of composers such as Palestrina) is the other form he specifically mentions.[15]

Coming back to Benedict's analysis of contemporary culture, the third response he cites in the passage quoted above is "resignation and cultural abstinence." Seeking refuge from all the unworthy art and music, the faithful gave up the fight and tried to disengage totally. They closed their eyes and went on an inward retreat from all outside stimulation. Unfortunately, closing your eyes doesn't negate the imagination, which feeds on the imagery supplied by the senses and stored in the memory. Once seen, there is no escaping modern culture, unless it is supplanted by something better and more powerful. This means that we cannot afford to abstain from the debate.

Although the separation of secular culture from the culture of faith began in the 18th century, by the 19th century the effects were well-established in contemporary culture (although the differences might not even be obvious to us today when the effects are even more marked). Catholic culture became an emasculated, paler version of what it had been, although not yet overtly adopting secular forms. In general, the sacred art, for example, of the 19th century is only a dim shadow of the 17th-century Baroque from which it is descended.[16]

By the beginning of the 20th century the split was more obvious, and even the pale remnants of Christian culture were thrown out. Move-

---

15. Ibid.

16. Those who are interested in a fuller account of the differences might read John Rupert Martin, *Baroque* (Boulder: Westview Press, 1977).

ments such as the Bauhaus in architecture, Expressionism in art, and the dissonant music of composers such as Schoenberg broke much more obviously (and deliberately) with the old Christian order. These styles began to move into our churches, and by the 1950s we already have plenty of examples of architecture, art and music associated with worship that spoke boldly of the secular worldview. This was not necessarily liked at the time. But even when this fad for ugliness was recognized and rejected, the ability of artists to produce truly beautiful art was limited and their efforts to work in more naturalistic styles were even more degraded and superficial than in the 19th century. This is the saccharine or "kitsch" art that Benedict refers to in the quotation above.

People today are still trying to cross this gap between the sacred and the mundane. But without a firm foundation in beautiful culture of faith, it becomes very difficult. Many of these attempts are very often crudely conceived in-your-face statements of the Faith or the gospel, rather than what a Christian contemporary culture used to be, a more subtle reflection of the priorities, beliefs and values that rest upon an assumed faith. This gap can never be crossed unless we try to bridge it from a starting point of well-established and beautiful liturgical forms. Only now, as the true intentions of the Second Vatican Council are implemented, can we see hope for this happening.

Liturgical reform in this spirit is right at the center of this process. As the liturgy reflects more and more the true intentions of the Council, as articulated by people such as Benedict, we are beginning to see an improvement also in the artistic and musical forms associated with it. We are not there yet, but I dare to say, albeit guardedly, that I can see it happening.

What Can We Do?

By the 19th century (and perhaps earlier) it was clear that the Church had to do something in response to the new worldview that was taking hold. Its response was not only intellectual, through figures such as Blessed John Henry Newman, but also liturgical. This was the period of the beginning of the liturgical reform movement. We are still in the period when the Church is responding. The Second Vatican Council was a recent part of it.

There may be arguments today among Catholics about the value of this Council, but, regardless of where one stands on this, it seems that going from where we are now, a true reflection of what the Council gave us in regard to liturgy is at least the first move in the right direction. Liturgical reform today is a controversial topic, the discussion of which is mostly beyond the scope of this book. However, for those who are interested in knowing more I refer readers to several books that contain useful information on the topic as starting points.[17]

While lay people can have little influence on what goes on in the Mass, each of us can strive to develop the right interior disposition in our participation in it. This points again to the actions we advocated earlier: development of an authentic liturgical piety and an immersion in the traditions of liturgical cultural forms of the Church.

Universality and Noble Accessibility

In seeking to evangelize the culture, we are trying to make it universally Christian. Catholic culture, therefore, is that culture which speaks of that Good which is universal. This goes beyond what is explicitly sacred and includes all that is universally good; and it participates in a universal Beauty.

Some might interpret the intention to evangelize the culture as one to impose a European culture on the whole world, most of which will not relate to it. This is not so. First of all, there is no suggestion of any imposition. It is something freely offered, and those to whom it is offered are free to accept or reject it. Second, to the degree that what we offer is truly Catholic in the way just described it will be compellingly beautiful; that is, people will want it. Catholic culture like the Catholic Faith that it reflects is universal; that is, it manifests qualities that appeal to all people and excludes no one. The very word *Catholic* means universal, and the Church calls itself Catholic because it has a message that is intended for all people.

Universal is not the same as uniform, nor does it mean culturally neutral or *acultural*. The timeless qualities that make it good, true, and beautiful and which are common to all aspects of Catholic culture are always manifested in particular instances that characterize particular times and places as well. It is always by looking at the particulars that we discern the general. So, every work of art, every piece of music is a product of its time and place and can be recognized as such, but that art which is good is a particular expression or application of values that are universal. It is the underlying principles that are true for all times and all places. A work of art that is universal is therefore *both* timeless *and* time-bound, it is *simultaneously* of one place *and* of all places. While we may recognize a work of art as representing Western European culture of the 17th century, for example, it still bears the marks that give it appeal to all people.

---

17. Benedict XVI, *The Spirit of the Liturgy*; Benedict XVI, *The Ratzinger Report* (San Francisco: Ignatius Press, 1987); Fr. Thomas Kocik, *The Reform of the Reform? A Liturgical Debate: Reform or Return* (San Francisco: Ignatius Press, 2003).

The most powerful combination is an absolute harmony of the timeless and time-bound. When a work of art or music expresses well the timeless principles that appeal to all men, but in a way also that characterizes the time and place of those who experience it, the result is irresistible. The need for the creation of these modern expressions of the traditional are at the forefront of culture. This is the challenge we are placing before the gifted and creative today.

So, if we go to a new place that has no Christian culture, we may introduce first forms that we know reflect the universal beauty—these will be the established liturgical forms that very likely will be, through the accident of history, European in origin. However, if we do not do so in a way that immediately allows these forms, even Gregorian chant, to engage and assimilate with the local culture of that time (without compromising in any way its universality and changing only those aspects that characterize time and place) then our attempt to evangelize the culture, and ultimately to evangelize the people, will fail. This cannot be overemphasized. These new forms do not replace those that they grew from, but sit alongside them, casting them in a more penetrating light, helping us to see the mysteries that they reveal. Each nourishes our appreciation of the other and both direct us to the saving Beauty of God more powerfully.

This is why we can never rest on our cultural laurels as Catholics. There is an absolute imperative to create anew and make Catholic culture a *living* tradition. It is also why, in the later section on education, I emphasize so strongly that any Catholic education that is limited to teaching people to appreciate what is good is crucially deficient. It must train us to create beauty as well. Every single one of us, through our daily activities, no matter how mundane, contributes to the culture in some way. Whether we like it or not, we are creating a culture that is either a living secular culture, a dead and ultimately ineffective Christian culture that survives only in the margins, or a beautiful, Catholic culture that is simultaneously both new and traditional. This latter is the highest level of culture that we must strive for.

Benedict XVI refers to this in another book on culture and liturgy, called *A New Song for the Lord*:

> The level of a culture is discernible by its ability to assimilate, to come into contact and exchange and to do this synchronically and diachronically. It is capable of encountering other contemporary cultures as well as the development of human culture in the march of time. This ability to exchange and flourish also finds its expression in the ever-recurring imperative: "Sing the Lord a new song." Experiences of salva-

tion are found not only in the past, but occur over and over again: hence they also require the ever-new proclamation of God's contemporaneity, whose eternity is falsely understood if one interprets it as being locked in decisions made "from time immemorial." On the contrary, to be eternal means to be synchronous with all times and ahead of all times.[18]

We can think of the iconographic tradition of painting to illustrate this. As discussed, every painting conveys information through what is painted (its content) and how it is painted (its style). It is the stylistic features of an icon that characterize it as an icon and unite it with the tradition of which it is a part and differentiate it from others. Each characteristic element participates in the essential timeless and "place-less" principles that make an icon what it is. Nevertheless, every icon speaks also of a time and a place, even to the extent of bearing the individual stylistic marks of the person who painted it. They may not be deliberately imposed upon it by the artist, but they are there because at every brush stroke he must decide how to apply the principles that define the tradition. It may surprise some to learn that even in the iconographic tradition, which allows barely any room for conscious self-expression, someone who knows icons well can identify the geographical region and time-period of an icon to within about 50 years just by looking at it.

Every living tradition remains vibrant by developing contemporary forms. If it relies on its past only, then it will die. This is why we paint icons now and never rely exclusively on the canon of past works.

The Pattern of Organic Growth of a Beautiful Culture

Accordingly, Christian culture should be offered to all throughout the world as part of that process of evangelization. This may mean offering traditional European culture initially. As already discussed, if what we have is good, it will be desired and accepted and take root in people's hearts. Once it has taken root then, as a living tradition, local variations will develop organically in way that reflects the particulars of that society, but without deviating from its core principles.

We can see this pattern if we study art and music of the past. Gregorian chant developed from the Middle Eastern forms of the Jewish chant, and from Roman culture. Some of these melodies remain to this day; for example, the *tonus peregrinus*, which is the melody for Psalm 113 in plainchant, is a pre-Christian Jewish melody; and the most familiar tune used for the famous hymn for Compline *Te Lucis Ante Terminum*

---

18. Pope Benedict XVI, *A New Song for the Lord, Faith in Christ and Liturgy Today* (New York: Crossroads 2006), p. 127.

("To You before the End of Day") is that of a lullaby that Roman mothers sang to their children.[19] However, Gregorian chant is neither Jewish nor ancient Roman but distinctively Christian, because it built on the universal principles contained within the forms it took from elsewhere to create something distinctive to its time and place. Sometimes this involved minimal development, sometimes more, as gradually and organically Christian culture took from other cultures and incorporated what is good, transforming it into its own. We must never feel that we have finished the job, even in chant. We must sing a new song, even in chant, that sits alongside these glorious expressions created by the masters of the past. The only legitimate reason for casting Gregorian chant aside is if something new is created that surpasses it in universal beauty, in holiness, and goodness of form. We should be cautious, I suggest, in making such a judgment.

We see a similar pattern to the development of chant in the development of visual art. If we consider Christian art, when it began to develop, its starting point was that of the ancient Roman art (which was itself an adaptation of Greek art). Just as with the development of music, it was transformed into something distinctively Christian, in this case the iconographic tradition. Then the style spread across the whole of Christendom as the universal principles of iconography prevailed, but local variations always appeared: some still looked like the Greco-Roman art from which it was derived in Hellenistic areas, such as Egypt; while in the extreme West on the Celtic fringe a very different form of iconography developed (that we see in the representational art of the *Book of Kells*, for example).

The development of Russian iconography is interesting in this regard. The very famous Vladimir Mother of God (the eye of which is used in the logo of the Icon Productions film company) came to Russia in the 12th century. Stylistically it is Greek, with its highly modeled form, employing subtle transitions from light to dark and from one color to another. This icon is venerated in Russia perhaps more than any other because of its connection with prayers for the successful repulsion of invading forces over the centuries. It became, therefore, the prototype for a standard iconographic representation of the Mother of God and Our Lord, named after the original. Over the centuries since, many Vladimir Mother of God icons have been painted based upon this prototype. Most of these are painted in the characteristic Russian style, which is distinct from the Greek. The Russian style describes form with strong line and light washes of flat color and has much less obvious modeling of

19. Dr. W. Fahey, private communication.

form in paint than the Greek. There are two points that come from this. First, the starting point for a Russian icon is in fact one that is characteristically Greek; and, second, the production of Russian-style icons of the Vladimir Mother of God did not diminish the passion of Russians to venerate the original Greek-style icon. Rather, each subsequent portrayal of the type points to it by the common universal elements and reinforces the power of the original in the minds of the faithful.

This pattern of organic growth can be reflected in all aspects of the culture and is the basis of an inculturation for the good.

The dominant contemporary culture of the West today is the secular culture of anti-culture. It defines itself not by what it is, but by what it isn't. It is founded on a reaction against Christianity. Therefore, it is a distortion of it and as such is parasitical upon it. As with all parasites, if the host dies, so does the parasite: and if Christian culture were to fall altogether, modern secular culture would fall too.

Should Christian culture disappear altogether, it is not modern secular culture that would dominate, for it would have lost its host. Something different, perhaps Islam, would be sucked into the vacuum. Secular culture would be unable to defend itself against it, and would go down with its Christian antithesis.

Western Pop Culture

There is a tendency today to assume that popular culture is low culture, but I say that if we truly had inspired composers and artists creating new works that are universal (thinking now of the contemporary culture, not the culture of faith), they would outshine the existing lowbrow works of the secular pop culture and create a noble Christian popular culture. It would appeal to many people and not just the *cognoscenti*[20] and chattering classes. This is a point that all who wish to be creative in the arts should take to heart. Popularity is not the only criterion by which we judge something, of course, but it is a measure of some good. It is our failure thus far to create forms that appeal to many people that has left the arena open to lesser forms. Bad popular culture can only flourish if there is no good popular culture to compete with it. Pope Benedict put it thus in *A New Song for the Lord*: "It is precisely the test of true creativity that the artist steps out of the esoteric circle and knows how to form his or her intuition in such a way that the others—the many—may perceive what the artist has perceived."[21]

---

20. For our purposes, we will classify the cognoscenti as the sort of people who know what cognoscenti means!

21. Pope Benedict XVI, *A New Song for the Lord*, p. 134.

Tolkien is a model of the creation of high-quality popular forms. Here was a brilliant scholar for whom it would have been easy to write prose that baffled most people and impressed his friends at dinner parties. However, he chose to write stories that subtly reflected a Christian worldview, could withstand analysis at all levels, and had a broad popular appeal. In the same way, Shakespeare and Mozart were part of the popular culture of their day. Every generation should strive, at least, for its Tolkien, Shakespeare, Mozart, and Velazquez who can create the noble and accessible popular culture of their day. This will be made most easy and most powerful when it relies on the elevated liturgical forms for its inspiration. We need great works from the past, too, of course, and the study of them is a vital part of the formation of those who will create the noble, popular works of today.

Objections to the Idea That the Liturgy is the Most Powerful Force for the Formation of Culture

Many people, even committed Catholics, suspect that the institutions of the modern age, and not man's worship, have created modern culture. Some of these look back wistfully to a pre-industrialized age because they blame the ugliness of modern culture on industrialization and mass production; others think that unfettered free market capitalism is the problem. I find nothing in history or Catholic social teaching to back up this assertion.

That is not to say that each is always a good thing. Rather, that to the degree that they are bad they reflect the same flaws that appear in the rest of the culture. For the most part these are now aspects of a post-Enlightenment society that, although they pre-dated it, have grown significantly during the period when the contemporary culture was already separated from the culture of faith. Consider first industrialization and mass production.

Industrialization and Mass Production as a Cause of a Culture of Ugliness?

There is plenty of evidence that mass production can be the agent of the creation of beautiful objects. We just need examine the products made in factories before the Enlightenment took hold very strongly. For example, if we go back to the early industrial revolution in England, right at the heart of it in late 18th-century Staffordshire, there were the porcelain and china factories, for example, of Wedgwood and Spode, which mass-produced objects of such beauty that they are still sought after by collectors and museums today.

In point of fact, I would use these examples to assert that mass production of beautiful objects is actually desirable. If an object is beautiful, then mass-producing it means that more beautiful things are available to us than would be if we stuck to limited editions or only handmade items.

The reason, I believe, that we associate mass production with ugliness is that since the rejection of traditional values in art and design, which really started to take hold in the 20th century, most designers simply haven't known how to make something that participates in the timeless qualities of beauty. The quality of the article that is mass-produced is dependent upon the quality of the original design of the template from which all the artifacts are made. If the design is bad, then we have ugliness in great quantity. If it is good, we have beauty in abundance. Most design today does not incorporate the traditional ideas of proportion and harmony and so if it has merit it is through the individual intuition or lucky whim of the designer. There is nothing to suggest that traditional principles of harmonious proportion cannot be incorporated into the design of mass-produced goods, mass housing, industrial buildings or any other emblem of modern ugliness that you may care to mention.

Socialism and Capitalism?

There are some who will assert that economic or political forces shape culture as powerfully as or even more powerfully than the liturgy. This attitude has its roots in an atheist-materialist worldview that does not acknowledge the spiritual dimension of existence and therefore will not believe that worship or faith in God can affect the culture except to the degree that it impacts the things that it does acknowledge: politics and economics.

I do not deny some influence here, but I would always place the influencing power of the liturgy higher than that of political or economic systems, *provided that they do not interfere greatly with the exercise of personal freedom* to worship and relate to our fellow man in love. This means that the preservation of personal freedom is a vitally important aspect of the reestablishment of a Christian culture.

If political or economic systems are based upon some restriction of personal freedom, then they *will* tend to stifle the creation of a new culture even if all else is in place. So socialism and communism will have this effect, as will some forms of capitalism.

However, capitalism is not inherently bad. John Paul II (who is writing in the line of Popes, since Leo XIII especially, who have articulated Catholic social teaching) is my guide here. He clearly states that the forms of capitalism that preserve freedom and are bolstered by rule of law according to the principle of justice are the optimum for the flourishing of man. He posits that the primary force that affects culture is the attitude of man to God and not economic or political systems that govern class membership—here we repeat the quotation already given in a fuller context:

> It is not possible to understand man on the basis of economics alone, nor to define him simply on the basis of class membership. Man is understood in a more complete way when he is situated within the sphere of culture through his language, history, and the position he takes towards the fundamental events of life, such as birth, love, work and death. At the heart of every culture lies the attitude man takes to the greatest mystery: the mystery of God. Different cultures are basically different ways of facing the question of the meaning of personal existence. When this question is eliminated, the culture and moral life of nations are corrupted. For this reason the struggle to defend work was spontaneously linked to the struggle for culture and for national rights.[22]

In the same encyclical, he states explicitly that where there is a compromise of personal freedom it will push that society into decline:

> Nevertheless, it cannot be forgotten that the manner in which the individual *exercises* [my emphasis] his freedom is conditioned in innumerable ways. While these certainly have an influence on freedom, they do not determine it; they make the exercise of freedom more difficult or less difficult, but they cannot destroy it. Not only is it wrong from the ethical point of view to disregard human nature, which is made for freedom, but in practice it is impossible to do so. Where society is so organized as to reduce arbitrarily or even suppress the sphere in which freedom is legitimately exercised, the result is that the life of society becomes progressively disorganized and goes into decline.[23]

In regard to the question as to which economic/political system is best for human flourishing, the answer is clear, he says: capitalism in which personal freedom is maximized, which he terms the "free economy":

> It would appear that, on the level of individual nations and of international relations, the free market is the most efficient instrument for utilizing resources and effectively responding to needs. But this is true only for those needs which are "solvent," insofar as they are endowed with purchasing power, and for those resources which are "marketable," insofar as they are capable of obtaining a satisfactory price. But

22. John Paul II, *Centesimus Annus*, 24.
23. Ibid., 25.

there are many human needs which find no place on the market. It is a strict duty of justice and truth not to allow fundamental human needs to remain unsatisfied, and not to allow those burdened by such needs to perish.

In simple terms this is saying that the free market is the best means of distribution for those goods that money can buy. But, he points out, it is a form of distribution based on price and so cannot help in the distribution of those things that do not command a price. We have a duty in love, therefore, to provide what the market cannot and to strive to help our fellow man. This last point is not a criticism of free markets or an argument for an alternative economic system. Rather, it is saying that the scope of the free market should be maximized and that capitalism is the best system to do this, but even then there is a limitation to what it can achieve and more is needed. In making this point, he stresses that it is only capitalism that is backed up by strong legal framework that protects personal freedom that will allow the flourishing of a society in which many people are inclined to contribute the things that the market cannot supply.

That is not to say that all forms of capitalism are good. It is possible, he states, to have forms in which personal freedom is compromised so that the values of a religious culture cannot permeate fully. These are not desirable, he says:

> Returning now to the initial question: can it perhaps be said that, after the failure of Communism, capitalism is the victorious social system, and that capitalism should be the goal of the countries now making efforts to rebuild their economy and society? Is this the model which ought to be proposed to the countries of the Third World which are searching for the path to true economic and civil progress? The answer is obviously complex. If by "capitalism" is meant an economic system which recognizes the fundamental and positive role of business, the market, private property and the resulting responsibility for the means of production, as well as free human creativity in the economic sector, then the answer is certainly in the affirmative, even though it would perhaps be more appropriate to speak of a "business economy," "market economy" or simply "free economy." But if by "capitalism" is meant a system in which freedom in the economic sector is not circumscribed within a strong juridical framework which places it at the service of human freedom in its totality, and which sees it as a particular aspect of that freedom, the core of which is ethical and religious, then the reply is certainly negative.[24]

24. John Paul II, *Centesimus Annus*, 34, 42.

Popes since the 19th century, when socialism appeared, and right up to Pope Francis today have been strong in their condemnation both of socialism and of forms of capitalism that stifle personal freedom. However, we must understand that personal freedom is not, as many today think, just a lack of restriction to choose what we want (although it is part of it). Rather, true freedom lies in being able to exercise the power of choice well. That is, no one is truly free unless he has capacity to choose the practicable best; and that is what is *objectively* the best for that person.

We can see from John Paul II's description of the free economy above that we cannot even talk of a flourishing economy without consideration of the distribution of goods that have no price. This requires a distribution network based on loving interaction between people. The two networks of distribution—loving interaction and the market—are not totally separate. Even what might be viewed as a purely economic exchange is not, as is sometimes characterized, the interaction of two purely self-interested people; for at some level each must consider the needs of the other in order to be able to respond to them. Furthermore it is found in practice that even the most basic economic interaction requires each party to trust the other, for otherwise very little trade will take place. This requires, therefore, a supporting culture based on freedom, properly understood, which is characterized by a general picture in which people on the whole behave honestly and justly without compulsion and are to some degree, at least, habitually given to loving cooperation with each other. This culture described here, a culture based on love, will be a beautiful culture.

When I look at modern art, architecture and high culture and I see aspects I dislike, my reaction is not to want to abolish painting, building, literature, and music. I argue, as I think most would, these things are intrinsically good and lack something in their modern forms. Therefore, I seek to add to them so that they might be complete, so that they might be more Catholic and more fully what they are meant to be.

Similarly with mass production, industrialization, and capitalism. I am not happy with all that is mass-produced today, nor with the nature of industry, nor with the forms of capitalism that are most commonly seen today. And, like my reaction to bad art, my reaction to them is not to conclude that they are intrinsically bad and should be abolished. I say that they too in their current forms are manifestations of a flawed culture, and that the answer, in general terms, to the question of what to do about it is the same for all aspects of it. It is a transformation of the culture, which will in turn lead to a transformation of industry and of capitalism.

It is the culture of beauty, a Catholic culture rooted in worship of God, that will allow for the greatest flourishing of man and society, by *any* measure.

3

Liturgy, Culture, and Education

The proper and immediate end of Christian education is to cooperate with divine grace in forming the true and perfect Christian, that is, to form Christ Himself in those regenerated by Baptism. . . . For precisely this reason, Christian education takes in the whole aggregate of human life, physical and spiritual, intellectual and moral, individual, domestic and social, not with a view of reducing it in any way, but in order to elevate, regulate and perfect it, in accordance with the example and teaching of Christ. Hence the true Christian, product of Christian education, is the supernatural man who thinks, judges and acts constantly and consistently in accordance with right reason illumined by the supernatural light of the example and teaching of Christ; in other words, to use the current term, the true and finished man of character.[1]

Pius XI

I N THIS CHAPTER, we are considering how one can educate so that inculturation occurs and what the place of such an education is within a general Catholic education.

In a traditionally Catholic culture so much would have been introduced naturally in the home, so one might argue perhaps that this is something that we transmit predominantly by teaching Catholic parenting skills. Certainly this is a priority, and to the degree that we can do this it will have a profound effect.[2]

But should this be part of the aim also of a formal Catholic education in high school or college? Is inculturation intrinsic to Catholic education? Or is it something that should be aimed at certain people only?

---

1. Pius XI, *Divini Illius Magistri*, 60.
2. Leila Lawler and I have written a book with this in mind. See David Clayton and Leila Lawler, *The Little Oratory: A Beginner's Guide to Family Prayer* (Manchester: Sophia Institute Press, 2014).

Should we offer a Masters in the Evangelization of the Culture, perhaps, that is designed only for those whose unique personal vocation is to follow the path of the New Evangelist? In order to answer this, we must consider first what characterizes a Catholic education in general and see how this relates to the question of the evangelization of the culture.

In this next section I reference the Church documents on education and the liturgy heavily in order to reinforce the key points: the general aim of Christian education and the place of inculturation within that; and the means by which the person is formed in accord with that aim.

What is a Catholic Education?

The aim of all Catholic education is to offer students a formation that might lead to supernatural transformation in Christ, that each might be capable, by God's grace, of movement towards their ultimate end, and of contribution to the good of the society of which each is a member:

> For a true education aims at the formation of the human person in the pursuit of his ultimate end and of the good of the societies of which, as man, he is a member, and in whose obligations, as an adult, he will share.[3]

> Every form of pedagogic naturalism which in any way excludes or weakens supernatural Christian formation in the teaching of youth, is false. Every method of education founded, wholly or in part, on the denial or forgetfulness of original sin and of grace, and relying on the sole powers of human nature, is unsound.[4]

The Church's documents on education state other aims for education, all of which are ordered to this ultimate end. These include the formation of students so that they are capable of the re-ordering of society's culture, forming them so that they are capable of bearing witness to Christ in their surroundings; and the training of skills to enable the student to earn a living. They also make it plain that these are achieved in their fullest measure by this supernatural transformation. Furthermore, we are told that formation of students so that they are capable of changing contemporary culture is not just a legitimate goal, but is intrinsic to Catholic education:

> No less than other schools does the Catholic school pursue cultural goals and the human formation of youth. But its proper function is to create for the school community a special atmosphere animated by the Gospel spirit of freedom and charity, to help youth grow according to

---

3. Paul VI, *Gravissimum Educationis*, 1.
4. Pius XI, *Divini Illius Magistri*, 60.

the new creatures they were made through baptism as they develop their own personalities, and finally to order the whole of human culture to the news of salvation so that the knowledge the students gradually acquire of the world, life and man is illumined by faith.[5]

The true Christian does not renounce the activities of this life, he does not stunt his natural faculties; but he develops and perfects them, by coordinating them with the supernatural. He thus ennobles what is merely natural in life and secures for it new strength in the material and temporal order, no less than in the spiritual and eternal.[6]

This transformation, made possible by baptism, is made real by an encounter with the living God. This encounter can happen in many ways but occurs most profoundly and most powerfully in the Eucharist, and by it we are made capable in a new way, through God's grace, of loving Him and our fellow man. Schools should therefore seek to promote this transformation: "First and foremost every Catholic educational institution is a place to encounter the living God who in Jesus Christ reveals his transforming love and truth."[7] Furthermore,

A mystagogical[8] catechesis must be concerned with bringing out the significance of the rites for the Christian life in all its dimensions— work and responsibility, thoughts and emotions, activity and repose. Part of the mystagogical process is to demonstrate how the mysteries celebrated in the rite are linked to the missionary responsibility of the faithful. The mature fruit of mystagogy is an awareness that one's life is being progressively transformed by the holy mysteries being celebrated. The aim of all Christian education, moreover, is to train the believer in an adult faith that can make him a "new creation," capable of bearing witness in his surroundings to the Christian hope that inspires him.[9]

A Christian education does not merely strive for the maturing of a human person as just now described, but has as its principal purpose this goal: that the baptized, while they are gradually introduced to

5. Paul VI, *Gravissimum Educationis*, 8.
6. Pius XI, *Divini Illius Magistri*, 60.
7. Benedict XVI, Meeting with Catholic Educators, Catholic University of America, Washington, DC, April 2008.
8. Mystagogy is a form of catechesis which takes place after the rites of initiation into the Faith such as baptism and confirmation. Its purpose is to deepen the understanding of the mysteries of the Church and so lead to an ever deepening spiritual life. In the context from which this quotation is taken, it is a passage which states that education should be directed to a more fruitful participation in the liturgy by greater conformity to "the mysteries being celebrated."
9. Benedict XVI, *Sacramentum Caritatis*, 64.

knowledge of the mystery of salvation, become ever more aware of the gift of Faith they have received, and that they learn in addition how to worship God the Father in spirit and truth (cf. John 4:23) especially in liturgical action, and be conformed in their personal lives according to the new man created in justice and holiness of truth (Eph 4:22–24).[10]

These ultimate goals of man, to which a Catholic education is directed, summarized as love of God and love of our fellow man in all its forms, are inseparably bound together: the encounter with God in the Eucharist renews our capacity for love of neighbor; and love of neighbor tends to deepen our participation in the worship of God in the Eucharist:

> The saints—consider the example of Blessed Teresa of Calcutta—constantly renewed their capacity for love of neighbor from their encounter with the Eucharistic Lord, and conversely this encounter acquired its realism and depth in their service to others. Love of God and love of neighbor are thus inseparable, they form a single commandment. But both live from the love of God who has loved us first.[11]

So profound is this connection between love of God and love of neighbor that there is no authentically human activity—thought or deed, sacred or mundane—that cannot be formed by and ordered to the Eucharist for the better of each person and society and the Church. In this sense the Eucharist is the form (as in guiding principle) of every aspect of the Christian life including all those pertaining to a Catholic school: "There is nothing authentically human—our thoughts and affections, our words and deeds—that does not find in the sacrament of the Eucharist the form it needs to be lived to the full."[12]

How Would This be Implemented in a School or College?

Such a school or educational institution, therefore, should ensure that all that goes on is in accord with the end of all education. Accordingly, it should ensure that students are aware that their capacity to be educated and that every aspect of their lives as Christians, whatever their personal goals, will be enhanced when they participate actively in the Eucharist and live a liturgically formed life. This applies to just about any subject that can be taught at school: vocational skills and servile arts, humanities, liberal arts, philosophy, or theology, each considered in its broadest definition. Each will be enhanced if the student is aware of the connection that these, in common with all human activity, have with the litur-

10. Paul VI, *Gravissimum Educationis*, 2.
11. Benedict XVI, *Deus Caritas Est*, 18.
12. Benedict XVI, *Sacramentum Caritatis*, 71.

gical life. This knowledge will help to motivate students in their studies and order all their activities to their personal goals in life, which in turn are ordered to their ultimate end.

Each student should be instructed, I suggest, so that they are clearly aware of the profound desirability of a supernatural Christian transformation and, therefore, the need for grace in their education, as in all human activity; and that Sacred Liturgy is *the* optimal encounter with Christ in this life that provides for this need. There are many ways that Christ can be encountered, and every activity of a school should be such an encounter of one form or another. However, each encounter, if it is real, derives its meaning from that optimal encounter in Sacred Liturgy to which it directs the students. Students should be aware that the fruits of such a transformed Christian life, which are promised to us, are precisely those that a Christian education aims to provide in the ideal.

As well as imparting an understanding of the primary importance of the Sacred Liturgy as the form of their everyday lives and in their education, students need to be given religious instruction so that each, in accordance with his personal situation, might develop a sacramental life that will make the transformation possible. This religious instruction includes principles by which they can develop a harmonious balance of liturgical prayer, devotional and personal prayer in which the non-liturgical elements are derived from and point to participation in Sacred Liturgy. By this instruction they will know, in theory at least, what is necessary to continually deepen their participation in the sacramental life, with the Eucharist at its heart; and continually to renew and increase their capacity for love of neighbor.

While it may be appropriate for the instruction of what is just described to be given to all in the classroom, the actual participation in the liturgically-centered sacramental life must always be one that is voluntary. We must respect each person's God-given freedom to choose. Transformation itself can neither be taught nor enforced: it is derived from a personal and free response to God's love for us. The participation, therefore, should be encouraged. Accordingly, the role of the college is to increase the freedom of each person to choose well by enhancing their knowledge of what is good in this regard and giving them, where humanly possible, the power and opportunity to do so. In accord with this the college should make it a priority to make beautifully and appropriately celebrated Sacred Liturgy available to the students in a beautiful place of worship. Ideally the faculty will lead by example, such that their actions speak of the centrality of the Eucharist in a life well lived.

All subjects included in the curriculum, while not all relating directly to the subject of the Sacred Liturgy, must nevertheless be consistent with these twofold and inter-connected aims of love of God and love of man, consummated in a freely chosen, liturgically oriented piety.[13] Each faculty member should be able to explain the reason for the inclusion of the subject taught in the light of these principles and willingly direct the students to its liturgical end. Moreover, beyond the classroom the college should strive to encourage a culture in which any aspect of community life is in accord with and reinforces its ultimate goals for the students.

Education and Inculturation

These documents tell us, therefore, that it is intrinsic to Catholic education to offer a formation that makes possible a supernatural transformation so that we become people who, in turn, are capable of transforming contemporary culture into a Catholic culture of beauty. This is not limited simply to an understanding or even appreciation of the culture. It must go beyond that and train the person to be one who *forms* it—one who is capable of ordering the whole of human culture through a living encounter with a cultural inheritance. An "education in beauty" is, therefore, at the very heart of every Catholic education.

The next question is: what are the implications in regard to the curriculum and how it is taught?

A "Liberal Arts Program"

The program that I am about to describe is often referred to generically as a "liberal arts" program. This can be somewhat confusing, because although they are contained within it, there is much more to it than simply the seven Liberal Arts. To get around this ambiguity some refer instead to a "great books" program, the idea being that the student works from original texts rather than commentaries. The problem here is that it can become a dogma of education that commentaries are always inferior, not allowing for new texts—"great" often being identified with "old." This narrows the scope of study unnecessarily: in fact, in certain fields of study written commentaries (or comments from the teacher in class) can be very helpful; and sometimes there are great new texts.

I tend to refer to this education as a "liberal arts" education, and I hope it will be clear to the reader when I am referring to the whole program, or just the part of it that gives its name to the program.

13. This life, governed by love, is liturgy in its widest sense; cf. *Catechism of the Catholic Church*, 1070.

The Beauty of the Culture is the First Stimulus

Even before the first seeds are sown, the ground must be prepared. The student must be stimulated so that he is receptive to such an education. The first step, I suggest, is a development of the natural and personal response to the divine beauty which is present in creation and in the beautiful works of man in both the culture of faith and the contemporary culture. This should be a natural and joyful experience.

In the ideal this would just happen naturally as the person is growing up. It would be modern expressions of the culture of beauty that speak most powerfully, and these would then open the door naturally to the more traditional forms. In a world in which a child growing up encounters a living Catholic culture at every turn, as might have been the case in Medieval Europe, this would just happen to all by osmosis, as it were. In some homes today, the parents are aware of this and they create little islands of Catholic culture in a small controlled environment. It is wonderful that they do this; but even then, this influence on any children would not compare with a world of the past in which the whole society was so obviously Catholic. For many it is the school or college at which this occurs first today.

We begin the education by exposing the students to art, literature, and music, and potentially any aspects of the culture that are clearly linked to the creation of beauty; this could include as well, for example, arts such as gardening or tapestry.

Very few people enjoy all aspects equally: some respond more readily to literature, some to art, some to music, and so on. While all should be introduced to a basic canon of works in each selected discipline, once people discover their natural preference, they should be encouraged to focus on what they enjoy and delve more deeply into it. From these people will emerge those who will contribute creatively to contemporary culture through the arts. Right at the beginning, the student should be learning to create these forms through imitation.

Each of us has a personal and unique way of responding to the beauty of the Divine Logos. This should be nurtured, developed, and drawn out by educators. We each have our personal *via pulchritudinis*—way of beauty—by which we can enter into the mystery of the Trinity and thereby accept God and give of ourselves in the dynamic of love in union with Him. This is the path by which our creativity can blossom.

The impression I have in general of the institutions that are faithful to the Magisterium (who in the current climate are to be applauded and supported in all they do) is that they are quite good at forming *consumers* of Catholic culture, but not good at forming *creators*.

The caricature of a group of artsy intellectuals who delight in having interesting conversations with their peers at dinner parties, reciting works of poetry from memory, or talking about great works of art knowledgeably is not so far off the mark. The point is that this is not a bad thing in itself, but that it does not go far enough; for this group, as described, does not touch people beyond its own circle.

Even if this principle of creativity is acknowledged, the works of art that are made are too often intended to appeal only to a narrow group of people. The result is a small self-contained group that has refined tastes yet communicates little to those who are not trained to understand the specialized coded vocabulary that it employs. Again, this is not a bad thing in itself, but it is not enough. Our goal here, consistent with the goal of re-ordering contemporary culture, is the formation of inspired creators of popular culture who, like Tolkien, can touch the lives of many.

When the student has been exposed to enough of the culture to be "wounded by the arrow of beauty," he is directed towards formal study of the Liberal Arts. This is a Liberal Arts education that incorporates and elevates this essential aspect of creativity.

The Liberal Arts

The exact reason for naming this array of subjects "liberal" can vary from commentator to commentator. The most convincing is that traditionally these were thought of as the studies which are directed towards training man in the right use of his freedom (*liber* is Latin for free) and by which man can become fully what he is meant to be.

The Liberal Arts are complemented by the Servile Arts. This is not a pejorative term, but indicates those studies that are directed towards practical ends, such as drawing and painting, architecture, medicine, agriculture, and so on.

The Liberal Arts are a preparation for the higher "sciences"—study of philosophy, law, medicine, and then theology. The fields of study can be traced back to the ancient Greek philosophers, especially Plato and Aristotle. In the first century AD they were ordered into nine fields of study by a Roman pagan, Marcus Varro. This was then refined and reduced to seven by the Christians Augustine, Boethius, and Cassiodorus in the 5th century. They classified them into two groups. The first three were together referred to as the *trivium* or "three roads." The second grouping, of four, was called the *quadrivium*.

The *trivium* is a focus on teaching the skills of language and communication of truth: logic (or dialectic), rhetoric, grammar. Grammar traditionally incorporates analysis of great works of literature and literary form (if the student has been primed, as described, he will have an appetite for this). The skills and knowledge learnt here have application all the way through the rest of his education.

The study of literature, as with all aspects of the wider culture that open us up to beauty, is a preparation for the liturgical forms, and so stimulates the liturgical instincts of man that lead ultimately to our ordered acceptance of love in the Eucharist. While licit but ugly liturgical forms in the liturgy do not invalidate the point (for Christ, who is Beauty incarnate, is at the center of every Mass) it does reinforce the point that this study of contemporary culture should be an accompaniment to beautiful liturgy. The benefit of having the external forms of the liturgy beautiful as well were highlighted by Benedict XVI:

> The liturgy is a radiant expression of the paschal mystery, in which Christ draws us to himself and calls us to communion. As Saint Bonaventure would say, in Jesus we contemplate beauty and splendor at their source. This is no mere aestheticism, but the concrete way in which the truth of God's love in Christ encounters us, attracts us and delights us, enabling us to emerge from ourselves and drawing us towards our true vocation, which is love.[14]

The quadrivium is the analytical study of mathematics and the order of the cosmos, described mathematically: geometry, arithmetic, astronomy, and harmonious relationship/music.

Even by medieval times the field of knowledge was great enough that different universities would teach different content in each of these fields, and the further studies each led to might vary. Theology was always considered the highest, but a student might specialize in law, natural science, or medicine before that.

A liberal arts education is given not so much for the usefulness of the information gained, but rather for the way it forms the student to think in a particular way (towards the higher ends already described), especially as he progresses up through them to think creatively.

Ironically, for all that its primary reason for study is not practical, this is a training that is useful in all practical aspects of life, including the Servile Arts. Whatever else it is that one does in life, he will do it better for a liberal arts education, for, if nothing else, he now understands how these activities harmonize with the ultimate purpose of life.

There are many articles and books on the nature of a liberal arts education already at large, and it is the recognition of the importance of the traditional liberal arts education that has led to the establishment of the Great Books programs of many American colleges and universities. I do

---

14. Benedict XVI, *Sacramentum Caritatis,* 35.

not intend to offer a detailed curriculum, which is a topic discussed in many other places.[15] Rather, I wish to emphasize aspects of it that seem to me to be neglected by some commentators. One book devoted to the subject is an exception, Stratford Caldecott's *Beauty for Truth's Sake*.[16] I would recommend very strongly that any who are interested in this subject and have not yet read his book do so. His analysis is valuable in this context for two reasons in particular. First, he explains how an education in beauty was always considered a vital part of both the mathematical and literary studies of a liberal arts education. In doing this he seeks to reconstitute an aspect of traditional wisdom that is not currently present in many modern liberal arts programs. Second, he stresses the importance of teaching this in the light of the modern understanding of the world. It seems to me that in our approach to the modern world and modern Western secular culture, we must add to what is good so that it might be better, rather than seeking to dismantle it altogether. We cannot turn back the clock by trying to either ignore or undo the Enlightenment. We must counter the negative effects of individualism, but not at the expense of the benefits gained from rationality and self-consciousness.

Caldecott emphasizes the points that we have been discussing in this book in regard to an education in beauty. He talks of the study of beautiful prose and poetry to develop the faculty of grasping the whole. He talks also of the point I made in the introduction of the importance of consideration of the *qualitative* aspect of mathematics, that is, its symbolic meaning, as well as the *quantitative*. It is this aspect particularly that I intend to enlarge upon here.

Mathematics and geometry are generally presented today as a form of practical logic. This employs the quantitative aspect, which of course is important, but it neglects this vital aspect of the qualitative. In ignoring the qualitative aspect of number, it is missing an important part of the study of geometry that would have been present in the traditional quadrivium. This is the use of geometry, for example, to reconstruct the order that reflects the patterns and rhythms of divine beauty. This more complete approach is the geometry that would have been put to practical use by the medieval cathedral builders, or by the craftsmen who made the beautiful patterned *cosmati* tiled floors (named after the family that was most famous for making then in the 13th century) such as the Westminster pavement, and which also prepared the mind of the

---

15. I would refer the reader to Dr. Ryan Topping's books on Catholic education and Catholic culture.

16. Stratford Caldecott, *Beauty for Truth's Sake* (Ada: Brazos Press, 2009).

future philosopher or theologian to synthesize all that he learned in the context of the whole body of learning.

If we taught astronomy so that students understood the cosmic symbolism, for example, by relating the patterns of motion of the visible planets to the passage of time—the year, weeks, and months—and how this relates to the seasons and the feasts of the Church's year, then students would learn to see the night sky with even greater wonder and integrate it with their lives, deepening their participation in the liturgy. If in addition to the study of scientific biology or particle physics we consider the beauty of symmetry and harmony that they display, and see how those patterns relate to the mathematics of musical harmony and the patterns of the liturgy, then we are adding something extra to the good work of the modern scientist.[17]

To study Euclid or Ptolemy without developing an appreciation for the beauty of what is seen, which can happen, is to sell our students short. When I taught Euclid, my instructions were to require the students to memorize five proofs for each class, for three classes a week. I was asked to test them by selecting students at random to demonstrate the proofs on the board from memory. This struck me as creating unnecessary work and making the class artificially difficult with little justification, wasting time and memory on things that didn't need to be committed to memory (time that for these students would have been more usefully spent memorizing Latin or Greek vocabulary). This grind of memory work distracted them from focusing on the beauty of what they were learning.

There are different aspects to the beauty of geometry: there is an abstract beauty to the pattern of logic that gradually unfolds as these subjects are studied. There is a visible beauty to it, as well. The proofs are directed towards the actual construction of geometric shapes and examination of their properties, not simply as an academic exercise, but also as a means to the manifestation of sensible forms that reflect the harmony of the cosmic order.

In some ways the students of today are getting the worst of both worlds, ancient and modern. On reflection, I felt that my Euclid class was offering remedial-level math and science (by modern standards) imbued with a false air of profundity by the quaintly archaic Victorian English of the translation; and it fell short of the standards of the past, too, in that it neglected the symbolic element of geometry. It struck me that they would be better going to a modern university and learning

---

17. See the appendix "Liturgical Science."

these subjects in a modern context in such a way that at least they would pick up the *strengths* of modern math and science, if nothing else.

If, however, these subjects (talking now of the whole quadrivium, including geometry) are done well, passing on the strengths of both the quantitative and qualitative components of number, then it will benefit the student enormously. It brings together natural scientist and artist. The modern scientist describes the order of the universe mathematically. The artist describes it visually in conformity to those same mathematical laws, but their conformity is reproduced intuitively. In a single graceful line, the calligrapher and artist combines intuitively and uniquely ellipses, parabolas, hyperbolas, sine waves, and bell curves, each transitioning smoothly into the next. These mathematical functions are the stock-in-trade of the scientist, but the precise combinations used to describe the flowing line that describes a forearm might well be a more accurate reflection of the way that nature is than a precisely drawn mathematical function produced by the scientist.

The ancient is not pitted against the modern here; science is not the enemy to be destroyed by poetry or art. The artist or poet who despises modern science is as limited in his thinking as the scientist who despises the liberal arts. As Newman pointed out, both scientific analysis and poetic (or artistic) synthesis are necessary aspects of human thinking. Our aim, therefore, is to add this ancient wisdom to the modern way of looking at things so that we gain the best of both the ancient and the modern modes of thought while removing the worst.

Developing Creativity

As already mentioned, the study of the *trivium* and the *quadrivium* ought to include, essentially it seems to me, the practice of beauty-in-the-making. We are incarnational and learn by imitation and doing, and ultimately, as this progresses, by the creation of new works. So as part of the study of "music," as well as the theoretical study of harmony and proportion expressed mathematically, the student will create designs for buildings with harmonious proportion and study audible music, first in the performance of music and, finally, for those who are gifted, in its composition. The student should not only analyze geometrically patterned art or the great paintings of the past, but should strive to create works like them. All students can benefit from some experience of trying to do this. In the end, they will focus on those aspects of creativity in the field in which their talents lie. This develops the habit of using the faculty of human creativity and directing it towards the common good. Once developed, this habit can be used in all other aspects of life.

The Higher "Sciences"

After the seven liberal arts, the traditional path in education is to study the higher "sciences," as they are called, philosophy and theology. The word "science" today is most commonly used to refer to the study of the physical world. Traditionally it was used to relate to any field of knowledge or study (including the physical sciences) in which there is a body of truths or facts systematically arranged and showing the operation of general laws. The grasping of these in accordance with wisdom requires the student to employ *both* forms of learning: he must understand and be able to articulate reasoned conclusions—analysis; and he must grasp intuitively the beauty of it—synthesis.

As the student progresses, he will see all that has been done in the past in a new light. It deepens and broadens his natural enjoyment of the contemporary culture. This is recreation. Make no mistake, recreation is important. The enjoyment of these aspects of the culture is important in maintaining, nourishing and strengthening this already-existing faculty, but it is not the main end to which this education is directed.

The study and enjoyment of literature of the wider culture can never be higher than the study of philosophy and theology. Some educators do talk as though the study of the higher sciences is the final preparation for a return to literature, which now reveals more and constitutes the highest "science." To me, this would be like a newly qualified brain surgeon returning to pre-medical studies to see what new insights it will give him. Pre-med studies were good at the appropriate point in the student's education, but at this later stage (unless his purpose is to design or teach a pre-med course for others) focusing on something less when the need is for something greater will be detrimental to his ability as a surgeon. Instead, the newly qualified brain surgeon continues his development by practicing brain surgery. By applying what he has learned in the abstract (including his pre-medical studies) and directing it in love by working to cure the patient, he gathers together all he has learnt at all levels, including the pre-med, and he becomes a better surgeon for it.

The consummation of this Christian training is not a return to anything, but rather the participation in the liturgical life in its broadest sense. The more detailed and the more precise the analytical pursuits of our education, the better the final picture will be, provided that the synthesis is sound. It is in the liturgy that the final synthesis of all knowledge occurs and the picture of the single, simple Truth, the Logos, is assembled. Then one might look back, but in such a way that what preceded it is drawn into the whole picture of the field of study now seen in a new light. When viewed from the hilltop of the liturgy, the education as a whole is seen in a new way, but not such that the hierarchy of learning is inverted. Rather, within this complete picture, each detail is clearer, each color is brighter, the contrast is sharper and the harmony of each in its properly ordered place is more complete. This repeated cycle of exit and return reinforces the hierarchy of learning by clarifying the whole.

Directing Our Creativity to the Common Good

Each of us is called to be creative in a special way and to contribute to the culture. Our formation also, therefore, ought to involve a process of discovery of personal vocation. When we know our own unique path we find that the way opens up before us and we are more effective and fulfilled.

Does everyone need to become a Doctor of Theology? The program we have described could involve many years of study; the study of the liberal arts, culminating in a Master of Arts, then a Doctorate in Philosophy and finally a Doctorate in Theology. I am not, however, suggesting that every person spend ten or more years in higher education before they are capable of participating fully in the liturgy and contributing creatively to the culture.

Not everyone needs such a deep and broad knowledge of theology or philosophy in order to fulfill their personal vocation. Professional theologians, who are contributing creatively to the field of theology, might well need this, but it is not necessary for everyone. All can go through a pattern of education that follows this structure, but in a narrower focus, as appropriate to their personal vocation.

Consider the method of learning to paint icons. The fact that this is a focus on a narrow field of study does not preclude the possibility of penetrating right to its heart. This begins with a joyful appreciation of icons which is deepened, perhaps, through prayer. As the skills of painting are taught, beginning with a process of copying of works of masters in the field, the teacher explains the content of what is being painted. Even within a single class they might learn the principles of compositional design in accordance with traditional proportion, then in simple terms the natural source of these proportions, and finally the theology that justifies their presence in the icon. Almost every class contains in microcosm that dynamic of analysis and synthesis that was described by Newman. All of this is done in accord with the end to which icon-painting is practiced: the creation of a beautiful painting that will draw others to God in accordance with an ideal that is conceived in the mind of the artist.

In the description I have given, the student is taken through each stage in the hierarchy of learning in a single lesson. This principle of taking the student through the hierarchy of learning can be applied as widely or narrowly to a field of study as we wish, and we can do so in many areas of study, as appropriate to different people according to their capacities and interests. Through this principle a reduced program of study for those specializing in any field (for example, in science or engineering) could be developed so that each is ordered to its proper end within a Catholic education.

Always, the student should be aware of how what he is learning is in accord with the end to which all education is directed. Right from the beginning he should be participating in the liturgy (or at least encouraged to do so) and the connection with what is going on in the classroom should be made. If we teachers can't make a connection between the two (even those teaching something such as engineering), we should start to question if this subject ought to be taught at all (or if I am the right teacher). Each new lesson learned by the student, potentially, feeds into his ability to participate in the liturgy even if only indirectly (remembering the connection between the wider culture and the liturgy). This understanding of context is crucial. First, it will motivate the student to learn. Second, it will motivate the teacher to teach well and to order his thoughts properly.

A Liturgical Focus Engenders a Balanced Education, Avoiding Overemphasis of One Aspect Over Another

A repeated focus on the liturgy as source and summit of education helps mitigate against the danger of different modes of learning become competing rather than complementary elements. For example, if we were not careful we might find the poetic form pitched against the prosaic; emotion or intuition pitched against formal logic and reason; mathematics and science pitched against the humanities; the Liberal Arts pitched against the Servile; rather than each being complementary to the other.

If all study is placed in the context of the liturgy, then even if the student's education is cut short he will still have traveled far along the path that points to union with God in those aspects he has studied; it may not be the broad highway, but at least he has forged a narrow and personal path that will lead potentially to the glorious open plain on its summit. It is almost the case that even a single class might cut a path that leads all the way to our final destination, but it will be the narrowest of paths, fragile, and easily disrupted. Subsequent classes broaden, reestablish, and straighten that path so that it is sound and permanent. So, rather than thinking of education as a process of building an edifice, block by block, it is better to think of it as a cord that connects us to

God. That cord starts as a single thread and gradually thickens and multiplies until, strand by strand, it becomes a rope.

Another, traditional example of teaching at all levels quickly is that of the teaching of literature to medieval monks in the study of "grammar" in Greek, *grammatica*, translated into Latin as *litteratura*.

In his book *The Love of Learning and the Desire for God: A Study of Monastic Culture*, Jean Leclercq describes how the classical approach of literature was modified by the monks so that alongside the study of classical literature, right from the start, they would study scripture and the psalms. He tells us first that the Roman pagan Varro gave this definition of grammar in the first century BC and quotes him directly: "The art of grammar, which we call literature, is the science of things said by poets, historians and orators: its principle functions are to write, to read, to understand and to prove."[18] Thus, Leclercq tells us:

> Grammar is the first stage and foundation of general culture and the two synonymous terms *grammaticus* and *literatus* designate a man who "knows how to read"—that is not only how to decipher letters but also how to understand texts. For the Romans of the classical period grammar is a truly logical analysis of the categories of understanding. The procedure is used in connection with texts of the great writers. The analysis and explanation of the authors, above all of poets, is done in connection with and by means of a prepared expressive reading selection. To express a text and make it give up its full meaning by reciting it to oneself is to have understood it. No doubt in St. Benedict's time this method was elementary; its aim was to satisfy immediate needs. It is concerned less with reading the great authors and writing in their style than learning the Bible or at least the psalter, if possible, by heart. During the Merovingian[19] period it was reduced practically to the psalms; and instead of beginning by the grammatical analysis of letters, then of syllables, words, and finally sentences, the child is immediately put in contact with the psalter, in which he learns first to read verses, and then whole psalms. But nothing proves that such was already the case when the *Rule* of St. Benedict was written, and the fact remains that for St. Benedict as for all monastic legislators of his time, the monk was expected to have some knowledge of letters and a certain proficiency in doctrine. In the monastic school, teaching is concerned mainly—but not exclusively—with Scripture and its

18. Jean Leclercq, OSB, *The Love of Learning and the Desire for God: A Study of Monastic Culture* (New York: Fordham University Press, 1982), p. 18.

19. The Merovingians were a dynasty that ruled the geographical area largely corresponding to ancient Gaul for 300 years from the middle of the 5th century, and therefore includes the period in which St. Benedict lived but was largely after his life.

commentaries. Thus the monastic school resembles at once the classical school, because of the traditional method of *grammatica*, and the rabbinical school because of the nature of the text to which this is applied. Furthermore, education is not separated from spiritual effort. Even from this viewpoint, the monastery is truly a school for the service of the Lord.[20]

Tensions within the Liberal Arts

In this next section I will discuss the tensions that are more likely to appear in the provision of a Catholic education when the liturgy is not made central: between dialectic and grammar; between prose and poetry, and finally between the written word and other incarnations of beauty, especially music and visual art. These tensions arise because of different views on the relative importance of each in education.

Dialectic versus Grammar—Scholastic versus Monastic Schools

This tension is described by Leclercq and relates to the study of logic, sometimes called dialectic, which is one of the three liberal arts of the *trivium*. This is at its core the study of the method of ascertaining truth by reasoned discussion or dialogue. As such it requires an understanding of logic and the technical language of logic. The difference arose between two kinds of school, the monastic and the town *scholastic* schools. The word "scholastic" is derived from the Latin word meaning "school" and is applied to distinguish it from the monastic setting. One of the principle methods of teaching in the Schools that distinguished them from the monastic is that of debate—the systematic raising and overcoming of objections.

The monastic schools of the medieval period recognized its value but were suspicious of scholastic Schools, in which some saw a trend in which dialectics dominated to the detriment of the other liberal arts, and especially those concerned with the beautiful expression of what is true and good. As Leclercq puts it,

> The Scholastics were concerned with achieving clarity. Consequently they readily make use of abstract terms, and never hesitate to forge new words which St. Bernard [as an example of an authority from the monastic school] for his part avoids. Not that he refuses to use the philosophical terminology which through Boethius had come down from Aristotle . . . , but for him this terminology is never more than a vocabulary for emergency use and does not supplant the biblical

20. Jean Leclercq, OSB, *The Love of Learning and the Desire for God: A Study of Monastic Culture* (New York: Fordham University Press, 1982), p. 18.

vocabulary. The one he customarily uses remains, like the Bible's, essentially poetic. His language is consistently more literary than that of the School.

This does not imply that Bernard himself does not possess a technical language. There are terms which he and other monastic authors use, as the Fathers formerly before them, to describe with precision experiences and realities for which ordinary language has no exact equivalent. But—and this is one of the problems with monastic theology—these terms, instead of being borrowed from an abstract language forged for the need of the case, are drawn from the language in general use and from a book intended for all: the Bible. It has been said that the element of such very appealing images and descriptives ought not take anyone in . . . we are dealing with real technique, rigorous technique. And in the use of this traditional technical vocabulary there also exists a certain diversity: each monastic author chooses from the Bible and the Fathers his favorite expressions and gives them the shade of meaning he prefers. Within the overall unity there remains a variety which is characteristic of a living culture.[21]

The strength of this great flexibility is a noble accessibility and beauty that open the door and draw in the ordinary reader to receive the wonders described; the weakness is its technical imprecision, allowing the text to become ambiguous and thus leading to a greater possibility of misinterpretation. It is the desire to remove that weakness that led to the development of the precise scholastic language. This had the advantage of opening up a precise discourse that allowed for the development of thought. This has its own beauty, that of the order and symmetry of the underlying truths that it seeks to convey; and it should not be underestimated. But there were disadvantages, too.

The criticism of scholastic discourse is that it is dry, inaccessible to any who have not studied its methods, and leads to a cold, detached understanding of what is true rather than a full knowledge in love. I suggest that this is not inherent to scholasticism, although it is a danger. Another criticism is that scholastics can become so enamored with the process of dialectic itself, and with the authority figures within it, especially Aristotle and St. Thomas, that they might forget the end to which it is directed. When this happens they have greater interest in the power of the method to express truth, and those who said it, than they have in the truth itself. The goal then becomes one of making all truth conform to scholastic descriptions. Things that they cannot express in this way or which have not already been said by the respected authorities are

21. Ibid., p. 201.

rejected, on the assumption that if it can't or hasn't already been said in the scholastic way it can't be true.

Furthermore, it can engender an inflexibility of thought, to the extent that some of those formed scholastically are unable (or perhaps unwilling) to accommodate any form of expression that does not conform to the precise scholastic use of vocabulary. Consequently, they will tend to assume that those whose mode of communication is not precisely scholastic are imprecise in their thinking. This will cause a damaging prejudice against the work of great Fathers of the Church, as well as shut the door on contemporaries whose education is non-scholastic. When this desire to fit everything into a scholastic-shaped box is so strong, the scholastic education has become an impediment to wisdom rather than an aid.

As a general principle, I suggest, the way to avoid extremes of an overemphasis on the poetic form on one hand and an overemphasis on dialectic on the other is to make prayer and the liturgy the central, harmonizing principle of the life of the student and professor alike, whether monastic or scholastic in form. True wisdom, understanding in love, is the goal:

> St. Bernard has stated in a few words that "we search in a worthier manner, we discover with greater facility through prayer than through disputation."[22] The reverence for God's mysteries which characterizes the monks' theology devolves from what St. Benedict calls the reverence of prayer. This is the additional value which is superimposed on the scientific method; it is the source of all understanding and all love.[23]

Even Leclercq, a 20th-century Benedictine monk who for the most part advocates the monastic form of education, acknowledges that where the education is consummated in the liturgy, that the scholastic education is very powerful. Talking of the mendicants Bonaventure and Aquinas, he says:

> They [monks] are no doubt not the only ones to unite speculation with a certain experience of love and so the difference between the scholastic and the monastic milieu must not be too sharply opposed. As later with St. Thomas, St. Bonaventure, and with the greatest of the 12th century masters, a significant role is played by religious experience and knowledge through love, sometimes referred to as wisdom or "philosophy." "The latter," writes Thierry of Chartres, for instance, "is

22. Bernard of Clairvaux, *De Consideratione*, v. 32.
23. Jean Leclercq, OSB, *The Love of Learning and the Desire for God*, p. 211.

love of wisdom, and wisdom is the integral comprehension of truth: without love it cannot be attained or at best barely attained." But altogether the great difference between the theology of the schools and that of the monasteries resides in the importance which the latter accord the experience of the union with God. This experience in the cloister is both the principle and aim of the quest.[24]

Provided that union with God through worship of Him remains the aim of a scholastic form of education, then all will be well there too.

Those seeking to offer a Catholic education today are likely to draw on both the monastic and scholastic influences in offering an education to lay people, and this danger of the two competing against each other is always there. Even in the few Catholic Great Books programs that exist today, we can see how a polarization develops, each tending to favor one or the other—emphasizing the superiority of either St. Bernard's more literary approach on the one hand or a formal Thomistic training on the other. This needn't be so, for to the degree that each is a community with the liturgy at its core these become complementary rather than competitive influences.

Prose or Poetry?

Is poetry inherently superior to prose? Some think so and suspect, therefore, that the scholastic educational approach is deficient. My belief is that clear, elegant, and precise prose is as capable of communicating what is beautiful as powerfully as formally structured poetic form. St. Augustine, for example, was always admired and seen as "the model of artistic prose in which all the procedures used in ancient rhythmical prose were put to the service of his Christian enthusiasm."[25]

It seems that we cannot conclude that one form is always inherently superior to another in every case and for all people; for, if it were so, Holy Scripture would have written exclusively in either prose or poetry. It seems that some truths are best said in prose, some in poetry, and that God in his wisdom chose the form for each truth when inspiring the writers of scripture.[26]

Whatever the means by which it is communicated, prose or poetry, the truth we seek to grasp is the same one. Each of these paths of learning leads potentially and through God's grace to the one highest form of

24. Ibid., p. 212.
25. Ibid., p. 97.
26. Although we note that the Book of Psalms, which contains "all of theology" according to St. Thomas (ironically, the greatest scholastic!), is poetic in form.

knowing, which is the same for each of us, and that is love. And we cannot love anything unless we see the whole and its beauty. Whether or not we are able to do this will depend on our ability to see the whole, that is, to think synthetically. While we might use the poetic language to train the mind to think synthetically, once we have that ability, we do not always need another poet to articulate it for us (save for one poet, that is, the Poet, the Holy Spirit speaking through those inspired texts that He chooses to express poetically.) We are both the scientist who analyses and the poetic thinker who synthesizes and places the parts together in the mind beautifully, each part in right relation to the other.

As an illustration of this, in his little book *Thomas Aquinas and the Liturgy*, David Berger discusses how St. Thomas's precise, scholastic approach, rather than restricting him, enabled him to grasp mystery and so prepared him for a full participation in the liturgy. In this section of text he concludes with a quotation from 20th-century theologian Réginald Garrigou-Lagrange:

> In order to be able to encounter the liturgy in an appropriate manner, man needs a certain sense of mystery. St. Thomas was endowed to a high degree with such a sense and with the ability to communicate it. It is rightly said of him that he feared neither logic nor mystery in any great measure: "It is in fact the precision of his logic that by necessity brings him to perceive mysteries in nature which speak of the creator in their own specific way. And it is precisely this logical perspicacity which enables him to make other far more sublime mysteries powerfully visible: the mysteries of grace and God's inner life which would have remained unknown to us without divine grace."[27]

St. Thomas's analysis is not poetic, but is good and beautiful to the degree that it accurately reflects the particular aspect of the truth he is communicating. If one is to benefit from study of St. Thomas, one must be trained subsequently to be able to synthesize all his analysis in the context of the liturgy. It is an education in beauty, the formation of the person through inculturation as we have described, that trains the mind to do this.

What enabled St. Thomas to synthesize as well as analyze? Perhaps it came naturally to him; but we can say, without even knowing precise details of the form of his early education, that St. Thomas would have said Mass and prayed the Liturgy of the Hours and led a life that was liturgically centered from an early age. Furthermore, he lived at a time

---

27. David Berger, *Thomas Aquinas and the Liturgy* (Washington, DC: Sapientia Press, 2005), p. 48.

when the whole culture was Christian and perhaps the integration of the culture of faith and contemporary culture was as complete as it has ever been. Simply to grow up and live in this environment would have been a powerful education in beauty that would have engendered an ability to synthesize and analyze. We are not so fortunate today. And I suggest that it would be unwise for those who study St. Thomas not to develop the synthetic faculty for seeing the whole picture, so to speak, as well as to think analytically. The *Summa* is a reflection of an analysis by St. Thomas. However well the student understands each part of it, he does not truly grasp its meaning unless he is also able to synthesize and place each item in its true context.

What we have been describing here are three operations of the mind. First is the initial grasping of the object to be known as something that is true, beautiful, and good. Second is the detailed analysis by which we seek to know more of each part of what we know as a whole, up to this point perhaps only dimly. The more detailed this analysis is, the better it is, provided the third operation is present: the act of knowing in love, by which the product of our analysis is reassembled, each part in right relationship to the other. Now we see the whole again, but our love for it is greater because our vision of it is brighter, clearer, more complete. As before, for this last stage we need no other poem or poet to say this for us save for the Poet, God himself, who speaks beautifully (whether prosaically or poetically) to us and for us in a personal encounter within the sacred liturgy.

Primarily a Culture of Language, But Not Only

Each person tends to respond most readily to different aspects of the culture, whether linguistic, musical, or artistic. Inevitably this leads to an overemphasis of the relative importance of the particular field favored by them. Because it is the nature of academia today that education and teaching are book-based, there tends to be a prejudice which says that true study is based upon reading and writing. Make no mistake: language is the central and most important medium, but it should not be overemphasized at the expense of the visual and musical. In the liturgy, the art and the music that accompany the words add another dimension of beauty that raises understanding. This is why sung Mass is the intended norm; it is not simply that a beautiful setting helps with concentration or makes the focus on the language, poetic or prosaic, easier. It adds to our understanding. There are levels of understanding that cannot be said in words alone, that can only be communicated visually or through words when they are sung beautifully. The harmony of forms of the language, music, and art that engages us in the liturgy gives us a deeper understanding than could be given to us by words, music, and art in isolation.

Considering music, St. Augustine describes how it communicates things beyond what words will ever be able to do. What he says is equally applicable to art:

> Will you ever, do you think, offer a perfect performance so that you need know no fear of jarring the perfect listener's ear? This is the way of singing God gives you; do not search for words. You cannot express in words the sentiments which please God: so praise Him with your jubilant singing. This is fine praise of God, when you sing with jubilation. You ask, "What is singing with jubilation?" It means to realize that words are not enough to express what we are singing in our hearts. At the harvest, in the vineyard, whenever men must labor hard, they begin with songs whose words express their joy. But when their joy brims over and words are not enough, they abandon even this coherence and give themselves up to the sheer sound of singing. What is this jubilation, this exultant song? It is the melody that means that our hearts are bursting with feelings that words cannot express. And to whom does this jubilation most belong? Surely to God who is unutterable. And does not unutterable mean what cannot be uttered? If words will not come and you may not remain silent, what else can you do but let the melody soar? What else when the rejoicing heart has now words and the immensity of your joys will not be imprisoned in speech? What else but "sing out with jubilation"?[28]

Just as music can express things that words cannot, so can art. The Catechism tells us that the beauty of sacred art expresses aspects of Truth that are beyond words: the depths of the human heart, the exaltations of the soul, the mystery of God.[29] Also, any good book on holy icons will emphasize this point in regard to sacred imagery.

Not Just for Monks or Mendicants

It would be a mistake to interpret what has been said so far as indicating that the aim of union with God is the preserve of the monks and mendicants, or priests and religious. On the contrary, every person is called, and every person has a community which he can pray for (if not always with) and with which he can lead a life centered on the Mass, and the Liturgy of the Hours if he chooses to follow it. What is proposed here is not necessarily a monastic or even semi-monastic life. It can be the holy

---

28. St. Augustine, *On Psalm* 32, *Sermon* 1, 7–8; quoted in the Office of Readings for the Feast of St Cecilia, November 22.

29. *Catechism of the Catholic Church*, 2500.

lay life that is the calling of most of us. It is a communal life, based upon the communities of which we are part—family, work, recreational. No matter how busy any person is, this life of religious devotion with liturgical piety at its center is a reasonable goal. St. Francis de Sales put it thus:

> The practice of devotion ... makes the care of family peaceful, the love of husband and wife more sincere, the service of one's king more faithful, and every task more pleasant and a joy. It is not only erroneous, but a heresy, to hold that the life in the army, the workshop, the court, or the home is incompatible with devotion.[30]

Some of us may need spiritual guidance to understand how a busy lay life can be permeated with the rhythms of the liturgy in such a way that it lightens the load rather than adds to it, but nevertheless it can be done and is within the capabilities of every single one of us, for it is part of every unique personal vocation. It is worth striving for. It gives us a joy that surpasses the rewards of anything else that is offered to us in this life; and yet is still only a pale version of what is promised to us when we experience it in full, by the grace of God, in the next.

It will not infuse everyday life on any scale until we can make this ascension of Mount Sion part of the little lessons in life as much as the underlying schema for a 10-year graduate and post-graduate education.

What of Those Who Will Not Go
to a Liberal Arts or Great Books College?

Some are not meant to go into tertiary education at all. For these we should ensure that the habits of worship and analysis and synthesis have been ingrained, at some level at least, through their high school education.

Those who are headed for college but who are not literary and incline instead towards the natural sciences will go to colleges that offer majors in these subjects rather than a liberal arts college. There, ideally, they will have a reduced form of liberal arts. This might be a Catholic Studies program that is a slimmer but nevertheless penetrating slice of the program described. It will cover aspects of each of the previously mentioned subjects in such a way that it ensures that the student knows how to integrate the skills he is learning with his Christian vocation.

As well as the study of Catholic culture in general, their education should include the study of the beauty of the best work in their own

---

30. St. Francis de Sales, *Introduction to the Devout Life*, taken from the Office of Readings of his Feast day, January 24th.

field. A civil engineer, for example, might look at Roman aqueducts or the bridges of Brunel or Thomas Telford in England. Even the brick-built sewers of Victorian London, which still serve the city today, have a grace to them that the modern concrete sluice does not; and so this might be brought to the attention of civil engineers.

In medicine, there should be studies in Christian anthropology and consideration of the beauty of the human person through works of art and poetry, both through the study of past masters and the creation of new works.

Even in what might seem to be highly abstracted and dry disciplines such as accountancy,[31] consideration of how a "beautiful business" contributes to the common good and can become a community that adds beauty to society will be beneficial. Those who are going to go into manufacturing can study, perhaps, the beautiful objects that have been mass-produced in the past, for example, 18th-century porcelain and china in England, or even elegant cars.

Catechesis and the Simplest Religious Education

These principles are applicable in the simplest religious education as well, when the hope is to impart the basics of the Faith: when teaching children about the Faith, for example; or catechizing teenagers or adults prior to baptism or confirmation; or, subsequently, any sort of instruction that seeks to deepen the Faith of those who are already Catholics and for which the available time is limited.

We should remember that the liturgy is the most powerful force for catechesis. Therefore, whatever basic information is considered essential should be presented so that it is ordered to the end of teaching the individual to worship God and to increasing his motivation to do so by explaining why the liturgy is central to what is being given to them. This simple approach, I believe, would be the single most powerful way of ensuring that those who have reached this point remain firm in the Faith and that after instruction has finished they continue to develop in the Faith and pass it on to others.

Once we have established our curriculum and what we offer in the classroom, we must go further and consider how we can create a college in which the environment is such that it becomes an educational community. That is the subject for the next chapter.

---

31. With apologies to any accountants who feel that I am unfairly representing their chosen career.

Excursus 1

Teaching Skills of Concentration and Listening

Part of any education should involve, I suggest, the development of skills of communication: oration, recitation, chanting, and the receptive corollaries of these: how to listen and concentrate. One can see quite easily, I feel, how oration, recitation, and chant could be taught, with the latter practiced in liturgical settings. But how does one teach concentration and listening? I suggest that one way would be via the technique of *lectio divina*. (This meditation technique is encouraged for all as part of their spiritual lives, of course.)

Lectio divina is a technique described by St. Benedict in his Rule and presented in a more formalized way, in four stages, in a book called the *Ladder of Monks* written by a 12th-century Carthusian called Guigo II. It is a way of praying with scripture (the words are Latin for "divine reading"). The four stages are termed *lectio, meditatio, oratio*, and *contemplatio. Lectio* is the careful reading of the text. *Meditatio* is a process of actively thinking about what it means and mulling over and developing any thoughts that might occur to you. *Meditatio* is not meditation in the way that many people think of it today, which usually involves an elimination of conscious thought. *Meditate* is another word for "think"; Christian meditation is directed thinking, an active process of conscious thought. The third stage is *oratio*—prayer: generally this means prayer arising from meditation—perhaps a request for help (or at least prayers in which we praise God for giving us this chance to hear his Word). The fourth stage is *contemplatio*: in contrast to *mediatio* this part *is* passive. We are in a state of readiness during which there may be direct communication from God to our spirit, unmediated by the senses; and which only occurs if He should choose it. If so we "see," or experience, God directly unmediated by the senses, through the "eye of the soul," as St. Teresa of Avila describes it. We sit quietly and in the stillness of the moment. The first three stages have prepared us for this receptiveness. Beyond this there is nothing one can do actively to pursue it. Contemplation, therefore, is not a reward or goal of the first three stages well done; rather, it is something that might happen or might not, over which we have very little control. It is, to my knowledge, not common. However, this is not wasted effort by any means should contemplation not occur. The discipline of regular practice of *lectio divina* will develop wisdom through well-directed study of scripture, and will develop a natural habit of attentiveness to God. Furthermore, this preparation of the spirit that takes place in the first three stages of *lectio* will prepare us also for full receptiveness of God's love in our practice of the liturgy, I suggest, where, as discussed earlier, consideration of the spirit is so important.

St. Clare of Assisi developed a very similar technique that involved meditation upon visual imagery rather than scripture, or in conjunction with the reading of scripture or holy works that are linked to the image. This would enable us to meditate on the truths not expressible in words, communicated to the spirit through the beauty of sacred art. For the more fidgety among us, it also would serve to engage the sight or the inner sight (the imagination) during the *contemplatio* stage of *lectio divina.*

Excursus 2

The Principles of a Traditional Artist's Education

This is a traditional artistic training as it might be offered to a student today. It is appropriate both for those who wish to become artists and those who are not training to be artists but wish to develop their capacity to apprehend beauty. This education sets out to train in the practical skills of the art in question. It is for the most part a process of learning by creating in humility. The student follows the directions of a teacher in imitating the work of a past master, or the Master. By requiring the humble following of directions, it tends to increase in the individual an ability to apprehend beauty and to engender a humility that opens him up to inspiration from God.

1. The drawing and painting of works of accepted past masters in the tradition—imitation with understanding.

2. The drawing and painting of nature—studying the work of the Artist.

3. The study of the above should involve not only consideration of how we perceive them with our senses directly, but also developing an understanding of what it is we are looking at. As they draw and paint, the students need to understand the visual vocabulary they are learning and how it relates to a Christian worldview. This will include Christian anthropology. Much of this can be introduced by the teacher in conjunction with the drawing or painting of past works, but it might also mean formal academic study.

4. The study of the *quadrivium*—as an aspect of the seven liberal arts, this is the part that describes beauty mathematically. This would include the practice of creating geometrically patterned art based upon harmonious proportion and "sacred" geometry.

5. Spiritual development. So much of seeing what is beautiful is a response in love. Our ability to love is derived from our love for God. At the core of this is a spirituality centered on the liturgy, which involves the Mass and Divine Office essentially. While it is appropriate to include instruction on the spiritual life, the fruits come from taking this instruction to heart and actually practicing what is taught. But this must be freely assented to; it cannot be forced.

One question that arises from this will be discussed here, and that relates to how we choose which works of Old Masters to study. The objectivity of beauty implies a certain transcendence of time and fashion. To identify works that are worthy of study and imitation as a basis for training, we must look, I suggest, to those artists whose work has by common consent outlived their own time. Fashions and trends do not necessarily point to beauty, and their influence will be greatest in the work of contemporary artists. For this reason, we look—to begin with, at least—at the acknowledged masters of the past.

This is not to say that there are no masters of good modern styles in existence. It is very likely that there are. It is simply saying that the uncertainty involved in identifying them is great because they cannot (by definition, if they are modern) have passed any test of time. It will be difficult, therefore, to obtain the necessary consensus to select, with sufficient confidence, artists of contemporary styles for our core repertoire of masters. I do not see that we lose anything by this, for we do not need to agree upon an exhaustive canon of great art before we can make any progress. We only need enough examples to allow the students to learn what they need to know.

Eventually, in the case of those who wish to be artists, the students or apprentices will become in turn masters of their craft, able to demonstrate the true originality that flows from submission to a reality beyond oneself: to objective truth, goodness and beauty. Once firm foundations in skills and, one hopes, powers of discernment have been laid, the student, inevitably, will begin to follow his intuition and look to incorporate any influences that he judges to be good. These could be from any time, including the present.

4

Art, Grace, Education, and Prodigious Drinking

How a College Can Become an Educational Community

Lord, what love have I unto thy law! All day long is my study in it. Thou, through thy commandments, has made me wiser than mine enemies; for they are ever with me. I have more understanding than my teachers; for thy testimonies are my study. I am wiser than the aged; because I keep thy commandments.

Psalm 118(119):13

PART OF MY ARTISTIC TRAINING involved the study of painting and drawing at a school in Florence, in Italy. I went there to receive a traditional academic training. The "academic method" is named after the art academies of the seventeenth century. The most famous of these was the academy opened by the Carracci brothers, Annibali, Agostino, and Ludivico, in Bologna in 1600. Their method became the basis of art education right through to the last part of the 19th century. This consisted of the study of Old Masters (including the drawing of casts of Greek and Roman statues), traditional proportion and compositional design (sacred geometry), and drawing and painting from nature (including the human figure). Under the influence of the Impressionists the method fell out of favor. By 1900 nearly every school teaching the academic method had closed down, though a few remained in the United States for about 30 years after that.

Within the last 30 years there has been a small but growing re-establishment of the academic method in both Europe and America. The founder of my school was trained by an octogenarian in the 1970s who had studied in Boston about the time of the First World War. By the

time of my attendance there in 2005, there were four schools in existence in Florence, each teaching a similar form of "classical naturalism."

Along with all of the students who attended, I am immensely grateful
for the excellent education in technique and the stylistic elements of
seventeenth-century Baroque naturalism. Despite this, pretty much
everyone at this *atelier* agreed on one thing: although there were some
good contemporary artists, no one in the modern era was producing
work of anything like the quality of the Old Masters (Velazquez was the
standard we aspired to). This realization cast a cloud of pessimism over
Florence. Something seemed to be limiting the standard of the students.
If classical naturalism was to become a mainstream art form again, the
students would have to be getting steadily better and surpassing the
work of their teachers. But it didn't seem to be happening.

The pessimism was exacerbated when one looked at the work done
by the students once they had left these schools. Some were happy doing
precisely what they had been taught. They could make a good living as
society portrait painters, or paint traditional still lives of high-enough
quality to sell in the alternative "realist" art market of the US. There is a
valid place for this sort of art today, in my opinion, but it would never
be the basis of the required "new epiphany." Others who left felt the
need to use what they had learned and develop it. The mark of any truly
living tradition is an evolution of style that nevertheless remains faithful
to the timeless principles that define it. The problem was that no one
seemed to know how to change anything without eroding what we had
learned.

I saw a number of people struggling with this. They might introduce
some exaggerated and expressive brushwork, or some heightened color.
Guided only by their own gut feeling of what was right, they traveled on
their own little personal journey through the artistic styles of the later
centuries: Romanticism, Neo-classicism, Impressionism, Fauvism,
Expressionism. Some settled for a style somewhere along the way, perhaps with an expressionist or a fauvist influence dominating. Others,
sometimes the most talented, knew this was a path that was leading
them to the place that they had sought to escape, and after a struggle
gave up painting altogether in disillusionment. It seemed that whatever
was being given to us contained the same fatal flaw that had allowed the
tradition gradually to decline and then finally to collapse when challenged by Monet *et al.* 100 years before.

How could students break out of this downward spiral?

It seemed to me that there were two things missing in our education.
The first was an understanding of the fact that the style we were learning
was the product of a Christian worldview and could only be understood

once this was accepted. With a few exceptions, the Old Masters, even those who were not conventionally Christian, accepted the worldview that the stylistic elements of Baroque art were developed to communicate.

In my training, there was some acknowledgment of the historical part that Platonic philosophy and the Catholic Church had played in the creation of this style, but it was not presented as the visual representation of a living truth. The atmosphere was essentially secular. The presentation of the tradition was detached from its Christian ethos. This is precisely what had happened in the academies and *ateliers* after the Enlightenment, and it is what made the tradition vulnerable to attack. It is difficult to defend the use of traditional methods if you have no idea why they are good beyond an appeal to respect of the past. It was the Impressionists who despised the past methods who destroyed the *ateliers*, because no one could argue coherently why those methods should be retained.

Grace in Education

The second reason is one that was apparently ignored completely, and yet it is something that is important in all education: the necessity of grace. If Velazquez was the standard we were aiming for, then something must have allowed him to be greater than his own teacher. Perhaps the answer lay not just in Velazquez himself, but in the education he received.

Velazquez's teacher was his father-in-law, a Spaniard named Francisco Pacheco. He published an instruction manual for painters called *El art de la pintura* in 1649. This articulated what an accepted authority on the Baroque, John Rupert Martin, called "the clearest definition of the transcendental significance of Baroque naturalism."[1] Pacheco clearly sees the role of the artist as being to imitate nature in order to bring glory to God. In doing so, he asserts, he will be practicing a virtue. Therefore, the act of painting will serve to lead both artist and those who see the painting to "contemplation of eternal glory, and as it keeps men from vice, so it leads them to the true devotion of God our Lord."[2] In doing this the artist will achieve his principal goal, which is "to achieve a state of grace through the study and practice of his profession."[3]

Velasquez's training was as much an education in humility and apprehension of beauty as an education in skill. It was designed to open him up to any inspiration that God might choose to give him. He was

1. John Rupert Martin, *Baroque* (New York: Harper and Row, 1977), p. 289.
2. Ibid.
3. Ibid.

taught to study nature and the work of recognized masters with self-discipline and under the careful eye of his teacher, who corrected him along the way. But if the process of education were limited to passing the knowledge of the teacher on to the student, then, because no teacher can hope to pass on everything he knows to his pupil, it would necessarily involve a diminution of knowledge. Clearly, in the case of Velasquez something had enabled the pupil to surpass his teacher.

The obvious answer is sheer talent—the genius that enables one person to excel when another cannot. We live in an individualistic age, and the post-Renaissance obsession with artistic genius makes it hard to conceive of any other factor. But talent is a gift from God, and not necessarily the most important element in producing truly great work. Artistic inspiration itself is a gift, as any artist will tell you. The beauty of nature is a gift, when we recognize that all things come from God. The deeper answer, therefore, is grace. Velasquez surpassed Pacheco partly because of how he responded to the grace of God.

Of course, not every great artist is a Christian, or even a virtuous person. God inspires whomsoever he pleases. But when it comes to opening ourselves to the grace of God, participation in the sacramental life of the Church is likely to help dramatically. "All true human art is assimilation to *the* artist, to Christ, to the mind of the Creator. . . . When a man conforms to the measure of the universe, his freedom is not diminished but expanded to a new horizon."[4] I do not know how fervent a believer Velasquez was, but, as part of the court of seventeenth-century Spain, he would at least outwardly have been a Catholic conforming to the liturgy of the Church. Through that liturgy we can become attuned to the deepest of all sources of inspiration.

How the Consideration of Grace Can Affect the Organization and Physical Structure of an Educational Institution

Once one accepts the importance of grace as a factor in the education process, it can affect the design of the curriculum. In fact, it can be a factor in the design of the institution right from the administration through to the layout of the buildings and the living arrangements, not to mention the liturgy. The question that can always be asked is: are we inviting God's grace, or working against it? The college system at Oxford University can be used to illustrate this. Everything was set up so as to create an educational community of teachers and students. This aspect of the community is vital, as we will see.

From the thirteenth century, residential educational institutions were

---

4. Benedict XVI, *The Spirit of the Liturgy* (San Francisco: Ignatius Press, 2001), p. 153.

founded by the new orders of friars, the Dominicans, the Franciscans, and the Carmelites, as well as the older monastic orders such as Benedictines and Cistercians. The community was infused with the rhythm of the heavenly liturgy through participation in the Mass and the Divine Office. The full Office was sung each day, if not by the whole community each time, then by some of its members on behalf of everybody within it.[5] I have seen this same pattern in Dominican communities today.

The liturgy is a source of grace for those who pray it, and in these colleges the whole community would have benefited from living in accordance with a divine rhythm, making the whole greater than the sum of its parts. The sense of a community was reinforced by the practice of communal eating. Eating in community is a quasi-liturgical event echoing the divine banquet at the Mass and the Last Supper which binds together a family as much as a college. It is interesting to note when looking at the colleges of Oxford how much energy was devoted to making the whole college a beautiful place and how nearly as much energy went into making the dining hall beautiful as was used for the chapel.

The library, the place of inspired learning, was also created as a room of beauty. When designing the buildings, it was not left arbitrarily to each architect to come up with something original. The proportions of the building followed traditional ideas of harmony and proportion that created a physical manifestation of the beauty of the cosmos and liturgical principles.[6]

This is more than creating a beautiful environment to sooth the soul. The beauty of the cosmos was considered a physical manifestation of divine wisdom: "Through his own wisdom God is the governor of the universe of things to which he is compared as an artist to his artwork. The pattern of divine wisdom, in so far as all things are created through it, has the character of art, exemplar, or idea."[7] This is consistent with what scripture tells us in the Book of Proverbs: "The Lord by wisdom founded the earth; by understanding he established the heavens; by his knowledge the deeps broke forth, and the clouds drop down the dew."[8] If the man-made environment participates in that pattern of divine wisdom too, then we have an environment that will be a constant influence that educates those who live there whether they are aware of it or not.

5. I am indebted to Rev. Fr. Jerome Bertram of the Oxford Oratory for this and much of this information given in a private tutorial about college life in pre-Reformation Oxford. Any errors that occur are in my note-taking, not his instruction!

6. For a fuller discussion of what these proportions were and the connection with the liturgy, see later chapters.

7. St. Thomas Aquinas, *Summa Theologica*, I-II, 93, 1.

8. Proverbs 1:20, taken from the Office of Readings, Monday wk. 6.

As the University expanded, it did so mainly by the establishment of new colleges, rather than by the growth of existing ones. This meant that it remained a series of communities so limited in size that each was able to pray and eat together regularly. Even after the Reformation in England, the liturgical rhythm continued in Oxford through adherence to daily Anglican offices and services. Daily Mass did not continue unbroken, but as the practice of Catholicism began to be tolerated again in the 18th century and finally legalized in the 19th, the Real Presence in the Eucharist has been there for much of the period since. Even today Matins and Choral Evensong is sung daily in the university and the colleges during term time (even though many students never attend); and students are required to attend formal meals in hall.

The academic year is still organized according to sacred time, just as it was then, and the terms are named accordingly. There are three terms. Michaelmas term begins in the Fall around the time of this feast ("Michaelmas" being the old English name for the Feast of St. Michael the Archangel). There would be a break for the Christmas season. The second term, after Christmas, is Hilary term, named for the Feast of St. Hilary of Poitiers in January. Then there is a break for Easter. After Easter, studies resume again, and the third term is called Trinity term. It is named for Trinity Sunday, the first Sunday after Pentecost. Each term was short, only eight weeks long. (I do not know if this is coincidental, or even if it is both reflective of cosmic beauty and harmony, and liturgically significant in that it represents the Octave.)

Oxford and Cambridge are perhaps unique in Western Europe in retaining to such a large degree both the physical structures and the living patterns and arrangements of a medieval university today. Under the influence of the French Revolution and then Napoleon, the medieval structures of the European universities were removed. The standard in Europe became the German model of a university, subsequently adopted by most US colleges and universities, in which the institution became a single entity, centrally organized, and the subdivision was by department (e.g., mathematics, physics, English literature, and so on); this was for the purposes of administration rather than consideration of what might allow a community to develop. In principle, each department can grow indefinitely, and there might be hundreds of students showing up at giant lecture halls. As each department grows, so does the degree of isolation and anonymity of each student.

How important is the existence of the right environment and of a community to the education process? Isn't it far more important, some might say, to have a well-designed curriculum, good teachers, and students showing up to class and doing their work as required? Surely, one might say, quadrangles and fancy names for the academic year are just minor details that evoke an aura of old-fashioned academia; but they don't actually deliver anything concrete, do they?

It is worth reading the opinion of one who attended Oxford and who wrote extensively on education. John Henry Newman attended Oriel College, Oxford in the early 19th century. He wrote the talks and lectures that are contained, for the most part, in *The Idea of a University* in response to a request from the Bishop of Armagh to create a Catholic University for Ireland. He drew heavily on his Oxford experiences. In his opinion, the right environment would create an educational community in which the students would teach themselves. He was in no doubt that enough of this was present in post-Reformation Oxford to form the leaders and great figures of British history that made the country what it was. This is a long text, but it is worth quoting:

> I protest to you, Gentlemen, that if I had to choose between a so-called University, which dispensed with residence and tutorial superintendence, and gave its degrees to any person who passed an examination in a wide range of subjects, and a University which had no professors or examinations at all, but merely brought a number of young men together for three or four years, and then sent them away as the University of Oxford is said to have done some sixty years since, if I were asked which of these two methods was the better discipline of the intellect,—mind, I do not say which is *morally* the better, for it is plain that compulsory study must be a good and idleness an intolerable mischief,—but if I must determine which of the two courses was the more successful in training, moulding, enlarging the mind, which sent out men the more fitted for their secular duties, which produced better public men, men of the world, men whose names would descend to posterity, I have no hesitation in giving the preference to that University which did nothing, over that which exacted of its members an acquaintance with every science under the sun.
>
> Universities and scholastic establishments, to which I refer,[9] and which did little more than bring together first boys and then youths in large numbers, these institutions, with miserable deformities on the side of morals, with a hollow profession of Christianity, and a heathen code of ethics,—I say, at least they can boast of a succession of heroes and statesmen, of literary men and philosophers, of men conspicuous for great natural virtues, for habits of business, for knowledge of life, for practical judgment, for cultivated tastes, for accomplishments, who

---

9. He is talking here of the Oxford of the latter part of the 18th century before he himself attended.

have made England what it is,—able to subdue the earth, able to domineer over Catholics. . . .

I am not taking into account moral or religious considerations; I am but saying that that youthful community will constitute a whole, it will embody a specific idea, it will represent a doctrine, it will administer a code of conduct, and it will furnish principles of thought and action. It will give birth to a living teaching, which in course of time will take the shape of a self-perpetuating tradition, or a *genius loci*, as it is sometimes called; which haunts the home where it has been born, and which imbues and forms, more or less, and one by one, every individual who is successively brought under its shadow. Thus it is that, independent of direct instruction on the part of Superiors, there is a sort of self-education in the academic institutions of Protestant England; a characteristic tone of thought, a recognized standard of judgment is found in them, which, as developed in the individual who is submitted to it, becomes a twofold source of strength to him, both from the distinct stamp it impresses on his mind, and from the bond of union which it creates between him and others,—effects which are shared by the authorities of the place, for they themselves have been educated in it, and at all times are exposed to the influence of its ethical atmosphere. Here then is a real teaching, whatever be its standards and principles, true or false; and it at least tends towards cultivation of the intellect; it at least recognizes that knowledge is something more than a sort of passive reception of scraps and details; it is a something, and it does a something, which never will issue from the most strenuous efforts of a set of teachers, with no mutual sympathies and no intercommunion, of a set of examiners with no opinions which they dare profess, and with no common principles, who are teaching or questioning a set of youths who do not know them, and do not know each other, on a large number of subjects, different in kind, and connected by no wide philosophy, three times a week, or three times a year, or once in three years, in chill lecture-rooms or on a pompous university.[10]

Newman's assessment, therefore, is that the creation of the community is an immensely powerful force in the development of the intellect of the person (for good or ill), and the strength of Oxford University was that it consisted of a series of such educational communities. This is not an argument for an education with no curriculum, no lectures, no exams, or no moral guidance; rather, he is stressing the importance of creating the right environment for education as a priority. The task, it seems, is to harness the power of the community in such a way that the

10. J.H. Newman, *The Idea of a University*, Discourse VI, 9.

benefits are retained, but where the atmosphere is moral and what is taught is directed towards better ends than the domination of Catholics! Newman's description of the 18th century is consistent in many ways with my own experiences at Oxford in the early 1980s.

I studied Metallurgy and Science of Materials, which is the physics of solid materials. Although I walked from the college to the departmental building, near the University Parks, for lectures and tutorials most days, I didn't consider myself primarily a member of the metallurgy department. My community was my college, St. Edmund Hall. I lived in the college, ate and socialized with the other college members, and played sports for its teams.

From memory, there were about 350 students at the college and only four of them studied Metallurgy. This meant that when I socialized it was with a whole range of people from different subjects—sciences, engineering, humanities, medicine, law, philosophy, and so on.

When I compare my Oxford education with what I have experienced or seen at other institutions, the first difference that strikes me is the volume of work we were required to do. Considering the amount of time I spent studying in comparison with students at Michigan Technological University, where I did my Masters, or Thomas More College, where I now teach, I would estimate that I did somewhere between a third and a half of the amount of work that they do in order to get my degree. I was not the greatest student, I will admit, but I came out with a creditable grade. Also, as I studied science, which was generally more hardworking, there were plenty of people who worked even less than I did. Geography and PPE (Politics, Philosophy, Economics), I remember, were notoriously low-work degrees.

For the most part, nobody checked to see if you attended lectures or not, and my attendance was sporadic. We were expected to hand in three essays every two weeks, which we defended in tutorials. Tutorials consisted of two students and a tutor. The work we did for the tutorials was critiqued, but not graded. There were no end-of-term or even end-of-year exams that counted towards my degree. Provided we maintained a minimum level, we were allowed to stay as part of the university. The only examinations that counted were taken at the end of the three years of your time at Oxford; and, in principle, you could be asked about anything that you had covered in that time. I had six three-hour papers over three days, called "Finals," and the final grade of my degree was based on performance in these exams.

Although the volume of work was low, the degree of difficulty was very high. Quite often I would be given a set of problems to tackle for the next tutorial and at first look I could not do any of them. At this point I would go to my friends who were studying the same subject and we would work together. We taught each other and, between us, we did the best we could. Collaboration between students was not discouraged by our tutors provided you could understand what you had done and could explain your answers to the tutor. I firmly believe that I couldn't have managed at all if I hadn't been allowed to work with others.

For two and a half years, most in my circle of friends (which included three who were eventually awarded First Class Honors) all enjoyed the student life outside the classroom, played sports, and had active social lives. It was great fun. Then, six months away from Finals, I panicked and started to knuckle down and study. From that point on I studied just about all my waking hours, going systematically through every subject I had taken, or was supposed to have taken, over the last three years. When I walked into my Finals I was expected to be able to know all the material that we had covered.

As I revised, I noticed at some point that nearly all of the material could be reduced to a small number of methods of inquiry. Once I noticed this, learning the material became much easier. The questions in the Finals required us to spot those common threads that ran across the different topics. In principle, a single question could ask us about one topic in the first year and relate it to a different topic learned in the third year. As we practiced on past papers, it trained us to look for these lateral connections within the corpus of knowledge. The way I characterized it at the time was that they gave us information at the lecture hall in columns, and then asked us to present it back to them in exams in rows. This was teaching us to think in a particular way that would never have occurred if we had been tested at the end of each class, as is the standard in American universities. We had to understand how each piece of information related to all others within the whole degree. It was forcing us to think synthetically. This generated a habit of lateral thinking that engendered original thought and creativity.

Social Life

When I tell people of my time at Oxford, they expect accounts of prodigious levels of study and hard work, or perhaps of spare time spent in activities that might characterize gentlemanly leisure—cultured soirees consisting of music and poetry recitals, perhaps—rather than the tales of prodigious drinking with which I usually regale them (I am not proud to say). I did attend occasional concerts and plays put on by students, but those are not the abiding fond memories of my time at Oxford, and I don't think they were the most important in my extracurricular education.

What formed me most profoundly was conversation. At the college, in which there was a strong community feel, people used to refer to the "Teddy Hall spirit." This eclectic mix of people passed leisure time together; we talked and joked about just about anything, constantly. If we had pride in connection with this, it was desire to be admired for being witty. The things we talked about were the things that were happening in our lives, and that included the subjects we were learning. The unspoken rule was that you could talk about any topic as long as, somehow, you made it funny and entertaining; or at least interesting and understandable to people who weren't studying the same degree. If you weren't interesting enough, there were plenty of people who were, and you wouldn't hold your audience. It wasn't a nastily competitive environment—it was stimulating, and interesting, and very funny. I loved it. As we joked, there was much that was superficial but, inadvertently, we taught each other about what we were learning in the classroom.

For example, I learned about volcanism of all things by listening to someone who studied geography telling me about it. But he didn't just give me an hour-long tutorial about the subject. My friend told me a long story about how all the geography students in the college had challenged each other to put the phrase "raging inferno" into their essay on the subject ten times without the tutor noticing. In the story he told us afterwards, when he read out his essay at the tutorial everything was flowing quite nicely right up the final paragraph. At this point he had only got through six of the required ten "raging infernos." This meant that his conclusion included the phrase four times. The humor of the story was in his explanation of how he tried to fit them into the flow of the text, and in order for me to understand the joke, he had to explain to me what the technical terminology meant.

In fact, in my circle of friends the social pressure was against graft and obvious participation in high culture; if you did the latter you risked being called a "pseud." It was okay to be clever and good at your subject and even heading for a First (first class honors) but you didn't want to be seen to be trying. Similarly, it was good to be aware of high culture, but if ever you looked as though you were trying to be cultured, it was the greatest social faux pas. So it was permissible to make references to Mozart's operas as incidental information in a story about falling into the river Thames while engaged in some student jape,[11] but to organize an evening recital of Mozart arias or a poetry recital would be considered a dreadful affectation that would cause you to be teased

11. As long you could somehow make the telling of it sound spontaneous and not contrived or rehearsed.

mercilessly. So, secretly, I strove to become cultured in order to partici-pate in the humor of the group.

The essence of humor is to connect two facts in a surprising but nev-ertheless legitimate way. To be funny requires you to think laterally and creatively. Through the attempt (it is for others to judge how successful I was), we were comparing and contrasting all subjects and relating them to each other. In other words, it was teaching us how to think and how to connect all subjects together by searching for unifying themes. In order to do this, we were, again, thinking synthetically and moving beyond the boundaries of the subject we were there to learn. And it was fun!

Everything that Newman says about the lack of a moral compass was true here, too, unfortunately. Eighteen-year-olds are considered adults in England, and (although I didn't really feel like an adult) we were left to entertain ourselves; the college administration had little interest in our moral or religious lives. The was a bar in the front quad, between the chapel and the dining hall; and, as the drinking age in England is eighteen, this was the focal point for social activity . . . or mine at any rate. I didn't go into the chapel once the whole time I was at the college.

We organized all our own social events, such as balls and dinners, to mark any occasion that it seemed to us was worth celebrating. I loved sports, and played for the college third soccer team, the first tennis team, the first hockey team, and the second cricket team if they were short; I was even, believe it or not, selected as traveling reserve for the college second darts team's weekend tour of Cambridge University col-lege bars. Every single team would have its annual dinner, in which we self-importantly dressed up in black tie and invited a speaker (usually another student), who was expected to be entertaining and witty. Din-ner was punctuated with formal toasts and we drank too much. We aspired to be popular enough to be voted in by our peers to run these events, perhaps as club secretary; and we wished to be regarded as entertaining and witty enough to be an invited speaker at dinner of a club of which we were not a member.

The competition for places at Oxford and Cambridge was high. When I went there, only 10% of the population went into tertiary edu-cation at all, and the state not only paid the fees for every single one of them but also gave a grant for living expenses. So no one in Britain who was offered a place would be unable to take it. For those who passed the Oxbridge Entrance Exams, there would be a follow-up interview. We were told that amongst this pool they would always look for people who were likely to contribute to the "college spirit" by being good at relating to others, and who had wide interests, including sports. They felt such students would generate the right sort of educational community.

Final degrees offered were in three classes: a First, which very few obtained; a Second, which perhaps 95 percent obtained; and a Third which, again, very few obtained (you had to do quite badly to get one). The joke was that unless you got either a First or a Third, you had wasted your time at Oxford. The assumption was that if you got a Third it was because you spent huge amounts of time seriously devoted to leisurely pursuits and so participating in the college culture. I don't think anyone seriously advocated aiming for a Third, but the joke reflected a recognition that exams and lectures were not the only formation that was important.

What Can We Learn From This?

My memories of my time at Oxford are very happy. I made firm friendships that still exist. However, I am not presenting this as a model that should be replicated in every detail. My point in passing on these tales is this: even when you have a student with a poor attitude, such as I was, and an educational institution that is just like the Oxford Newman described, non-Catholic and morally dubious, when that institution is an educational *community* it still delivers real results. How much better it would be if the community created had an atmosphere that was both moral and Catholic—with the liturgy and the Mass setting the pattern for the rhythm of life.

I am convinced now that the medieval structures and pattern of living contributed to the culture of community at the Oxford I attended. The beauty of the place opened up our hearts to grace and conviviality in a way that a brutalist concrete dormitory and cafeteria could never do. Even the formal dinners which were the one common social event attended by both faculty and students had the mark of quasi-liturgical activity: the principal and faculty at high table, the students at long bench tables arranged in longitudinal rows. While it might look stiff and intimidating, it was also very practical, for it actually encouraged conversation by ensuring that each person was in close contact with just a few people: your neighbor on either side and three opposite you. (In contrast, circular tables with perhaps eight people sitting at them discourage proper conversation as each person has only two very close, one at each elbow, and can only talk to one at a time, or else has to address the whole table. This encourages the flamboyant storyteller to dominate by addressing the whole table.) After coffee at dinner, those who wished to were permitted to smoke, and the speakers would address the college from the top table.

Also, the impact of the presence of the Liturgy of the Hours in the colleges cannot be underestimated (in some it was a weekly event, in some daily). This is the prayer of community, and when it is taking place all benefit, not just those who attend. I never once went into the chapel of the college the whole time I was at Oxford, but I believe now that the prayer of community was acting to bind us together, all of us, even immoral freeloaders like me.

My impression of the American system where I now work is that generally students are overloaded with a high volume of analytical study that stifles synthetic thought and creativity, to the detriment of a truly Catholic education. There is a deeply held conviction that a good education must involve a high volume of work and that students must be kept busy as much as possible. Furthermore, I wonder how many students, even those who do well because they know and understand what they have been taught, really know *why* they were taught it. It is the why that will tell them how to use what they have learnt.

Those who design the curriculum and the pattern of daily student life should also think carefully about *how* students learn, and especially about the need for grace. I am suggesting that a priority should be given to the creation of an environment which fosters the development of a community with a culture of learning. That culture of learning exists primarily outside the classroom, lecture hall, or tutorial. That is, it happens via the personal interaction of peers.

Creative leisure is not something that can be timetabled into the curriculum for credit, but the workload and class load should not be so large that they mitigate against it. For the most part, it must develop naturally and spontaneously, free from the direct influence of teachers. If I were designing such a college, I would program formal events that involve students and faculties, such as commemorative dinners, but beyond that I would not get too involved in organizing students' social life for them. To my mind, students must not only have time to devote to worship and recreation but also the freedom to decide badly and to waste it if they choose. The college may set boundaries in regard to how the students behave, but I would be less inclined to specify what the students actually do. This is a risk that might worry parents, I realize, for some will not use their time well. But it is how a healthy culture of creativity will emerge.

I side with Newman and say we should create the environment of an educational community first, striving to make it a Catholic environment, and then worry about the structure and content of classes, lectures, exams, and a curriculum, ensuring that whatever form these take, they follow a pattern that is in harmony with that of the culture of the educational community and not in conflict with it.

PART TWO

What Does Such a Culture Look Like?
How the Forms of the Culture Reflect the
Patterns of the Liturgy:
Ordering Time and Space Numerically

5

The Music, Art, and Architecture of the Spheres[1]

He made the moon also to serve in its season, to mark the times and to be an everlasting sign. From the moon comes the sign for the feast days, a light that wanes when it reaches to the full. The month is named for the moon, increasing marvelously in its phases, an instrument of the host on high shining forth in the firmament of heaven.

Sir 42(43)

Wisdom calls aloud in the streets, she raises her voice in the public squares; she calls out at the street corners, she delivers her message at the city gate.

Proverbs 1

MOST CHRISTIAN ART has been, so to speak, "representational." Whether stylized or naturalistic, it has attempted to represent people and material objects in a recognizable fashion. However, Christians are not bound to paint or sculpt representationally. The practice of non-representational art, usually called abstract art, is a perfectly legitimate pursuit for a Christian, provided that truth is not compromised in the process. But what is the relationship to truth implicit in abstract art?

To *abstract* means, literally, to draw out. Abstract art was given its name because it was felt to draw out a truth, the essence of something that is not immediately apparent when looking at it. In fact, to be authentically Christian, any representational art must have a degree of

1. This is a slightly extended and updated version of an article, "The Art of the Spheres: Mathematical Ideals in Christian Art," that first appeared in *Second Spring: International Journal of Faith and Culture,* Issue 8 (2007), ed. Stratford and Leonie Caldecott and Philip and Carol Zaleski.

abstraction. The artist is attempting to show the invisible through visible means.

By the same token, it would be wrong to represent anything that is material by nature and to ignore its materiality altogether. "Truth" in representational art corresponds to its degree of resemblance to a model. We can modify the appearance of things as they are seen in order to reveal metaphysical truths, but it must be a limited modification that does not distort the image beyond the bounds of truth.

Mathematics is an important link between representational and abstract art (including art with a mainly decorative function). The language of mathematics straddles the physical and the metaphysical realms. The number six, for example, can be used to denote a number of material objects—six apples. It also has a scriptural, and so metaphysical, significance—the creation of the world over a period of six days. And we can also conceive of the number six apart from anything else, without applying it to any material objects or investing it with any spiritual significance. The fact that number can be conceived in the abstract and represented visually means that works of art based upon mathematical forms do not contravene the principle of conforming to truth. This provides the key, then, to one type of abstract art that is perfectly legitimate within a Christian milieu—or any milieu where truth is paramount.

The art of geometric pattern generally takes two forms (although most examples of abstract art contain elements of both). First, the representation of number as geometrical shape produces "hard" or "crystalline" works of art—examples of which would include the Islamic tiled patterns of the Alhambra and the Cosmati pavement in Westminster Abbey. Sometimes such designs are created as works of art in themselves, and sometimes as decorative borders around a piece of figurative art (and both forms of abstract art have been a basis for compositional design in figurative art).

The second form is "soft" or "fluid" art. This is calligraphic art—the art of line. As the artist draws, he uses the circular arcs of flexing joints in fingers, elbows, and shoulders to produce parabolas and eccentric curves. These are in fact graphical representations of mathematical functions that describe the order of the natural world. However, the artists who produced these shapes are not necessarily aware of this correspondence. This type of art tends to be more intuitive and less prescriptive than the other.

We see this in Celtic illuminated manuscripts, in Islamic calligraphy and art based on "arabesques," in Chinese characters, and in Baroque scrollwork. The beauty here is derived from an intuitive imitation of the natural order in the shapes of these curves. Baroque scrolls that appear in room decorations, picture borders, and picture frames are very abstracted, but are nevertheless reminiscent of vegetation in the mimicry of growing vines with their twisting line and intertwinings, although this swirling decoration did develop into an overly ornate form in the later period. Unfortunately, it is this excess in the Rococo that in many people's minds typifies the Baroque and causes a negative reaction.

What is commonly described as "Baroque rhythm" is the imposition of eccentric curves and parabolas upon natural form. The sculptures of Bernini, in particular, are crisscrossed with these curves, at times forcefully and deeply applied, at other times as subtle as lacework across its surface. Bernini used them to introduce interest and vitality and to draw attention to particular aspects of form in his sculptures.

We talk about these lines as having a "natural grace." This is an appropriate phrase to use, for it reinforces the fact that God is the ultimate author of all beauty (grace being an undeserved gift from God). It is interesting to note that the production of a graceful line requires a graceful movement in the hand that holds the pen. This movement becomes an art form in itself, as, for example, in dance. It is also, in part, what draws crowds to watch sports and causes a cricket commentator to purr in appreciation when a batsman plays a "graceful" classic off drive!

In painting, it seems to be a general rule that the more naturalistic the rendering, the less will the composition withstand obvious symmetry. So whereas Romanesque art would happily allow an obvious symmetry of placement, the later naturalistic artists sought to conform to the natural order but to incorporate it more subtly, so that the figures do not look as though they had been pushed into what would otherwise appear to be an ill-fitting box. Either they would arrange the figures according to a geometric pattern and then break it up with the use of shadow and dynamic arcs moving in and out of the shapes, or they would arrange figures in natural poses that do not conform to the geometric pattern but then apply secondary forms, such as the impinging lines of shadow, drapery, limbs, and so on to trace the geometry across the surface.

As the production of this flow of line is a rather intuitive process, I will concentrate here on art and design based on geometric shape. After considering why number is seen as significant, I will discuss some numbers and how they relate to the physical, the metaphysical, and the mathematical world that exists apart from these. Finally I will discuss how number has manifested itself in works of art of the past.

The natural order can be described mathematically. Even before the advent of modern science, the ancients were aware of this, as they observed changes and movements of the constellations in the night sky.

Most ancient peoples (Babylonian, Egyptian, Chinese, Indian, Greek, Roman, Mayan, Inca, and Aztec) observed these in great detail. They believed that the celestial bodies and the seasonal changes were controlled by mysterious powers or gods. For Christians, a single God controls all, but the stars and the planets are signs of the rhythms of heaven, to which the material world points.

The focal point for the meeting of the material and the spiritual is in the liturgy. When thought of in this way, all of creation participates in a liturgy of praise to God. The book of Revelation describes the timeless heavenly liturgy; the Mass and Divine Office as prayed by us are an earthly participation in this same liturgy. The physical and the spiritual come together in a single point in the body and blood of Christ, in the Eucharist. Everything else unfolds from this. Creation, through its being, is seen as giving liturgical praise to God. As Erik Peterson writes:

> The worship of the Church is not the liturgy of a human religious society, connected with a particular temple, but worship which pervades the whole universe and in which sun, moon, and all the stars take part.... The Church is no purely human religious society. The angels and saints in heaven belong to her as well. Seen in this light, the Church's worship is no merely human occasion. The angels and the entire universe take part in it.[2]

The Canticle of Daniel,[3] which is chanted in the Divine Office, calls upon all of creation to bless the Lord, including the sun and moon, stars of the heavens, clouds of the sky, showers and rain. How can the conformity of the natural world to the patterns of heaven be interpreted as giving praise to the Lord? This becomes clearer when we consider why God made creation. He made it so that through our perception of it we might come to know Him. Creation is made for us and we have a special place within it. The study of Creation and how we perceive it can provide knowledge of its Creator, and it is, for example, the basis of much of the work of the ancient Greek philosophers on the subject. This knowledge is completed in the Christian Faith by God revealing the full truth to us himself, in the person of Christ. This revelation provides us with those truths that can never be known by reason alone, such as the Trinity, referred to as the "mysteries." Creation speaks to us of the Creator in a way that is perceived at a deep, intuitive, pre-conscious level when we recognize its beauty. When creation speaks to us in this way it

2. Erik Peterson, *The Angels and the Liturgy* (New York: Herder & Herder, 1964), pp. 22, 50.

3. Dan 3:57–88; and Divine Office: Lauds (Morning Prayer) of Sunday Week 1 and all Solemnities, Feasts and Memorials.

"gives praise" to the Lord. It is a praise that we are made to hear, and it directs our praise. As St. Athanasius puts it: "Because an impress of Wisdom has been made in us and is found in all the works of creation, it is natural that the true creative Wisdom should apply to itself what belongs to its impress, and say: 'The Lord created me in His work.'"[4] It is the underlying order of creation, the "impress of Wisdom," that we recognize as beauty.

As a part of God's creation, albeit holding a special place, mankind and the angels give praise through their existence too. But they have free will and the additional capacity to praise God and to offer him thanksgiving through choice. This capacity is something that marks mankind out from the rest of creation, including other animate beings. Man can choose, in cooperation with God's grace, to make any aspect of his work beautiful and graceful and so participate in the "glory of the Lord." In discerning how to harmonize everything from the mundane to his work of praise and gratitude to God—his liturgical activity—with that of heaven, man takes his cue from the cosmos.

This connection between the beauty of creation and our worship has long been understood. Writing in the 5th century, Pope St. Leo the Great, for example, says:

> For every one of us nature is full of instruction that we should worship God. The heavens and the earth, the sea and all within them, proclaim the goodness and the almighty power of their maker. The wonderful beauty of these inferior elements of nature demands that we, intelligent beings, should give thanks to God.[5]

Christian cosmology is the study of the patterns and rhythms of the planets and the stars with the intention of ordering our work and praise to the work and praise of heaven, that is, the heavenly liturgy. The liturgical year of the Church is based upon these natural cycles. The date of Easter, for example, is calculated according to the phases of the moon. The purpose of earthly liturgy, and for that matter all Christian prayer, cannot be understood without grasping its harmony with the heavenly dynamic and the cosmos. The earthly liturgy should evoke a sense of the non-sensible aspect of the liturgy through its dignity and beauty. All our activities within it—kneeling, praying, standing—should be in accordance with the heavenly standard. Likewise, the architecture of the

---

4. St. Athanasius, Or 2, 78–79, taken from the Divine Office: Office of Readings, Wk. 30, Thursday.
5. Pope St. Leo the Great, *Sermon 6 on Lent*, 1; from Office of Readings, Thursday after Ash Wednesday.

church building, as well as the art and music used, should all point us to what lies beyond it and give us a real sense that we are praising God with all of his creation and with the saints and angels in heaven. Pope Benedict XVI is sensitive to this dimension of Christian life, and his little book *The Spirit of the Liturgy* seems devoted to awakening us to this. He discusses the importance of orienting church buildings and the Mass to the East, to face the rising sun, the symbol of the Risen One:

> The cosmic symbol of the rising sun expresses the universality of God above all particular places. . . . But . . . this turning toward the east also signifies that cosmos and saving history belong together. The cosmos is praying with us. It, too, is waiting for redemption. It is precisely this cosmic dimension that is essential to Christian liturgy. It is never performed solely in the self-made world of man. It is always a cosmic liturgy. The theme of creation is embedded in Christian prayer. It loses its grandeur when it forgets this connection.[6]

But why would we want to have a liturgical life at all? One reason, as Leo the Great pointed out, is the desire of believers to worship Him well by giving Him thanks and praise, as an end in itself simply because we love God. Another reason is that if we participate in the liturgy fully, it becomes an ordering principle for the whole of our lives; that is, by participating in an earthly liturgy that is in harmony with heaven, we receive grace that flows through our lives and overflows into the world. The liturgy is a portal that ushers the presence of God into our lives and (through our participation) the lives of others around us.

If we want to increase our collective ability to conform to grace, we should strive to make our liturgy conform to that in heaven. Canon law and the rubrics of the Mass can guide us; they are gifts from God that can guide us so that we can love him more, and open us, and so the world, to the grace of God. And number is an essential part of this, through the rhythmical repetitions of prayers and words, through posture, and in the production of beautiful music, art, and architecture that are "liturgical" even when they have a secular use.

The patterns observed in the cosmos are described using number. The beauty of number is that once its significance has been discerned, that symbolism can transferred, so to speak, and applied to any aspect of our lives through the ordering of time, space, art, and music in accordance with it. This is its special mystery. When we apply the liturgical numbers of the cosmos to the rhythms and actions of our lives extend-

6. Benedict XVI, *The Spirit of the Liturgy* (San Francisco: Ignatius Press, 2000), pp. 70, 76.

ing beyond that part lived in the church building, the whole of life becomes infused with a liturgical rhythm. We can imbue all our activities and work with a heavenly grace and beauty if the application of this symbolism is appropriate to that to which it is applied.

In the sixth century, St. Benedict, the founder of the Benedictine Order, underlined an aspect of "liturgical number" in chapter 16 of his Rule by looking to the Old Testament: "the prophet says: 'Seven times daily I have sung your praises' [Psalm 119:164]. We will cleave to this sacred number if we perform our monastic duties at Lauds, Prime, Tierce, Sext, None, Vespers, and Compline." Man cannot address his attention to prayer constantly, but must attend to the needs of life. These seven occasions of prayer during the day are seven portals through which grace pours into daily life and, to the degree we cooperate, sanctifies the times between prayer by integrating them with the cosmic rhythm of the liturgy.

The Connection with the Mind of the Creator

There are three ways in which one can discern significance in number:

1. Revelation.
2. Observation of the natural world.
3. Consideration of numbers significant in the abstracted world of mathematics.

The second and third are Christian traditions that stem originally from ancient Greece and the philosopher Pythagoras. According to tradition, Pythagoras lived around 550 BC. His ideas were conveyed largely through the works of Plato, especially the *Timaeus*; and through those of Aristotle in works now lost but referred to by later Christian writers, such as Boethius.

The question does arise as to whether or not the symbolism is intrinsic to the number itself. To what degree is there a property of number itself beyond that of indicating how many?

The traditional view, it would seem, is that the symbolism *is* integral to the number in some way. The fact that there are 10 commandments and that the phrase "God said" appears 10 times in the book of Genesis is because 10 is a mathematical archetype for authority that is consistent with the logic of God and for which no other number would do in this precise context.[7]

Having said that, we cannot tell by looking at the number in isolation

7. Cf. Benedict XVI, *In the Beginning* (Grand Rapids: Eerdmans Publishing Company, 1995), Homily 2.

that this is the case. It is not until it is connected to something else, such as commandments, that this aspect of the number is revealed to us. We shouldn't be surprised at this, it seems to me. After all, this is true about the quantitative aspect of number, too. We know what 10 is first, when we are young and learning about mathematics for the first time, because we see 10 apples in a row. Then, as our understanding develops, at some point we are able make a mental leap that allows us to grasp the idea of 10 in the abstract, so that we can conceive of the idea 10 when it doesn't actually have anything to count.

Also, we must not confuse cause with effect. Use of the number 10 does not create an authority which would not otherwise be there—telling somebody to do something 10 times, for example, does not suddenly invoke the divine authority of God. It must a true outward sign of the mathematical archetype that exists in the idea that formed what it is revealing. It is analogous to our use of words as signs, or the outward appearance of any object. In the case of words: if I say that God said something, it doesn't make it true, even though the words "God said" always mean the same thing. If it is not true, I am misusing the words. In regard to the outward appearance: the soul governs the outward appearance of man, but you or I cannot create a man by making something that has the same outward appearance. If I make a sculpture of a man in wax that is perfect in every detail, I still have not created a man but only an image, for there is no human soul present.

When man does do something that has the authority of God, as with the inspired authors of scripture, then it would be appropriate for him to incorporate the number 10 into it in some way, as an outward sign of the underlying truth. And so this is what happened when the writer of Genesis wrote "God said" 10 times. It both reflects accurately the number of times that God spoke and communicates in some additional way the meaning of what He said. In this way the mathematical proportion he assigns it is appropriate, or due, to it. It is by this understanding of due proportion that we make our actions beautiful and true, by conforming to the measure of the universe, which manifests an idea of it in the mind of the Creator.

Pope Benedict XVI discusses how the mathematical ordering of time, space, and matter in conformity to the cosmos in his books *In the Beginning* (where he talks specifically about this aspect of the number 10 in a commentary on the book of Genesis) and the *Spirit of the Liturgy*. He describes how St. Augustine especially deepened the Greek, Pythagorean idea of number.

Anyone who has read the works of St. Augustine will be aware that they are run through with incidental references to number symbolism.

In his *De Musica*,[8] especially in the final section, Book VI, which is gen-erally thought to be the one part written after his conversion to Chris-tianity, he sets out the closest we have, that I am aware of, to an articulation of the basis of this number symbolism for Christians.

Benedict describes how, for the Greeks, the order and beauty of the cosmos presupposed intelligent actions, and how the Greeks personified the stars and connected them to deities:

> For Christians, there was a spontaneous turn at this point from the stellar deities to the choirs of angels that surround God and illumine the universe. Perceiving the "music of the cosmos" thus becomes lis-tening to the song of angels . . . a further step was taken with the help of the Trinitarian faith, faith in the Father, the Logos, and the Pneuma. The mathematics of the universe does not exist by itself, nor, as people now came to see, can it be explained by stellar deities. It has a deeper foundation: the mind of the Creator. It comes from the Logos, in whom, so to speak, the archetypes of the world's order are contained. The Logos, through the Spirit, fashions the material world according to these archetypes. In virtue of his work in creation, the Logos is, therefore, called the "art of God" (ars = techne!). The Logos himself is the great artist, in whom all works of art—the beauty of the universe—have their origin. To sing with the universe means, then, to follow the track of the Logos and to come close to him. All true human art is an assimilation to *the* artist, to Christ, to the mind of the Creator.[9]

So we see that this pattern of the universe is the template for our wor-ship. When we "sing with the universe" we sing with the choirs of angels in the heavenly liturgy. And when our culture participates in that beauty, too, the ordinary activities of life become part of that song of beauty, singing God's praises just as the cosmos does.

The Beauty of the Cosmos and the Beauty of God

An artist who seeks to tap into a creativity that draws on the beauty of the cosmos could do well to take the last point made by the Holy Father to heart. It is hard to see how any artist can truly reunite his art with the principle of liturgical number and, ultimately, all beauty if he is not himself living a life infused with liturgical rhythm so that his soul is conforming to that pattern. Abbot Suger, who built St. Denis, the first Gothic church, in France in the 12th century, said as much when he described the process of the design and creation of the building. He

---

8. This can be found in *The Fathers of the Church, Volume IV* (1947; reprt. Washing-ton, DC: Catholic University Press, 2002).

9. Pope Benedict XVI, *The Spirit of the Liturgy*, pp. 152–4.

drew on the theology of Dionysius the Areopagite as received through the works of John Scotus Erigena and Maximus the Confessor. As Otto von Simson wrote, Suger believed that

> the mystical vision of harmony can become an ordering principle for the artist only if it has first taken possession of his soul and become the ordering principle of all its faculties and aspiration. . . . For Suger, as to his master St. Augustine, this process is not so much the physical labour as it is the gradual edification of those who take part in the building, the illumination of their souls by the vision of divine harmony that is then reflected in the material work of art.[10]

For Catholics, the act of conformity starts with the Mass and the Divine Office. From that foundation in Christ, we may begin to integrate all the other aspects of life. Underlying this argument is the assumption that the cosmos is beautiful; and the beauty that it possesses points to an even purer beauty, the heavenly beauty, and ultimately to Beauty itself, God.

Octaves in Music, Liturgy— Tracing a Helical Path through Sacred Time

One example that illustrates clearly how beauty can connect the cosmos to the liturgy and then become a principle for ordering everyday life is the octave. Most will be aware of the octave connected to the musical scale. In the Introduction to this book we described how, starting with the Pythagoreans, the octave, the perfect fifth and the perfect fourth were considered important (and expressed by the numerical ratios of 1:2, 2:3 and 3:4 respectively).

Imagine plonking notes out on a piano. If we start on any note—for example, middle C—and then move up the white notes on the piano, we follow a major scale, and after seven notes we hit B. The eighth note is C again. Because this is the eighth note, the cycle is called an octave. The octave note is simultaneously the last note of the first octave and first note in the next. It is an amazing thing to me that by taking a series of steps so that each note is higher in pitch than the last, we get to a note that is different, in that it is higher, but the same in that it has the same quality of tone, which we call C (the same applying to any other tonic). This perception of the sameness of the note is purely the product of how people process the information sent to the intellect from the eardrum. The "mind's ear," so to speak, hears a consonant relationship between

10. Otto von Simson, *The Gothic Cathedral* (New York: Harper and Row, 1964), p.126.

the two notes. There is nothing in the physics of music that tells us that it will sound like this, or even that these two ought to go together in any way. Certainly, we can look at the relative frequencies and wavelengths of octave notes and find that they are always in the ratio 1:2; but there is nothing in physics that says that this should make the two notes we are describing sound as though they ought to be related to each other as they are. When the two notes are played together, it creates a harmonious relationship, and everyone hears it.

Even though the notes are set on a piano so that you move up a linear scale as you move higher, it might be more relevant to think of a musical scale as following a helical path. At each step of a note, we move along a bit, and we change direction a bit, and we move up a bit, like following the thread in a screw. After eight steps we have gone full circle, but the eighth has moved upwards a distance of the pitch of the thread (it is interesting to note that the description of screw threads uses a musical analogy of pitch!). Music, when viewed like this, follows a helical path upwards. At any point, directly below is a note that is eight behind it in the scale; and directly above is a note that is eight steps further on.

If there were not a general consensus that an aural relationship existed between notes eight steps apart, then we could not define an octave in such a way. It relies on this consensus for its force. Furthermore, it doesn't matter what society or culture we come from: all hear this similarity. (As we will discover, the octave is not the only one of a number of fundamental relationships in the scale for which there is a consensus of consonance.)

It seems that God made us to hear it in this way, but why? The traditional approach to understanding this is to see beauty as a signpost to direct us to what is good. Where there is a consonant relationship that can be discerned as a numerical relationship, it can also be a way of ordering our lives so that what we do is in harmony with what is good and the pattern of our lives is beautiful and good too. Then the activity of our very lives points others to God, too.

Consider now the cycle of time. Because of the biblical description from Genesis, we order time according to cycles of seven days in a week. But, in fact, this follows the same pattern as the octave in music. The eighth day is simultaneously the first day of one week and the final day of the last, and has the same name. We go from Sunday to Sunday, for example, and if you include both Sundays you have an octave cycle. When we consider the passage of time, we do not feel that we are starting the same week again. We have moved forward in time and so are starting a new, fresh week. The helical passage through time, day by day, mimics the helical motion up the musical scale, note by note.

The week as a cycle by which we order our lives is, of course, also the cycle by which we order our worship. This traditional recognition of the importance of cycles of worship to the human person may not be so widespread now; but, nevertheless, even in these secular times, we still follow a seven-day week. If it were not natural to do so, one would assume that by now someone would have suggested a new metric week to go along with the meter and the kilogram. There is a cosmic reinforcement here. The seven-day week fits nicely into the monthly cycle, which ties into the phases of the moon and ultimately the passage of the earth around the sun which defines the year. It is not a perfect fit (hence we have months of differing lengths, and even a longer year every four years) but we can conclude that it is still close enough to work well as a way of ordering our time. This suggests that the natural human cycle is the same as the natural cosmic cycle.

The octave is an even stronger ordering principle in the liturgical cycles. The so-called eighth day of creation, which symbolizes the incarnation, passion, and death of Christ, culminating in his resurrection on Sunday, is simultaneously the eighth and first days of the week. Eight, expressed as "7 + 1," is a strong governing factor in the Church's earthly liturgy. Sunday, the day of the Mass, is simultaneously the first day of the new seven-day week and the liberating eighth day of the previous week. It is the eighth day of the week that represents the new freedom from death through Christ. Without Christ, the passage of time could be represented by a self-enclosed weekly cycle sitting in a plane. The eighth day represents a vector shift at 90° to the plane of the circle that operates in combination with the first day of the new week. The horizontal circular motion is temporal, the vertical motion is supernatural. It demonstrates in earthly terms that a new dimension is accessed through each cycle of our participation in a temporal, liturgical seven-day week. This way time can be envisaged as a helix taking us forward to our heavenly destiny.

The 7+1 liturgical form operates in the Divine Office as well. For the psalmist, as quoted by St. Benedict in Chapter 16 of his Rule, says:

> As the Prophet said: "Seven times a day I have given praise to Thee" [Ps 118(119):164], this sacred sevenfold number will be fulfilled by us in this way if we perform the duties of our service at the time of Lauds, Prime, Tierce, Sext, None, Vespers, and Compline; because it was of these day-hours that he hath said: "Seven times a day I have given praise to Thee." For the same Prophet saith of the night watches: "At midnight I arose to confess to Thee" [Ps 118(119):62]. At these times, therefore, let us offer praise to our Creator "for the judgments of His justice"; namely,

at Lauds, Prime, Tierce, Sext, None, Vespers, and Compline; and let us rise at night to praise Him.[11]

The night office, Matins, is the eighth, sung in conjunction with the seven daytime Hours (in practice, many communities run Matins and Lauds together). This could be seen as paralleling the running together of the eighth and first days in the weekly cycle of the liturgy. Eight appears in the liturgy in the octaves, the eight-day observances, of Easter and Christmas. These are eight days of Eighth Days. They represent an overflowing of grace from these major feast days. So we can think of the passage of sacred time as a helix within a helix. There is a daily cycle sitting on a weekly cycle.

In fact, it runs more deeply than this, for there is too an annual cycle. Within the course of the year, Easter day is the central day, the Sunday of Sundays that takes one year forward into the supernatural and into a new, fresh period of sacred time. This is why we never complete the liturgy of the Church. Each year is fresh and new, taking each of us forward deeper into the heavenly dimension on our pilgrimage to heaven. In his book the *Wellspring of Worship*,[12] Jean Corbon describes how there is a seven-week approach to Easter, in Lent, and so Easter Week is the eighth week of eight weeks; Easter Week is then followed by the season of Pentecost. Pentecost is so named because it is 50 days long, that is, seven weeks or 49 days, plus an eighth Sunday to complete the final week.

Even within the structure of the texts of the liturgy, this pattern of seven and eight, the old and the new covenant, appears. In his commentary on the Psalms, St. Thomas Aquinas tells us that the book of Psalms is universal, for it contains the general principles of the whole of theology; and, quoting the ancient Eastern Father Dionysius the Areopagite, he tells us that this is why the book is especially suited to the liturgy. Then he goes on to say that there are 150 psalms because 150 is the sum of 70 and 80. Seventy comes from the number seven, which represents the old covenant, and 80 comes from the number eight, which represents the new covenant. As with the weeks before and after Easter in the seasons of Lent and Pentecost, this 7:8 ratio describes faithful anticipation followed by fulfillment.

In the Lord's Prayer, as given to us in the Gospel of Matthew, there are seven petitions. The first three relate to God and the last three relate to man. The seventh, which is fourth in order—"give us this day our

---

11. *The Rule of St. Benedict*, Ch. 16.
12. Jean Corbon, *Wellspring of Worship* (San Francisco: Ignatius Press, 2005).

daily bread"—relates to both God and man. It relates to man because it asks for food to sustain us physically, and it relates to God because it refers to the Eucharist under the appearance of bread. In this way, it is simultaneously the seventh and the eighth. We are told in the Catechism that the Our Father is not only the highest prayer, but is essentially liturgical. According to the apostolic tradition, the Lord's Prayer is essentially rooted in liturgical prayer:

> [The Lord] teaches us to make prayer in common for all our brethren. For he did not say "my Father" who art in heaven, but "our" Father, offering petitions for the common body. In all the liturgical traditions, the Lord's Prayer is an integral part of the major hours of the Divine Office.[13]

The Contribution of St. Boethius to the Tradition

The Church Father who is credited, along with Augustine, with bringing these ideas into Christian thought is a Catholic martyr, canonized as St. Severinus Boethius, but usually known simply as Boethius. Pope Benedict XVI made a special point of drawing our attention to Boethius in a general audience in Rome on March 12th, 2008. Boethius was born in Rome in about 480. As the Holy Father described, he was recognized as a brilliant scholar at an early age; he wrote manuals on arithmetic, geometry, music, and astronomy, the four liberal arts of a traditional education in the *quadrivium*. The manual on arithmetic and part of that on music survive. He used the categories of Greek philosophy to present the Christian faith, seeking a synthesis between the Hellenistic-Roman heritage and the Gospel message. Boethius has been described as both the last representative of ancient Roman culture and the first of the Medieval intellectuals. His most famous work is *De Consolatione Philosophiae* (*The Consolation of Philosophy*), written while he was in prison to help explain his unjust detention at the hands of the Ostrogothic Emperor Theodoric. In this work he draws extensively, though not exclusively, on the philosophy behind the *quadrivium*. His insight in applying the lessons of the study of something as abstract as arithmetic to the practical considerations of life—and adversity that, please God, few of us will have to face—can only be marveled at. Boethius was executed on October 23rd, 524. The date of his martyrdom is commemorated as his feast.

The influence of Boethius's work lasted well beyond his life. For example, his works are seminal in the rise of the 12th-century schools,

---

13. *Catechism of the Catholic Church*, 2768, quoting a homily of St. John Chrysostom.

especially that of Chartres. Dante, who structured his work according to number symbolism, read him.[14] Geoffrey Chaucer translated his work into Middle English, and thereafter he structured his literary works, including *Troilus and Creseyde* and *The Knight's Tale*, around the ideas that Boethius had proposed.[15] More recently, C.S. Lewis in *The Discarded Image* listed the *Consolation* as one of the few volumes that shaped his philosophy of life.[16] It has recently been proposed, and broadly accepted, that a unifying principle of Lewis's seven chronicles of Narnia is Christian cosmology.[17]

The reason for incorporating a Christian cosmology in these works is deeper than a superficial desire to conform to an ancient symbolism that only a few would recognize. The assumption is that human beings are hardwired to pick up information presented in accordance with the pattern of the divine mind. Nature appears beautiful because we recognize in it the thumbprint of the Creator who fashioned it. When the work of man is structured in the same way, we see the mark of inspiration from the Creator and we are drawn to it. This can occur at different levels. If the dimensions of the page of a book and the print within it conform to these proportions, then the eye finds it easier to take the information in. If the dramatic structure of the story being told within it conforms also to this divine model, then the author can decide to place the moments of high drama within the structure in such a way that they will have an even greater impact than the narrative alone would give. Lewis himself refused to explain these structures of his stories, although it is known that he employed them, saying that they should work for the story without the reader being aware that they are there.

For both Augustine and Boethius, number and due proportion—the appropriate and harmonious arrangement of the parts within something—hold a special key to the order of heaven and ultimately the "mind of the Creator."

Mathematics might be described as the science of pattern. As already mentioned, philosophically it is seen as a stepping stone that leads the mind to contemplation of the spiritual because it can be considered as a descriptor of the material world; and it can be conceived in the abstract without application to physical quantities in its own "world" of mathe-

14. Cf. Henry Chadwick, *Boethius: The Consolations of Music, Logic, Theology and Philosophy* (Oxford: Clarendon Press, 1990), pp. 223, 252.

15. Cf. P.G. Walsh, *Consolation of Philosophy* (Oxford: Oxford University Press, 1999), Introduction, p. xlvii

16. Cf. Ibid, p. 1.

17. Cf. Michael Ward, *Planet Narnia: The Seven Heavens in the Imagination of C.S. Lewis* (Oxford: Oxford University Press, 2008).

matics. Modern science makes use of its power to quantify. The ancients saw this, too, but they took it further. They equated sensible beauty (that is, beauty as perceived through the senses) with the symmetry and harmony of relationships in the non-sensible mathematical world. So for the ancients a beautiful harmony in music reflected a harmonious mathematical relationship (derived from the consideration of the relative lengths of string that produced the notes when plucked).

Number Reflecting Hierarchy in Creation

Many modern mathematicians see a beauty in the form of a perfect mathematical solution to a problem, regardless of whether or not it has a material application. The Church Fathers equated this with a natural hierarchy, consistent with the hierarchy of God's creation: the more perfect the symmetry or harmony in the relationship, the more beautiful. So this gave rise to special regard for certain numbers and certain mathematical relationships. This was confirmed for them by the fact that the writers of the Bible consistently highlight the number of days, the dimensions of buildings, the number of repetitions of acts. As God's revelation, the Bible can be considered an independent and authoritative source of significant numbers. These "governing" numbers could be used to classify and order the observed patterns in the universe. Indeed, the view was taken that the Bible could not be interpreted properly without knowledge of the hierarchical nature of number. St. Augustine wrote:

> An unfamiliarity with numbers makes unintelligible many things that are said figuratively and mystically in scripture. An intelligent intellect, if I may put it thus, cannot fail to be intrigued by the meaning of the fact that Moses and Elijah and the Lord himself fasted 40 days. The knotty problem of the figurative significance of this event cannot be solved except by understanding and considering the number, which is four times 10, and signifies the knowledge of all things woven into the temporal order. The courses of the day and the year are based on the number four: the day is divided into the hours of morning, afternoon, evening and night; the year into months of the spring, summer, autumn and winter. While we live in the temporal order, we must fast and abstain from the enjoyment of what is temporal for the sake of eternity in which we desire to live, but it is actually the passage of time by which the lesson of despising the temporal and seeking the eternal is brought home to us. Then the number 10 signifies the knowledge of the Creator and creation: the Trinity is the number of the Creator, while the number seven symbolizes the creation because it represents life and the body. The former has three elements (hence the precept

that God must be loved with the whole heart, the whole soul, and the whole mind [Matt 22:37]); and as for the body, the four elements of which it consists are perfectly obvious [fire, earth, water, air]. To live soberly according to the significance of number 10—conveyed to us temporally (hence multiplied by the number four)—and abstain from the pleasures of the world; this is the significance of the 40-day fast. This is enjoined by the law, as represented by Moses; by prophecy, as represented by Elijah; and by the Lord himself, who to symbolize that he enjoyed the testimony of law and the prophets, shone out in the midst of them on the mountain as the three amazed disciples looked on [Matt 17:1-8; Mark 9:2–6].[18]

Even though Augustine describes at length the root of the significance of the number 40 in the 40-day fast, he still assumes an acquaintance with the basic ideas of significant number beyond that of most modern readers! As we have seen, he is using the same number symbolism for 10 as that used by Benedict XVI in his interpretation of Genesis.

Does Modern Science Clash with the Ancient Symbolism?

The reader might assume that modern science has undermined the principle of symbolic number as understood by the Church Fathers. In fact, I am not aware of any situation where this is the case—if anything, it has reinforced it (see the appendix on Liturgical Science for an example). It is important that we do not ignore modern science. If sacred number is to be a truly living tradition it must be responsive and ready to adapt to what is known to be true at any particular time.

Sometimes, increased knowledge might lead to an adaptation of what was described without destroying the fundamental idea. Taking just one example: the four "elements" mentioned by St. Augustine are described also by Aristotle. The modern scientist, when considering the word "elements," would look to the periodic table and see more than four and so, perhaps, reject the significance of the number four as constituting the material world. But if one takes "element" to mean "fundamental part," then all matter might still be reduced to the four states, as best as the ancients were able to describe them, in Aristotle's four elements, in the form of solid, liquid, gas, and energy (or perhaps plasma).

A demonstration of how the symbolism is intrinsic to the number itself quite apart from whatever it is attached to is in the number six. Six has significance in arithmetic because it is a "perfect number." A perfect number is one that is numerically equal to the sum of its aliquot parts. The aliquots of six are those numbers that can be multiplied by a whole

---

18. St. Augustine, *On Christian Teaching*, Book 2, XVI, 24–25.

number to give six. The aliquot parts of six are 1, 2, and 3. Six is perfect because it is the sum of 1, 2, and 3. It has a higher degree of perfection in that it is also the product of 1, 2, and 3. It is both the product and the sum of its aliquot parts. Perfect numbers are rare; the next perfect number is 28, and then there is no other until 496, after which the next is 8,128. The number six has biblical significance as well, because the work of creation was carried out in six working days. St. Augustine notes the connection between the two and sees the arithmetic principle as the governing principle. In the *City of God*, he says: "Six is a number that is perfect in itself, and not because God created the world in six days: rather the contrary is true. God created the world in six days because this number is perfect, and it would remain perfect, even if the work of the six days did not exist."[19]

Invoking six does not cause the perfection. If I make something in six actions it does not make it perfect. God is the cause of the perfection of the world he created. However, six is the mathematical archetype of that perfection and so it is appropriate that the act of creation should be in conformity to it and reflect the *quality* of six.

Beauty and Love

There is an even deeper meaning of that "meaningful inner order" referred to by Pope Benedict XVI. For the Christian it is Love, or God— the two are the same. The poem in Book II of Boethius's *Consolation of Philosophy* is worth quoting. It describes how this ordering principle of harmony of both heaven and earth can be identified with the ordering principle of harmonious relationships, pure love—"Love"—that is God:

> *Why does the world with steadfast faith*
> *Harmonious changes put in train?*
> *Why do the ever warring seeds*
> *Eternal treaties yet maintain?*
>
> *Why does the sun in golden car*
> *Inaugurate the rose-red day?*
> *Appoint the moon to rule the night*
> *Once Hesperus[20] has led the way?*
>
> *And greedy sea confine its waves*
> *Within the boundaries it has set*

19. St. Augustine, *City of God*, Book XI, Ch. 30.
20. Hesperus is the Evening Star and Morning Star, Venus. In Christian cosmology, Venus is the symbol of the Mother of God, referred to, for example, in the Litany of Loreto.

Forbidding the encroaching lands
Extend the coastline further yet?

The power that contains this chain
Of nature's orderings is Love.
Love governs lands and seas alike
Love orders to the heavens above.

Should Love once slacken tight its rein
And cease to order near and far
The mutual love which all things show
Will in a moment turn to war.

With beauteous motions Nature's parts
In fond compact invigorate
The fabric of the universe
Which else they'd strive to dissipate.

Such love embraces nations too;
In hallowed pacts it them combines
With chaste affections man and wife
In solemn wedlock it entwines.

Love's laws most trusty comrades bind
How happy is the human race,
If Love by which the heavens are ruled,
To rule men's minds is set in place!

When we apprehend beauty, it stirs in us that which causes us to love. When they spoke of love, the Fathers were not referring so much to a feeling or emotion (although these are not unconnected), as to the inclination to act on behalf of others before oneself. A true loving relationship is one of mutual self-sacrifice rather than the alignment of self-interest. As well as defining the covenantal relationship with God, it applies to all human interaction, such as the love of a child by a parent, or even the service a public servant might give to the community. Romantic love, as we might term it, can be true love too, if directed towards the good of the other rather than the possession of the other for pleasure. Human love has no power or meaning if it is not intimately connected with our love for God and, more importantly, His love for us. God's love for us is already there, constant and unmoving. When mankind loves, one might describe rightly ordered love as free will in harmony with God's will.

Moral and Spiritual Beauty Reflects the Same Order

The principle of beauty relates as much to abstract principles of truth as it does to the proportions of a beautiful building. This leads to the idea that a good life is also a beautiful life for its possession of spiritual and moral beauty. The abstract world of arithmetic is seen as a stepping stone for the mind in its contemplation and grasping of morality. The mind that is formed through a good education in the symmetry and beauty of number is more likely to reach instinctively for objective moral truth because it will be attracted by its beauty as conceived in the mind.

There is a numerical symbolism running through the Church's presentation of the spiritual life. We have mentioned some instances already in the ordering of her liturgy, but we have also, for example, seven sacraments, seven deadly sins, and seven gifts of the Holy Spirit. The seven cardinal virtues can be divided into those revealed by God to St. Paul (1 Cor 13:13) and transmitted through scripture (faith, hope, and love), known as the theological virtues, and those deduced by reason after observation of the natural world (fortitude, prudence, temperance, and justice) and described by Plato in his *Republic*. This follows a common division of seven into three and four, where three corresponds to the spiritual or heavenly (and is indeed the number of the Trinity) and four corresponds to the earthly (characterized by the four rivers in Genesis taking water to the four corners of the world, just as the four evangelists, through the four Gospels, take the good news to the four corners of the world). The sum, seven, is the number of God's covenant with us and so it points to his love for us (we discuss this further later).

Catholic artists manifest these geometrically in the design of their paintings. Raphael, for example, in his *Transfiguration*, has the "heavenly" trio of the Christ and the two prophets arranged within a triangle, which is the geometric form of three, above the figures of the earthly onlookers, whose limbs and shadows trace out the shape of a square, the geometric form of four (though less easily discernible).

Consider another example of how numerical relationships can symbolize the moral life: in his *De Arithmetica*, Boethius's discussion of perfect numbers is not limited to how they are defined arithmetically; he says that they are significant in the spiritual life also:

> Concerning the generation of these in perfect number; there is in these great similarity to the virtues and vices. You find perfect numbers rarely, you may enumerate them easily and they are produced in very regular order. But you find superfluous or diminished numbers [those in which the sum of the aliquot parts is greater or less than the number itself] to be many and infinite and not disposed to any order.[21]

21. Boethius, *De Arithmetica*, Book 1, Chapter 20. This can be found in: Michael Masi, *Boethian Number Theory: A Translation of the De Institutione Arithmetica* (New York: Rodopi, 2006).

In these it seems he is drawing on Aristotle's idea of virtue as a mean between two extremes, in particular in Book II, Chapter 6, where Boethius says:

> Therefore virtue is a kind of mean, since, as we have seen, it aims at what is intermediate. Again it is possible to fail in many ways (for evil belongs to the class of the unlimited as the Pythagoreans conjectured, the good to that of the limited), while to succeed is possible only in one way (for which reason also one is easy and the other difficult—to miss the mark easy, to hit it difficult); for these reasons also, then, excess and defect are characteristic of vice, and the mean of virtue; for men are good in one way, but bad in many.[22]

Beauty: Why Bother?

This is all very well, one might ask, but why should I even seek to conform my life and work to the underlying harmony of heaven? The answer is that, with its consummation in the liturgy, it directs us on a path that leads to God. This is a joyful passage with a joyful end beyond our imagining. We find this message in another great Christian writer, whose writings, as much as Augustine's, are full of references to the beauty of creation and to number symbolism, the great Franciscan St. Bonaventure:

> Since therefore, all things are beautiful and to some measure pleasing; and [since] there is no beauty and pleasure without proportion, and proportion is to be found primarily in numbers; all things must have numerical proportion. Consequently, number is the principal exemplar in the mind of the Creator and as such it is the principal trace that, in things, leads to wisdom. Since this trace is extremely clear to all and is closest to God, it leads us to Him through the seven differences[23] and it causes us to know Him in all corporeal and sensible things; and while we learn that things have numerical proportion, we take pleasure in this numerical proportion and we judge things irrefutably by virtue of the laws that govern it.[24]

I shall give the last word on this matter to Pope Benedict XVI; in his address at Bagnoregio, Italy, on September 6th, 2009, speaking of St. Bonaventure, he said:

---

22. Boethius, *De Arithmetica*, Book 2, Chapter 6. This can be found in: Michael Masi, *Boethian Number Theory: A Translation of the De Institutione Arithmetica* (New York: Rodopi, 2006).

23. In his *Itinerarium*, Bonaventure classifies numbers in seven categories ("differences") that stimulate us in different ways, all playing their part in our journey to God.

24. St. Bonaventure, *Itinerarium mentis in Deum*, II, 7.

In addition to being a seeker of God, St. Bonaventure was a seraphic singer of creation who, following St. Francis, learned to "praise God in all and through all creatures," in which "shine the omnipotence, wisdom and goodness of the Creator" (*Itinerarium Mentis in Deum* [*The Journey of the Mind to God*], I, 10). St. Bonaventure presents a positive vision of the world, gift of God's love to men: He recognizes in it the reflection of the highest Goodness and Beauty that, following St. Augustine and St. Francis, assures us that it is God himself. God has given it all to us. From him, as original source, flow truth, goodness and beauty. To God, as on the steps of a stairway, one ascends until arriving and almost attaining the highest Good and in him we find our joy and peace. How useful it would be if also today we rediscovered the beauty and value of creation in the light of divine goodness and beauty! In Christ, observed St. Bonaventure, the universe itself can again be the voice that speaks of God and leads us to explore his presence; exhorts us to honor and glorify him in everything (cf. Ibid. I, 15). Herein we perceive the spirit of St. Francis, with whom our saint shared love for all creatures.[25]

25. Benedict XVI, *Address of His Holiness Benedict XVI, Piazza Sant'Agostina*, Bagnoregio, Italy on September 6th, 2009.

Number

God has arranged all things in number, sequence and proportion.

Wisdom 11:21

This section contains an account of some of most important examples of number symbolism in the Christian tradition.[1] This is not meant to be an exhaustive survey, but rather an indication of how number is viewed symbolically and qualitatively in the Christian tradition.

One ought to aim for discernment when interpreting the significance of numbers. When considering accounts in the Bible, for example, it is good to remember that when a writer refers to the number of times that an event occurred, it is possible that he is simply recording the observation without an intention of communicating any spiritual significance. Nevertheless, the words of the Book of Wisdom (11:21) should always be borne in mind: *"God has arranged all things in number, sequence and proportion."*

As with so many other things, the safest route is to allow tradition to guide us. The practice of the Fathers of the Church appears to be one of caution: there is greater confidence in the symbolic value of a number the more often it appears in the Bible or is confirmed by one of the other disciplines, for example, arithmetic, geometry, or music. Consider the number seven: its repeated occurrence in the Bible gives greater credence to the idea that it is especially significant, and comparison of the occasions on which it is mentioned has allowed for a greater understanding of what that significance is.

Zero does not exist as a number in traditional arithmetic. The first number was always considered to be unity. Zero came from India and was introduced to Europe through contact with the Arabs in the Middle

---

1. For those interested in this field, I would recommend Stratford Caldecott's booklet on the Book of Revelation, which I drew on for this article, particularly in discussion of the mathematical operators, e.g., addition and multiplication. See S. Caldecott, *Companion to the Book of Revelation* (London: Catholic Truth Society, 2008).

Ages. As Stratford Caldecott explains,[2] this is seen by some as a reason for rejecting it in the context of symbolic meaning. I agree with Caldecott, who suggests that the fault is a failure to read it symbolically. So, for example, he offers the idea that it could be the "ground of being and the symbol for the return to one."

One: Unity, First and Last

Unity, in philosophical context, means the unity of being—everything that is a "thing" can be considered as such, rather than as part of something else, because it is a unique entity. This number traditionally signifies the unity of being, transcending all that exists. It is often represented by a circle, or else by a point. Symbolically, the One is not merely the first in a series of numbers, but the number-beyond-number that includes all others, equivalent in that sense to the modern conception of Infinity. It has been suggested that the "tondos" or circular paintings of Raphael[3] are circular because of this principle: for example, the *Alba Madonna*, which depicts Our Lady, Our Lord, and John the Baptist, and hangs in the National Gallery in Washington, DC.

Two

This is the number of polarity and division. It is reflected in our language when we call someone duplicitous or two-faced. In a Christian

---

2. Stratford Caldecott, *Beauty for Truth's Sake* (Ada: Brazos Press, 2009), p. 63.

3. Cf. Hugh Honour and John Fleming, *A World History of Art*, 7th ed. (London: Lawrence King Publishing, 2005).

context it has a negative aspect as the dualistic separation of matter and spirit. It can also symbolize the beginning of the process of creation, which is described in the Book of Genesis as taking place through a series of polarizations (heavens and earth, light and dark, etc.).

Three

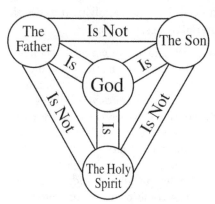

The Triad, of course, is the number of the Trinity and manifested as a triangle. This presents a graphic image of how the number three can be seen as returning polarity to unity. The triangle and the circle together are used to indicate one God in three persons. An equilateral triangle has a particular significance in the natural order, as it is the simplest shape that can be repeated on a two-dimensional plane without leaving any spaces between the triangles so that, for example, one could tile a floor completely with only triangular tiles (just as the tetrahedron can be stacked in three dimensions without leaving space between). As such, the triangle is one of the fundamental building blocks of patterned art, along with patterns based upon the square and the hexagon, for similar reasons. In the biblical context, a threefold repetition of a phrase represents an absolute. This is often reflected in the language of the liturgy, e.g., "Holy, holy, holy..." The Trinity shield design is shown here twice, first as a diagram, and then as it appeared on the shield of a 13th-century French Gothic illumination of a knight in armor.

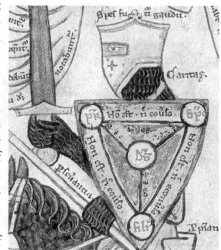

Four

Quaternity represents the earth, or the entire material order, and is manifested as a square. The four traditional "elements" of earth, water, air, and fire seem to correspond not to the types of atom described by modern science (hydrogen, helium, etc.) but to the four basic states of matter which we call solid, liquid, gas, and energy. (Sometimes plasma is given as the fourth state. Plasma is the state of matter in the sun, which is the source of our heat and light, i.e., energy, on earth.) St. Augustine affirms the significance of the four Aristotelian elements from a Christian point of view in his treatise *De Musica*. He then describes the geometric argument for the significance of four as the number of the sensible world that occupies space, applying it to the element of earth. Referring to all material things, he says:

> For which among them is more ordinary and lowly than earth? Yet first it has the general form of a body where a unity and numbers and order are clearly shown to be. For any part of it, no matter how small, must be extended from an indivisible point in length, third takes on breadth and fourth height, to fill the body. From where then is the measure of this progression from one to four? And where to from the equality of the parts found in length, breadth and height? From where a corrationality (for so I have chosen to call proportion), so the ratio length has to the indivisible point, breadth has to length, and height to breadth? Where, I ask, do these things come from, if not from the highest and eternal rule of numbers, likeness, equality and order? And if you abstract these things from earth it will be nothing. And therefore God almighty has made earth and earth is made from nothing.[4]

I have heard the art of geometry being linked analogously to the Creator's act of the creation of world, by a very similar argument. The geometer begins with a point which is extended into a line, and then a circle is drawn with this line as a radius. A plane has been created from three operations. Then, from the conjunction of the plane's different angles, a three-dimensional body has been created.

Looking at the Bible, in the book of Genesis,[5] the river of Eden split into four heads, supplying the world's rivers. Four is

---

4. St. Augustine, *De Musica*, Book VI, Ch. 17. Taken from *The Fathers of the Church, Volume IV* (Washington, D.C.: Catholic University Press, 1947), p. 377.

5. Gen 2:10.

also the number of the Evangelists, whose foundational writings are spread throughout the four corners of the world. Christ tells us in Mark's Gospel of the coming of the Son of Man, when he will "send out his angels, to gather his elect from the four winds, from earth's end to heaven's."[6] The symbols of the Evangelists—angel, bull, eagle, and lion—are derived from the four-faced figure described in the vision of Ezekiel. The fourfold nature of the Gospels was established as a canonical principle by St. Irenaeus in the second century. The traditional image of Christ in Majesty (a version painted by me is shown on the previous page) has the Word on His heavenly throne and the Four Evangelists in their symbolic form taking the Word out to the four corners of the world.

We see the number four represented in two-dimensional geometric patterns with four-fold symmetry. The Westminster pavement in Westminster Abbey in England (a 13th-century cosmati floor), for example, contains many; the example shown below is Sancta Croce in Rome. The shape below could be considered a geometric representation of the Christ Enthroned, in which the Word spins out in four directions from God at the center. Along with patterns based upon the triangle and the hexagon (six-fold symmetry), it is one of the basic units of repeated-pattern art.

Five

Five is traditionally seen as the number of the flesh, of life, and of love. It is manifested as a regular pentagon or a five-pointed star, and though the spiritual symbolism is strong in Christianity, it is perhaps more often used in Islamic art than Christian. Inanimate nature conforms to the order of four- and six-fold symmetry, as in crystal structures. Living

6. Mark 13:27.

nature, on the other hand, appears to be ordered more often by five. The traditional association is with the five senses and the five fingers on each hand (Bonaventure listed five spiritual senses in addition to the corporeal). There are numerous traditional devotions to the five wounds of Christ.

Six

Six is both the sum and the product of the first three numbers, one, two and three—the sum of its aliquot parts—and as such is the first "perfect" number. It is the number of days of the work of creation. It is represented geometrically as a regular hexagon. The hexagon, comprised of six equilateral triangles, is the third shape that can be repeated in a plane without leaving space. If equal-sized spheres are allowed to stack along any plane, they will form repeated patterns of either six-fold or four-fold symmetry. Six-fold patterns feature regularly in tiled floors or cosmati pavements and at Westminster Abbey. The photograph shown is a detail from the cosmati floor in Santa Maria in Cosmedin.

Seven

The seven days of creation (six days of work and one of rest) became the model for the seven days of the week. This number appears many times in Scripture, being a particular favorite of St. John. There are seven sacraments, seven deadly sins, seven virtues, seven gifts of the Holy Spirit. There are seven planets in the skies visible to the naked eye: the sun, the moon, Mercury, Venus, Mars, Jupiter, and Saturn. The tradition regarding the significance of these planets is not undermined by the subsequent discovery of more planets. To the medieval mind these were significant precisely because they are easily visible. One aspect of our humanity is that we are made to see the thumbprint of God, so what we are able to see with the naked eye is as important as what we know to be true otherwise of the heavens. It ensures that all men can see the glory of the Creator in His Creation.

The arrangement of tones in the Western musical scale is based upon the number seven also, with seven tones in the octave, the eighth being simultaneously the first note of the next octave.

Seven represents totality, since it is the sum of four, the number of the material order, and three, the number of the Trinity; and is related to twelve, which is the product of these same numbers. It appears in iconographic and Western naturalistic art as the combination of a square and a triangle as in Raphael's *Transfiguration*. The simple geometric design of Raphael's paintings conveys a sense of calmness. Raphael was well aware of the arithmetic of Christian cosmology. We know this because in his fresco in the Vatican, *The School of Athens*, we see on the lower left, amongst the great philosophers of the past, the kneeling figure of Pythagoras holding a diagram explaining the numerical basis of musical harmonies; also included in this painted chalkboard is representation of the tetractys—the triangular arrangement of 10 items. This will be discussed in greater detail in a later section on harmony and proportion.

Detail of Raphael's *School of Athens*, showing Pythagoras and the diagram of musical harmony along with the Tetractys, the triangular arrangement of the number 10

Seven also translates into the liturgy in the weekly cycles and in the daily Benedictine 7-times-a-day cycle of offices. St. Benedict took his inspiration from the Psalms. In each liturgy, most sevenfold repetitions are associated with an additional eighth motion that is crucial in our understanding of what the liturgy is. This will be discussed in our treatment of the number 8.

The fundamental significance of seven goes right back to God's covenantal relationship with mankind. The American scripture scholar Scott Hahn writes about this as follows:

> Where, precisely, does God swear his covenant oath? He does so in the very act of hallowing the seventh day (Gen 2:2). The seventh day itself is God's Great Oath.
>
> While etymologies do not often make for good exegesis, the etymology of the Hebrew word for "seven" is essential for our understanding of the Genesis text. For it is from the "seventh day" of creation that all subsequent covenant oaths took their origin and inspiration.
>
> The Hebrew word for the number seven, *sheva*, also has a verb form. Shava is the verb for swearing an oath. Its meaning is "to seven oneself." When human beings swear in this way, they follow the precedent set by God at the dawn of creation. Throughout the Old Testament, the num-

ber seven will recur many times in connection with the making of covenant sacrifices. For example, the place of Abraham's covenant oath with Abimelech was later named Beer-sheva, which is alternatively translated as "Well of Seven" or "Well of the Oath." It was there that Abraham swore his oath and gave seven ewe lambs as guarantee (Gen 21:22-34). In Genesis 2, the seventh day was the sign of the covenant that God had made with man and woman.[1]

What the Apocalypse shows is the definitive consummation of the covenant. Thus the number seven dominates the book: seven churches, the seven spirits and seven torches of fire before the throne, the seven lampstands, the seven spirits of the son of man and the seven stars in his right hand, the seven seals, seven angels that stand before God, the seven horns and seven eyes of the Lamb, the seven horns and seven trumpets, and seven chalices of God's wrath. The overwhelming message is that the son of man has definitively renewed the covenant. He has sevened himself by the liturgical offering of his body, once for all.[2]

Eight

As discussed earlier, the so-called eighth "day" of creation symbolizes the new order ushered in by the incarnation, passion, and death of Christ, culminating in his resurrection on Sunday, simultaneously the eighth and first day of the week. It is represented geometrically as a regular octagon. Traditionally, baptismal

fonts were created in octagonal shape. The baptistry of the Duomo in Florence (right) is an octagonal building that is separated from the main building. The number eight, expressed as "7 + 1," is a strong governing factor in the Church's earthly liturgy. Sunday, the day of the Mass, is simultaneously the first day of the new seven-day week and the liberating eighth day of the last. It is the eighth day of the week that represents the new freedom from death through Christ.

The night office, Matins, is the eighth, sung in conjunction with the seven daytime Hours (in practice, many communities run Matins and Lauds together). This could be seen as paralleling the running together of the eighth and first days in the weekly cycle of the liturgy. Eight

1. Scott Hahn, *Letter and Spirit* (Ignatius Press, 2005), p. 60.
2. Ibid., p. 154.

appears in the liturgy in the octaves, the eight-day observances, of Easter and Christmas, which represent an overflowing of grace from these major feast days.

Nine

As the sum of three threes, nine echoes the Triad, indicating the impress of the Trinity on creation. It features most famously in the nine choirs of angels in the celestial hierarchy of Dionysius the Areopagite. It also appears liturgically in the nine days between the day of the Ascension and Pentecost, and the medieval commentators connected the nine-fold invocation of Kyrie that has remained in the Extraordinary Form of the Mass to the nine choirs of angels. The Acts of the Apostles describes how Our Lady and the apostles prayed for nine days until the descent of the Holy Spirit (promised by Christ). From this comes the tradition of the *novena*, nine days of prayer.

Ten

The Decad or Tetractys is the sum of the first four numbers, and represented by an arrangement of ten points arranged in an equilateral triangle: one over two over three over four. This arrangement has been recognized as a significant as far back as the Pythagoreans. The word *tetractys* is Greek for Tetrad—a generic term for a fourfold grouping.

As a doubling of five, it echoes the form of the human being, or the symmetry of hands and feet. Stratford Caldecott describes how in the context of the Book of Revelation it represents authority, as it does in the Ten Commandments. The notes produced by plucking strings of relative length 1, 2, 3, and 4 are the basis for the fundamental musical harmonies in Western music (octave, perfect fifth and perfect fourth) and so for harmonic proportions in art and architecture. (The harmonious combination of numbers will be discussed in more detail in a later article on proportionality.) We do see it represented in Christian art, though less often than other numbers. For example, the late 13th-century fresco of *The Dream of Innocent III* by Giotto in the Basilica of St. Francis of Assisi has a tetractys painted on the gable end of a building.

The number ten provides an interesting demonstration of how the significance of numbers appears in different ways in different contexts. As we have already seen, in his commentary on the Creation story and the book of Genesis, Benedict XVI tells us first that the numbers are significant. They do not indicate the mathematical structure, as a scientific theorem might, but they point to another sort of truth that is every bit as associated with ten as its quantitative sense. He tells us that the words "God said" appear ten times. This is an anticipation of the Ten Commandments and make us realize that his words are signs pointing to the language and the meaning of creation, because they bear the pattern of the divine logic which constructed the universe. Analogous to this, Boethius tells us in *De Arithmetica* that there are ten harmonious proportions that were handed down to us from ancient Greece. He describes how the Greeks sought to establish ten significant proportions because of the significance of ten and thought that this was the number of proportions that there ought to be. In this sense, then, Christians might see them as mathematical commandments of beauty. However, it seems to me that although some of these are related to the beauty of creation, especially the first three and the tenth, which relate to music and human proportions, it is not clear how the others are derived; or how they are used practically other than to make up the full set of proportions.

Twelve

Outside the Decad, twelve is probably one of the most richly symbolic of numbers—especially in a Christian context. There are twelve lunar months in the year, and the heavens have been divided into twelve signs of the zodiac. This is a Christian "liturgical" division, if the stars in the sky are thought of as participating in the heavenly liturgy. This natural division of the year has been passed down in the division of the day and night into twelve hours each. It is represented geometrically by a regular solid with twelve sides, the dodecagon, or by a twelve-pointed star composed of equilateral triangles. Arithmetically, it is the product of 3 and 4 and as such is linked to $7 (= 3 + 4)$. This is the power of God, represented by the Trinity, being taken out to four corners of the world.

There are 12 apostles, 12 patriarchs, and 12 tribes. The signs of the zodiac do appear in Christian churches as a symbol of the universe participating in the heavenly liturgy. For example, one of the main designs on the tiled floor of the church of San Miniato al Monte, just outside Florence, contains a representation of each within a circle divided into 12 equal sectors, as part of an interior laden with geometric art. The photographs below are a broad view of the interior and a section of the central aisle, divided up according to the twelve signs of the zodiac.

Twenty-eight

Twenty-eight is the second perfect number, being the sum of its aliquot parts: 1, 2, 4, 7 and 14. In many ways, 28 can be thought of as the number of the moon. An idealized lunar month of 28 days is two phases (a waxing and a waning) and the seven-day week is half a phase. The moon is the symbol of the Church. When the Divine Office according to the Roman Rite was revised after the Second Vatican Council, it was ordered around this 28-day cycle. This revision, therefore, seems in accord with the traditional principles, even if new in application. The moon is linked to the cycles of the liturgy by the book of Ecclesiastes:

> He made the moon also to serve in its season, to mark the times and to be an everlasting sign. From the moon come the sign for feast days, a light that wanes when it reaches the full. The month is named for the moon, increasing marvelously in its phases, an instrument of the host on high shining forth in the firmament of heaven.[3]

1,000

1,000 is used to denote a very large number or eternity. St. Peter says, for example, that "a day with the Lord is like a thousand years and a thousand years as one day."[4]

Adding Numbers

The addition of numbers combines properties of each into a single entity. For example, seven is a special number in its own right and because it is the sum of three and four. Also, the addition of one to a number represents overflowing or further liberation beyond an initial

---

3. Book of Ecclesiastes, quoted from Thursday Week 1, Office of Readings.
4. 2 Peter 3:8

mark that is still identifiable, as in the case of eight, when considered as (7+1), which can be taken to mean that which is beyond seven.

Multiplying Numbers Together

This is an operation of expansion which is an abundant, unlimited extension of one number into another. So, 3 x 4 yields 12, which represents the celestial order, the spiritual animation of all that is material. In the Book of Revelation, there are 144,000 faithful in heaven. This number is derived from 12 x 12 x 1000, which corresponds to an unlimited extension of the Tribes and the Apostles.

Perfect, Superfluous, and Diminished Numbers

Perfect numbers are those that are the sum of their aliquot parts. Six and twenty-eight are the examples we have discussed so far. Those numbers for which the sum is greater or less than the aliquot parts are called superfluous and diminished, respectively. Boethius explains that "perfect" numbers are considered so as a consequence of their relationship with superfluous and diminished numbers: "Between these two kinds of number, as if between two elements unequal and intemperate, is put a number which holds the middle place between the extremes like one who seeks virtue."[5]

Triangular Numbers

These are numbers that can be arranged in a triangular patterns of dots: 1, 3, 6, 10.... Ten dots arranged in a triangle constitute the tetractys.

Square Numbers

These are numbers that can be arranged in square patterns of dots: 1, 4, 9, 16.... Any adjacent triangular numbers combine to form a square number: e.g., 6 + 10 = 16.

The Appearance of These Numbers in Geometrical Design

All of these numbers have regular application in different aspects of the Christian life. In geometry or art based upon geometric form the most

5. Michael Masi, *Boethian Number Theory: A Translation of the De Institutione Arithmetica* (New York: Rodopi, 2006) p. 96.

commonly occurring examples are 1, 3, 4, 6, 7, 8; circle, triangle, square, hexagon, square + triangle, octagon.

Take the example of four circles spinning out of a central circle, a common shape. It is called a quincunx, from the name of a coin that had the value of five parts of a denarius. The coin had a design of five dots arranged so that four surrounded a central one. It became a common decorative design, to be seen in Roman mosaics, for example. For the Christians it was used to signify the creation of the material universe by God, four spinning out of one. It has been suggested that it can also signify the end of time when all returns to God. This is the shape we see in the floor of Santa Croce on page 123. One could also consider it to be the geometric representation of the traditional iconographic image of Christ in Majesty (also called Christ in Glory) shown above and below, in which the four Evangelists take the Word to the four corners of the world.

The **vesica piscis** is a shape created by the intersection of two circles with the same radius, intersecting in such a way that the center of each circle lies on the circumference of the other. The name literally means "the bladder of the fish" in Latin. The shape is also called a mandorla (meaning "almond" in Italian). The fish is the traditional sign of Christ.

Some Christians believe that a second link between their religion and the fish symbol is seen in the Greek word for fish (*ichthus*, spelled: Iota Chi Theta Upsilon Sigma). That is an acrostic which has many translations in English. The most popular appears to be "*Jesus Christ, Son of God, Savior*." It is often seen enclosing Christ, especially when depicted in his heavenly realm. So, for example, Christ in Majesty, where he is depicted as King on his throne, uses this shape. Similarly, many depictions of the Transfiguration, in which Christ's appearance to the three apostles was transfigured in heavenly glory, will show Christ within a vesica.

Christ in glory,
illuminated manuscript, 12th century

6

Harmonious Proportion

Since God can only make things that are ordered according to their nature, since order presupposes number and number presupposes measure, and since only numbered things are ordered and only limited things are numbered, then God must needs have made things according to number, weight and measure.
St. Bonaventure, Commentary on the Four Books of Sentences 1, 43, 1

The awesome power of one sole and supreme Reason reconciles the disparity between all things of Heaven and Earth by due proportion: this same sweet concord, itself alone, unites what seem to oppose each other, because of their base origins and contrary natures, in to a single exalted and well-tuned Harmony.
Abbot Suger, builder of the first Gothic church, 12th century[1]

I N T H I S C H A P T E R we consider the beauty of numbers in combination and how these numerical expressions have been used in culture, especially in art and architecture.

Is This Art or Is This Science?

For many who are reading this section, there will be a suspicion that the adoption of a mathematics of beauty will stifle creativity and force all that is made to look the same. Those especially who hold on strongly to the modern idea that the human creative force is rooted in emotion and the unbridled passions of the individual will very likely feel that their freedom is being compromised.

In fact art, like most activities in life, benefits from the use of reason. We can illustrate how different the traditional attitude to beauty and

---

1. Suger, Libellus, *Alter De Consecratione Ecclesiae Sancti Dionysii*; quoted by Richard Foster, *Patterns of Thought* (London: Jonathan Cape, 1991), p. 132.

design was to that of the present by consideration of an account of a discussion that took place in connection with the building of a Gothic cathedral in 14th-century Italy. It is described by Otto von Simson in his book *The Gothic Cathedral*.[2]

A series of architectural conferences took place in Milan in 1391 and the following years. The minutes of these conferences are still in existence. Contained within them is reference to a debate that took place regarding the completion of the cathedral. The ground plan had already been established using a geometry based upon the square. A proposal had been made by the Italians that it should be completed using designs based upon the geometry of the triangle. No one questioned that the cathedral should follow a geometric form, but the proposal to switch during the process to a different geometry was disputed by the French architectural expert because, he argued, it would not allow for a harmonious design. There would be a clash of style between the ground plan and the elevation. There is a second point that has relevance in the consideration of the use of geometry:

> The second and even more interesting aspect of the Milan documents is that they suggest the reason for this reliance on geometric canons. The minutes of one particularly stormy session relate an angry dispute between the French expert, Jean Mignot, and the Italians. Overruled by them on a technical issue, Mignot remarks bitterly that his opponents have set aside the rules of geometry by alleging science to be one thing and art another. Art, however, he concludes, is nothing without knowledge: *ars sine scientia nihil est*. The word "art" in the medieval world has a broader meaning than in today's world. For the medieval the word "art" means everything that is made by man acting as a rational being. Artificial things (meaning "things made according to art") are all the products made by man according to a rational plan.[3]

In no way does "artificial" for figures such as St. Bonaventure, for instance, mean "fake" or "not real." When medievals claimed that art is "everything made by man acting as a rational being," they meant "everything made by man in a way that brings his products towards their true goals and fulfillment" (which would include what we would call art today). Von Simson continues:

> In regard to the Milan cathedral, Mignot's argument was considered unassailable even by his opponents. They hasten to affirm that they are in complete agreement as regards this theoretical point and have noth-

2. Otto von Simson, *The Gothic Cathedral* (New York: Harper and Row, 1964), p. 19.
3. Ibid.

ing but contempt for an architect who presumes to ignore the dictates of geometry. And it is taken for granted by both sides that the stability and the beauty of an edifice are not distinct values, they do not obey different laws but that, on the contrary, both are comprehended in the perfection of geometrical forms.[4]

Writing close to a thousand years earlier, St. Augustine reflected the classical approach to the creation of beauty and the importance of the use of mathematics. In this case he is talking of musical composition, but the principles are the same. He considers the creation of beauty a science as well. In the first book of his treatise *De musica*,[5] he acknowledges that music can be produced by instinctive use of practical skills, just as it can be appreciated by anyone who listens to music, even if they don't understand what they are listening to. But such understanding of music, according to Augustine, however creative or receptive, is but of a low order. In fact, there is little difference between man producing music in this way and an animal howling or bird singing. The true understanding of music, he says, which knows the laws of consonance and rhythm, is of a higher order. It applies them in composition of music, and discovers them in listening to it. This is what Augustine calls the *science* of music, and he explains that the nature of this science is mathematical.

If one considers how the creative process is taught today in most art schools, it has become exactly what the Gothic mason rejected and St. Augustine equated with the lowest order of human activity. The modern ethos seems to acknowledge predominantly emotion—gut feeling—as a guiding principle for individual expression. This almost exactly corresponds to the principle of *ars sine scienta* that was so abhorrent to the Gothic mind. What was referred to by the masons as *scientia* is now seen as the source of something cold and sterile that only constrains the creative process and so ought to be eliminated. Geometrical considerations in design have long been discarded.[6] The same philosophy dominates music and architecture, although musicians are still expected to understand, at least, the traditional musical forms, even if

---

4. Ibid.

5. There are six books in *De musica*, of which the first five were written before Augustine converted to Christianity. The fact that he wrote a sixth after his conversion seems to suggest that he did not wish to reject what he had previously written. We might consider this, therefore, reflective of the approach both of the Christian thinking and the classical that had preceded it.

6. In time, as the modernist ideas took a stronger hold, even the basic skill of drawing became steadily rejected on the basis that the discipline needed in order to learn to draw suppresses sincere expression of emotion. This is *ars sine ars*!

they then are directed to composing outside their domain. In architecture, there is a separation of aesthetics and functionality that did not exist for the medieval mason, so that the scientific element applies only to the practical considerations of the making the building fulfill the function for which it is designed without collapsing; the aesthetic considerations are considered subjective just as in visual art.

For my part, I do not reject the use of intuition. On the contrary, I would suggest that intuition is extremely useful in the creative process if employed in a spirit of humility and is potentially, therefore, open to guidance from God's inspiration. The true aim, I contend, should be to make the creative process a balance between the conscious application of reason and the use of intuition that is informed by reason. There is a danger always of rejecting one extreme and replacing it with another. In this case, if we reject the modern idea of unguided emotion as the sole principle by which we judge the good, the overreaction would be to eliminate personal judgment altogether. To my mind the laws of geometry are not an end in themselves, but a means to an end: creating works of art that reflect beauty, truth, goodness, and unity, which in turn bring glory to God.

This balance is most easily understood by considering how the rules of harmony are used in instrumental music: the principles of harmony and counterpoint ought to be followed in any composition, but conformity to them does not in themselves guarantee a beautiful piece of music. There is still the question of how those principles are applied, and this always demands an element of personal judgment. All faculties of the mind, including reason, can be used humbly in the service of God, and He can inspire us in our use of them. How the person feels during the process of composition is not necessarily indicative of inspiration or of how good the end product will be. The true measure of inspiration is the quality of work we produce.

Variety

To the man with a traditional outlook the idea that the use of harmonious proportion would restrict creativity would be puzzling. He would point to the seemingly endless variety of forms that exists in nature, each of which nonetheless conforms to a mathematically described order. Similarly, we might look at how rich and varied are the forms and styles in the art, architecture, and music that have employed harmonious proportion and observe that we can easily distinguish the work of particular periods, geographical areas, and even particular composers, artists, and architects, simply by recognizing a characteristic style.

It seems that just as the application of a moral code does rule out certain actions that are considered morally wrong, it still leaves an infinite range of actions that are good—nine-tenths of infinity is still infinity. So it is with the use of harmony and proportion: it does rule out the use of some proportions, but we are still left with an infinite range of beautiful options and combinations. It is in this spirit that we move forward and consider further the mathematics of beauty.

What Does Harmonious Proportion Look Like?

Harmony is a consonant relationship between two or more different magnitudes. We probably all know what harmonious music sounds like. We can hear when two notes sound good together. But what does harmony look like when you see it in a building? It is not always obvious why a building is pleasing—but one of the main reasons that people generally find old buildings attractive and modern buildings ugly is that nearly all traditional styles from before 1900 were built so that they conformed to traditional proportion.

Look first at this picture of Auckland Medical School, which is a modern building in a brutalist style.

The windows are evenly spaced. From top to bottom the windows and the stories are the same size. This is typical of most multi-story buildings built since the Second World War, when modernism really started to take hold.

Contrast that with this picture of the Hampshire House in the Beacon Hill neighborhood of Boston, which was built in the 18th century.

This uses traditional proportion. The first thing to notice is that the windows are different sizes. If you look particularly at those in the red-brick part you can see that they are arranged so that each story (and the windows within) get steadily smaller the higher up the building you go. There is a rhythmical progression as you move upwards—the first relates to second as the second relates to the third. This steady rate of change is a reflection of *harmonious proportion*. The house looks elegant because visually these three *different* dimensions work well together  (it is not arbitrary—you couldn't pick just any three different sizes for it to look appealing).

Harmonious proportion is reflected in many aspects of traditional culture, not just windows; but because they are an obvious and easily grasped manifestation of traditional proportion, they are an example we will use regularly to illustrate the principles we are discussing.

It is just like three notes in harmony, but displayed visually. This grouping of three is not accidental. For just as music theory tells us that you need three notes to complete a chord, so the architect seeks to portray visual beauty in a grouping of three different magnitudes. This chapter tells you something about the mathematics that helped the architect of the older house to decide how large to make those windows relative to each other.

How Did the Tradition Develop?

As already discussed, the starting point for the whole tradition in the West is ancient Greece and the Pythagoreans. When the ancient Greeks looked at the natural world, just like man today, they saw its beauty. The Greek word *cosmos* means simultaneously "order" and "beauty." The Greeks started to look at the patterns in the cosmos and all sensible beauty. This included the motions of the planets, for example, and an analysis of musical harmony. The tradition in the West, beginning with the ancient Greeks, is born of a consensus relating to two points. Firstly, that the natural world is beautiful; and secondly, that some musical combinations, such as the perfect fifth, are harmonious and beautiful.

This was accepted, to my knowledge, without question by the early Christians as they started to incorporate the classical tradition into their own thought. We have mentioned the very influential figures of Augustine and Boethius, but we can see it elsewhere too, even at this early stage—for example, in pre-Islamic Spain, when St. Isidore wrote: "In truth the Greeks named the world after ornament, for the diversity of the elements and the Beauty of the stars. In fact their way of calling it is *Kosmos*, which means ornament. For nothing more beautiful than the world may be seen with the eyes of the flesh."[7]

If these two points (the beauty of the cosmos and of certain musical intervals) had to be proved to a skeptic—and could not be taken as self-evident truths—then the whole basis of this discussion would fall. Just like the ancients, I appeal to consensus, the fact that most people see it that way, as a basis of its truth. Some might wonder if that consensus really is present today, but I would say that I do not know of a single person who has dissented from accepting either proposition. As far as I am aware, even in the most avant-garde, secular music schools today, which advocate dissonance in music as something good, it is acknowledged as a basis of music theory that there is such a thing as consonance, too. What *is* questioned is whether or not good music ought to be primarily dissonant or consonant, which is a different point altogether.

Once this consensus is accepted, it seems a small step to assert also that there is some property in the object of our attention which makes it beautiful; or, to put it another way, that beauty is an objective property. And, in turn, once we have accepted that, then it seems natural to try to analyze that beauty and describe it numerically.

Although modern man in the West generally follows the ancients in seeing the beauty of the cosmos and the consonance of certain musical intervals, he generally follows Enlightenment philosophers such as Burke in rejecting the hypotheses that beauty is objective and can be analyzed numerically. How do we convince others, then, or even ourselves, perhaps, of the rightness of the traditional view?

I would point to traditional culture and ask the simple question, is it beautiful? When I give lectures on harmony and proportion, I am aware that I might have people in the audience who hold the modern idea that beauty is completely subjective. I begin by showing slides of pre-modern buildings from many different centuries in which the pattern of the windows can be seen in all of them so that they can see the common

7. Isidore of Seville, *Etymologies* XIII.

patterns. Then I show some modern buildings in which this pattern is obviously not present. At this point I ask them if they can see that modern architecture has departed from the traditional pattern. So far they always have—they can see the difference. Then I ask which they prefer. At this point almost all say they prefer the traditional forms. Occasionally, someone will dissent and say they prefer modernity. Nevertheless, those who can see the difference and prefer the traditional to the anti-traditional are convinced.

The Sources of the Mathematics of Harmonious Proportion

There are four areas of analysis which reveal harmonious relationships that can be described mathematically. The first is in the abstract world of mathematics itself, separated into the disciplines of **arithmetic**, which is the study of number and answers the question, *how many?*, and of **geometry**, which is the study of continuous quantity and answers the question, *how much?* The mathematics of harmony arises from consideration of the patterns of number and shape and how they relate to each other.

Next is the analysis of the beauty of cosmos. This is called **music**. Music in this sense is a much broader term than in our use of it today. It considers the harmonious arrangement of things, both visually and aurally, and there are three sub-categories: instrumental, celestial, and human. What we would consider to be music today would be termed "instrumental" music. Celestial music is an analysis of the patterns in the relative motion of the heavenly bodies; and human music looks at the proportions of the human person. This analysis considers not only the physical proportions, but also the spiritual principle within man, as expressed by Boethius: "But whoever turns his attention to his own self, understands human music. For what is it that unites that incorporeal vital force of the reason with the body, unless it be a certain accurate joining together, and as it were, proportion, low and high tones, so producing one consonance?"[8]

The Christian traditions in these areas were, broadly speaking, received from classical antiquity. The crucial additional source for Christians, of course, was the Bible. As well as reading the book of nature, Christians read the Word as manifested in Holy Scripture.

My Sources

The *Timaeus* by Plato was highly influential in the Christian West because, unlike many other works of Plato (and Aristotle), it was avail-

---

8. Boethius, *Five Books on Music*, Bk. 1, Ch. 2.

able in the libraries of monasteries. Many other works that are now extant only became available in the second millennium, when the contents of Byzantine and Islamic libraries became available in the West. Two other influential texts were Boethius's *De Arithmetica* and his *De Musica* (of which the first five books are extant). These are highly theoretical in nature and rarely mention practical applications. In order to see how the proportions are used in practice, we need other texts: first, a first-century Roman textbook on architecture, Vitruvius's 10 *Books on Architecture*. This predates Boethius by several hundred years, and after the decline of the Western Roman Empire it was not widely available until the High Renaissance, when it was rediscovered (and thereafter was highly influential). But one can assume that it reflected in part, at least, what was commonly known to architects in the classical period, and afterwards passed down by tradition. For Vitruvius, the main principle for the construction of buildings is human music, that is, the idealized proportions of man. He does describe the mathematics of instrumental music, but only in the context of building acoustic resonance chambers in theatres. Nevertheless, it gives us an indication of the fact that musical proportion was translated into material form at this time.

Two architects in Italy, Leon Battista Alberti from the 15th century and Andrea Palladio from the 16th, wrote books on architecture that were clearly influenced by the newly rediscovered Vitruvius. Interestingly, Alberti gives a summary of musical theory and, now going further than Vitruvius, states that this is the basis for architectural design in the tradition.

Andrea Palladio is the architect after whom the "Palladian" style is named and who was influential throughout much of Western Europe. His style took various forms over time, becoming, for example, the basis of Georgian architecture in England and the American colonial style of the 17th and 18th centuries. By the 16th century, when Palladio lived, musical theory had advanced, due, as much as anything, to the improvement in the precision of tuning of musical instruments. As a result, the range of intervals considered harmonious had increased (with the basic Pythagorean harmonies still accepted). Palladio gives us the numbers in detail for his designs for the measurements he used in his building. The numbers he cites correspond to the basic arithmetic, geometric, and harmonic proportions—right down to the length, breadth, and height of rooms. Perhaps it is this detailed information that helped to make his style so influential in successive generations.

For the time between Boethius and the rediscovery of Vitruvius, we know that Boethius's works on arithmetic and music which described principles of harmony and proportion, and Plato's *Timaeus*, were still known and read. We can see musical proportions represented in architecture throughout this period. In the Gothic period, sources for our knowledge of their methods of their design and construction are the few Gothic mason's handbooks that exist. I have not used these directly but have relied for my information here predominantly on two books written in the 20th century.[9]

What is Proportion, Exactly?

Proportion is an essential element of beauty. St. Thomas Aquinas tells us that proportion has three attributes: *due proportion, integrity,* and *claritas.* To the degree that something is beautiful, all of these are present. I will explain them by using the example of a well-run church choir to illustrate.

Due proportion means that each part within the object under consideration is in the right relationship to the others. Taking the example of the choir, if all the different voices within it are to work together well, each singer must listen to the voices of those around him so that they can blend together. Even if a singer knows the piece perfectly, he cannot blend well unless he considers how his voice relates to the unified voice of the choir.

Integrity is the degree to which the whole conforms to the purpose intended for it. In a choir, even beyond the choice of the music and the words, there has to be a consideration of interpretation. In order for this to happen, the director must decide upon an interpretation for all to subscribe to. It would be hopeless if each singer interpreted individually and then sang accordingly. So aside from singing in unity, we must accept the authority of the leader to direct that unified voice to a purpose that is appropriate to the choir (this is also a good exercise in humility!).

Claritas can be thought of as the radiance of truth. For something to be beautiful it must communicate to us clearly what it is. So this means that if our choir wishes to sing beautifully, there must be a clear articulation of the words and music so that the congregation knows what is being sung. If the underlying idea in the mind of the composer is beautiful in its conception, but the choir does not clearly communicate it to

9. Rudolph Wittkower, *Architectural Principles in the Age of Humanism* (New York, St. Martin's Press, 1988). While this book focuses predominantly on the proportion of the Renaissance period, especially in Alberti and Palladio, the appendix includes a summary of the different sorts of proportion used, including during the Gothic period. See also Richard Foster, *Patterns of Thought* (London: Jonathan Cape, 1991). Foster's book is primarily about the principles of cosmati design in the 13th century, but also contains a discussion of general principles of design.

us in their singing of it, the result is not beautiful. We can see this reflected in another way. I used to show my classes a piece of complicated and exquisitely handmade metal medical equipment from Victorian times. It had a handle that turned, and intricate interlocking cogs and levers. It was not obvious to us non-medical moderns what its purpose was. Without explanation, I would show it to them and ask, "Do you think this is beautiful?" Almost always the reaction of the students would be, "I don't know. What is it?" It was revealing to me that, first, they always assumed that it had a purpose, and, second (and important to the discussion here), that they didn't feel able to answer the question regarding its beauty until they knew what it was for.

While St. Thomas is useful to us in that he clearly places the appropriate use of proportion in the list of the essential characteristics of beauty, he gives us only a general sense of what proportion is. He does not, as far as I am aware, discuss the mathematics of proportion. In order to do this, we must go back to Boethius.

We begin with the traditional definitions of two terms, *ratio* and *proportion*. While in common language we tend to use these terms interchangeably, traditionally they were distinguished from each other. If you have two numbers in relation to each other, they constitute a *ratio*. This would be expressed mathematically, for example as 1:2. *Proportionality* is something distinct from ratio and is defined as *a similar relationship of two or more ratios*. For example, the ratio 2:4 is said to be in proportion to 4:8 because in each case the second term is double the first. This is referred to as a "geometric" proportion.

Using mathematical symbols, the proportionality could be written as follows: 2:4::4:8. But when the largest number of the first ratio, in this case 4, is the same as the smaller number of the second ratio, the essence of this geometric proportion just described can be expressed using three numbers only. Accordingly, it is written 2:4:8. The middle term, in this case 4, is described as the "geometric mean" of 2 and 8, which are the "extremes." A geometric proportion could be expressed using many terms, to use this example, by continuing to double the number and produce a series: 2, 4, 8, 16, 32...; but the essence of this proportion, what defines it mathematically, is contained within any three consecutive terms.

Two numbers would not be sufficient to describe the proportion because we would not be able to tell the basis of the relationship. So, for example, if we are given the ratio 2:4 it might be part of a geometrically proportional relationship, but it might also belong to another kind of proportion. If the relationship is created by always having the second term greater than the first by two, then the next ratio in the series would be 4:6. This is called an *arithmetic* proportion by Boethius and can be expressed using three numbers, as 2:4:6. The number 4 is the arithmetic mean.

This means that if we see a 2:4 ratio, we do not know what proportion it participates in until the third term is present. It could be either an arithmetic or geometric proportion. It is not until the third term, 6 or 8 respectively, that we know.

Boethius tells us that he is reflecting the wisdom of the Greeks who preceded him and we can see how they also looked for this tri-numerate mathematical archetype to express the orderliness of even abstract concepts. Aristotle refers to the arithmetic mean in his account of justice in the *Nicomachean Ethics*. He describes how, as a general principle, virtue is a mean between two extremes. He relates justice to the arithmetic mean in particular, because he says that the just position exactly divides the line between the two extremes:

> In some states they call judges mediators, on the assumption that if they get what is intermediate they will get what is just. The just, then, is an intermediate, since the judge is so. Now the judge restores equality; it is as though there were a line divided into unequal parts, and he took away that by which the greater segment exceeds the half, and added it to the smaller segment. And when the whole has been equally divided, then they say they have "their own"—i.e., when they have got what is equal. The equal is intermediate between the greater and the lesser line according to arithmetical proportion. It is for this reason also that it is called just (*sikaion*), because it is a division into two equal parts (*sicha*).[10]

Another commonly occurring example is the *harmonic* proportion. In a harmonic proportion, the ratio of the difference between the mean and the first term to the first term equals the ratio of the difference between the final term and the mean to the final term. This is most easily demonstrated by giving an example. Consider the proportion 3:4:6. The difference between the first two terms is 1 (= 4−3). So the ratio of this to the first term is 1:3. The difference of the last two terms is 2 (= 6−4), and the last term is 6; therefore, the ratio of the two is 2:6, which is numerically equivalent to 1:3. So the condition described by Boethius is fulfilled.

The next number in this series is 12, and so 4:6:12 is another harmonic proportion. We can see now why it is called a *harmonic* proportion:

10. Aristotle, *Nicomachean Ethics*, Book V, 4 at http://classics.mit.edu/Aristotle/nicomachaen.5.v.html

within the series we have established—3, 4, 6, 12—are the ratios of the fundamental music intervals: 3:4 is a perfect fourth; 4:6 is the same as 2:3, a perfect fifth; and 6:12 equals 1:2, an octave.

Boethius describes seven more proportional relationships that have special significance, giving a total of 10 in all:

> It is testified to and known among the ancients who have studied the learning of Pythagoras, or Plato, or Aristotle that there are three ways to knowledge: arithmetic, geometric, harmonic.[11] After these relationships of proportions there are three others, which are conveyed to us without names but are called fourth, fifth and sixth and which are contrasted with the above. Then later thinkers, on account of the perfection of the number 10, which was pleasing to the Pythagoreans, added four other kinds, so that in these proportionalities they brought together the body of proportions 10 in number.[12]

Boethius described each proportion in prose, rather than with mathematical symbols. So, for example, arithmetic proportionality is described as follows: "We call that an arithmetic medial proportion in which as often as in three or any number of stated terms there is found the same and equal difference between all the terms."[13]

The words of Boethius have been converted into mathematical formulae (Table 1), as they will, it is presumed, be more easily understood by the modern reader. As three is the minimum number of terms needed to define the proportionality, we will define all the proportion using the three terms x, y, and z. Of these three, x and z are the two extremes, and y the mean. We will call the interval between x and y, that is $y-x$, a; and the interval between y and z, that is, $z-y$, b. This is represented diagrammatically as follows:

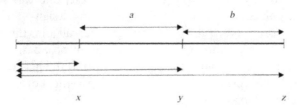

11. The word "harmonic" refers to a particular proportion and should not be confused with the generic term for a pleasing proportion that I have used, that is, "harmonious" proportion.

12. Boethius, *De Institutione Arithmetica*, Bk. 2, Ch. 41 from Michael Masi, *Boethian Number Theory: A Translation of the De Institutione Arithmetica* (New York: Rodopi, 2006).

13. Ibid.

The arithmetic proportion written as a mathematical proportion is:

$$y-x = z-y$$
$$\text{or } a = b$$

Table 1, at the end of this chapter, lists the 10 harmonious proportions of Boethius. They are ordered in five pairs. In each pair, the first established proportion is referred to as a "leader" or "major" proportion. The second proportion in each pair, derived from the first (for example, by the inversion of one of the ratios in the major) is termed a "follower" or "minor" proportion; sometimes Boethius refers to these as being "contrary" to a major.

The importance of the final proportionality, the Fourth of Four, is demonstrated by its appearance in the form 6:10:16, corresponding to the proportions of the idealized human body, and containing the ratios of the dimensions of the ark made by Noah in the Book of Genesis in the Bible and interpreted by St. Augustine as corresponding to the proportions of the figure of Christ It is noteworthy that this series is an earlier form of what was presented much later by the Italian mathematician Fibonacci in his famous series. As with the Fibonacci series, as the Fourth of Four progresses *ad infinitum*; the ratio of adjacent terms tends towards the ratio known today as the Golden Section.[14]

Geometry

The fundamental geometric representation of significant numbers, such as a square or a triangle, can be geometrically expanded and subdivided to form harmonic relationships. By constructing a grid that consists of a latticework of equilateral triangles, for example, one can selectively choose the points on the grid as key points in any design—for example, the corners of a room, or the point at which the wall joins the roof. This generation of design through the multiplication of a basic geometric shape is the basis for geometrically patterned art found in Christian culture, as with the "cosmati"-style Westminster pavement or in San Miniato al Monte in Florence.

Documents from medieval masons, such as the 13th-century Frenchman Villard de Honnecourt and the 15th-century German Matthew Roriczer, as well as a letter from the 15th century describing the design of Milan cathedral, describe these geometric processes as well.

---

14. For more information on the Golden Section see the chapter "Golden or Fallen?: A Note on Phi."

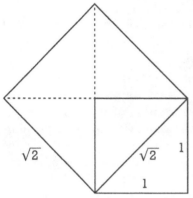

Quadrature and Moral Significance of Proportionality

One example of the geometric generation of form is the process known as "quadrature." Essentially, a square twice the area of another is created by constructing a second, based upon the diagonal of the first. Conversely, one can construct a square half the area of the first by joining the mid-points of sides of the first. In each case the ratio of the length of the sides of the larger to the smaller is $1:\sqrt{2}$.

The quadrature method for harmonious design, using only the traditional tools of set-square and compass, persisted throughout the medieval period. Sometimes the ratio was approximated to 17:12.

The number $\sqrt{2}$ is presents problems to Pythagoreans because it is an "irrational" number. That is, it cannot be described precisely as a ratio or fraction using whole integers (π is an example of another irrational number). However, the idea, at least, of $\sqrt{2}$ can be conceived as a precise relationship through geometry, in the form of a ratio of the lengths of two lines, as constructed in the diagram shown.

In this construction, the two squares defining the outer and inner dimension of the cloistered walkway around a quadrangle were built in accordance with this dimension, which meant that the walkway had the same area as the inner square.

The medieval cathedral builders were familiar with this ratio, which they constructed geometrically and employed in the design of spaces and arches to evoke a sense of harmony in the building. They saw $\sqrt{2}$ as representing the temperate mean between two extremes, 1 and 2 (the relative measures of each area), because the ratios $1:\sqrt{2}$ and $\sqrt{2}:2$ are numerically equal. That is, $1:\sqrt{2}:2$ constitutes a geometric proportion, as described by Boethius. So, symbolically, walking through the cloister to the church could be seen as treading the temperate path of virtue to heaven, between two sinful extremes. The rate of reduction of the width of the spire conforms to the same symbolic order—pointing upwards to heaven on the line of the temperate mean.

In fact, any of the beautiful proportions that are expressed arithmetically can be interpreted as a representation of moral beauty. In each case the mean corresponds to the temperate mean between two extremes. The symbolism is all the more poignant in the case of quadrature, however, because the two extremes 1 and 2 together represent separation and disharmony. They are harmonized by the geometric construction of their mean.

Music

Plato's *Timaeus*, which was so influential in the theory of harmony and proportion, is one of his later dialogues and in many ways confusing and difficult to understand. It is a description of the creation of the world by the "demiurge"—a god about whom we are given little information. Plato explains how the structure of the universe can be described mathematically, which provides the basis of its order and beauty. The actual mathematics that Plato offers is of less help, generally, than the general principles that later Christians saw in what he wrote, and interpreted in the light of Revelation: that is, that the cosmos is beautiful, that this reflects an order that can be expressed mathematically and implies an intelligence that created it. For Plato, the mathematics describes the "soul of the universe." For Christians, who cannot admit to a soul as a single animating principle within the cosmos itself, this becomes the form or ideal that exists in the mind of the Creator. This form exists as a mathematical archetype. We see this phrase in descriptions of the number in later commentators referred to here, such as Bonaventure and, in the present day, Benedict XVI—and this is a reflection of this Christianization of the *Timaeus*.

Plato's description of the generation of the musical scale in the *Timaeus* is purely mathematical, generated from the first three numbers: 1, 2, 3. He tells us that music is the principle that governs the soul of the universe and then gives us a very brief description of the generation of a musical scale. Even this might be puzzling and considered no more than a curiosity if it were not for two things. Firstly, we know more from other sources about the Pythagorean account of music, which this corresponds to, and so later commentators would understand what Plato was describing in relation to the Pythagorean account. For example, a commentary on the *Timaeus* dating from the 2nd century AD (by Plutarch) directly connects Plato's description to the wider Pythagorean theories of music and describes both. Secondly, this is one aspect of what Plato describes that can be verified very easily and directly by personal experience. His musical scale possesses (broadly speaking) the mathematical structure of the musical scale and musical harmony as we look at it today. (Although it would be generated not mathematically at first, but by investigation of how harmonious the relationships sound, and then those results would be analyzed mathematically.)

Plato starts with 1, 2, and 3, which are squared to give 1, 4, 9, and then cubed to give 1, 8, 27. From these numbers we generate the series 1, 2, 3,

4, 8, 9, 27. The first four numbers contain the fundamental ratios 1:2, 2:3, 3:4: the octave, the perfect fifth and the perfect fourth. In addition, the ratio 8:9 generates the interval of a single tone. From this it is possible, in theory, to generate a musical scale. Twenty-seven divided by eight is the interval of three perfect fifths. If this ratio is raised to the power of four $(27/8)^4$, then you have twelve perfect fifths combined to produce seven octaves, which is the limit of the Platonic scale (derived from the Pythagorean).

The general principle of the musical law as the source of beauty comes into the Christian tradition in detailed form from St. Augustine's *De Musica* and Boethius's 6th-century work of the same title. Another influential figure in this regard, who lived much later, is the 9th-century neo-Platonist John Scotus Eriugena. Eriugena's commentary on the *Celestial Hierarchy* of Dionysius the Pseudo-Areopagite was influential on Abbot Suger of St. Denis near Paris, who built the first Gothic church in the 12th century and pioneered the Gothic style that dominated Europe for the next 300 years. Eriugena describes the laws of harmonic proportion by which the different parts of the universe are reconciled. Suger placed this idea at the head of his treatise about the building and consecration of his church.[15]

For Boethius, as for Augustine before him, we are made by God to perceive the divine order. When we do so, we apprehend beauty. The fact that the beauty of certain musical intervals can be related to a harmonious order indicates that numerical order pervades all that is beautiful, including man himself. Our ability to perceive this numerical order exists because we are constructed similarly. The "structure" of the human person refers not only to his physical body, but also to his soul and its relationship to the body. The human order is compatible with the audible musical order through their common participation in the divine order. Boethius extends this point, arguing that we perceive beauty in the cosmos because it participates in this divine harmony, too. He calls each of these manifestations of the divine order "music":

> For since, in accord with what is united and adjusted harmoniously in us we take out [from the cosmos] that which is joined together in sounds suitably and harmoniously and delight in that, we recognize that we ourselves have been put together with the same likeness. For similarity is pleasing, but dissimilarity is hateful and opposed.[16]

15. Otto von Simson, *The Gothic Cathedral* (New York: Harper and Row, 1964).

16. Boethius, *De Institutione Arithmetica*, Bk. 2, Ch. 41 from Michael Masi, *Boethian Number Theory: A Translation of the De Institutione Arithmetica* (New York: Rodopi, 2006).

We have described already how the first four numbers (1, 2, 3, 4) can be used to generate the fundamental harmonies (1:2, 2:3, 3:4). These were referred to collectively by the Pythagoreans as the tetractys. In addition to these there are secondary harmonic ratios, 1:3 and 1:4, which are called "triple" and "quadruple," that can be made by the combination of an octave and a perfect fifth (1:2 x 2:3 = 2:6 = 1:3) and two octaves, 1:2 = 1:4. These were admitted as much for reasons of arithmetic completeness, I suspect, because they are the two remaining relationships that have not yet been accounted for, as for the harmonious sound they represent.

Incorporating the Musical Ratios into Proportionality

Because the tone in the ratio 8:9 cannot be expressed with the basic numbers of the tetractys (1, 2, 3, 4) another arithmetic presentation was developed. First, the octave ratio, 1:2 is multiplied by 6 to give the ratio 6:12. Then the arithmetic and geometric means of 6 and 12 are calculated: 9 and 8 respectively. This gives us a series of four numbers: 6, 8, 9, 12. The ratios generated by relating each number to the other three produces the fundamental Pythagorean harmonies: the octave (6:12), the perfect fourth (9:12), the perfect fifth (8:12), and the tonal interval (8:9). This is often represented in a diagram, shown below, which appears in Boethius's book and, several hundred years later, held by Pythagoras in a detail of Raphael's fresco in the Vatican, *The School of Athens*.

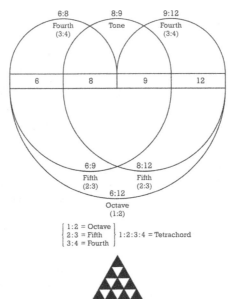

Each of these ratios is found in Vitruvius's textbook on architecture,[17] which also mentions the additional ratio 3:8, derived from an octave combined with a fourth. As music theory developed along with the improvement of musical instruments, the number of harmonious intervals considered beautiful increased. The 13th-century Gothic architect Villard de Honnecourt, who worked for the Cistercian order, included also the musical third, the ratio 4:5[18], and this was taken by commentators such as von Simson to be a regularly used ratio in the Middle Ages; as was 5:3 (which also occurs as a fundamental ratio in "human" music), which forms the major sixth.

By the time of the High Renaissance, things had progressed to the degree that the Venetian Gioseffo Zarlino published an account of music theory by which the scale was broken down into octave, fifth, fourth, major third, minor third (all of these now considered beautiful intervals), major tone, minor tone, and diatonic (semitone). He did this, just as Plato did with his scale, by arithmetic operation only, subdividing the octave using simply arithmetic and harmonic means, but clearly directed by his additional knowledge of which combinations were pleasing to the ear. His *Institutioni Harmonische* was published in Venice in 1558. This was immediately taken up by Palladio, who used the proportions generated from this in his buildings.[19]

Human Music: 6:10:16, the Ideal Human Proportionality

As we have mentioned, Boethius felt that study of the human person would reveal the cosmic order as much as study of the cosmos would. Although derived from ideas about the physical proportions of the body, this is only part of what the proportionality of the "human music" is trying to refer to. "Human music" refers to a divine resonance or harmony that is present when relating each aspect of the human person (physical, spiritual) to the other. It also reflects a participation of human nature in the divine order, and points, ultimately, to our destiny of partaking of the divine nature in heaven. The most commonly used source for the classical numerical proportions is Vitruvius, whose proportion coincides with that of the final one from Boethius's list, called Fourth of Four, which is 6:10:16 (or 5:3:8).

Among the Church Fathers, Augustine in particular describes the

---

17. Vitruvius, 10 *Books on Architecture*, Book 5, Ch. 4.

18. Otto von Simson, *The Gothic Cathedral* (New York: Harper and Row, 1964).

19. For a complete description of the proportions see Rudolph Wittkower, *Architectural Principles in the Age of Humanism* (New York, St. Martin's Press, 1988), p. 201.

Christian understanding of this "human music." He relates the human proportions to those of the ark built by Noah, as directed by God, which are based upon the proportions of the ideal man, Christ. Six and ten are seen as the perfect numbers that permeate the description of the human body:

> [The ark] is certainly a figure of the City of God sojourning in this world; that is to say, of the Church, which is rescued by the wood on which hung the Mediator of God and men, Christ Jesus. For even in its very dimensions in length, breadth and height it represents the human body in which He came, as it had been foretold. For the length of the human body, from the crown of the head to the sole of the feet is six times its breadth from side to side, and ten times its depth or thickness, measuring from back to front: that is to say, if you measure a man as he lies on his back or his face, he is six times as long from head to foot as he is broad from side to side, and ten times as long as he is high from the ground. And therefore the ark was made 300 cubits long, 50 in breadth and 30 in height.[20]

The Vitruvian ideal proportions of man are based upon the traditional measure of finger (*digitus*), palm (*palmus*), foot (*pes*), and cubit (*cubitus*), the length of the forearm. There are 10 fingers; 4 fingers make a palm; 4 palms make a foot; and, hence, the foot contains 16 fingers. The importance of 16 is confirmed for Vitruvius in his observation that 6 and 10, both perfect numbers, combine to make what he sees as the most perfect, 16.[21]

A survey of Christian art will quickly reveal that different traditions use a variety of proportions in the artistic representation of the human form. Even if a figure is sketched out by an artist in rough accordance with a cannon of proportion, unless the posture is a very stiff pose with all limbs in the plane of the painting (as with ancient Egyptian art), the problem of having limbs at different angles and different degrees of foreshortening mean that the artist will rely strongly on an intuitive sense of what looks right. If it is possible to generalize, the body proportions follow a general scheme that is used even by modern illustrators. However, there are exceptions in the detail: iconographic styles tend to have a smaller head in proportion to the rest of the body length (around 1:8 or even smaller), while in more naturalistic styles it is larger (around 1:7). The facial features of the icon and the size of the hands are modified slightly, also, relative to the natural proportions.

---

20. St. Augustine, *City of God*, Chapter 26.
21. Vitruvius, 10 *Books on Architecture*, Bk. III, Ch. 1.

An Intuitive Application of Proportion in Art Used by Artists

Artists use a similar device, created intuitively, to lend grace and rhythm to a composition. The progression of lines that define form will be made to conform to a format whereby a sense of proportion is created. I was first taught to use these when painting, for example, the lines that are used to define the folds of cloth in the robes of a saint. If you pick any well-painted icon and look, say, at the flexed elbow, you will see these rhythmical lines defining the bunching of cloth. You would employ this in the painting to give it grace, even if it is not precisely what you are seeing in nature in your model. Later, when I was student in Florence learning the Western academic method, I  was drawing a cast of a sculpture by the Italian baroque sculptor, Bernini. This is a very different style from the iconographic, but despite that I noticed that Bernini had these rhythmical lines tracing a lattice-work across the surface. In his sculptures of drapery, they are cut much more deeply than they would be in nature, so that this rhythmical effect is enhanced further. I exaggerated them in my drawing in accordance with what I had been taught by my icon-painting teacher. When the head of the *atelier* came to give his daily critique, he looked at mine and said: "You have natural baroque rhythm." I didn't have the heart (or perhaps cheek) to tell him that it was as much "iconographic rhythm."

The Bible

Just as there is a system of symbolic number that can be discerned from the Bible, so there are harmonious combinations of numbers. For example, when God directed the building or creation of something, He specified the dimensions. The Church Fathers analyzed the degree to which the biblical proportionality reinforced those relationships derived by observation of the natural world, especially those of the pre-Christian Greeks.

Right up to the High Renaissance, these dimensions were viewed as an important source of proportion for architects. We have already mentioned Palladio. Otto von Simpson discusses a document by a 16th-century French architect, Philibert Delorme.[22] Along with as the geometric and numerical principles already referred to, he asserts that the dignity

---

22. Otto von Simson, *The Gothic Cathedral* (New York: Harper and Row, 1964).

of the architect's profession is proved by the fact that God himself has instructed him, in the biblical models, about the measures and proportions to employ. He proposes that architects study the "sacred proportions" God gave to Noah, Moses, Solomon and Ezekiel.[23] These are the dimensions of Noah's Ark, the Ark of the Covenant, the tabernacle of Moses, Solomon's temple, and the celestial temple of the vision of Ezekiel. Another example is the heavenly city in the vision of St. John in the Book of Revelation.[24]

Some of these biblical passages, especially the final two from Ezekiel and Revelation, are very complex, and to someone (such as myself!) who is not an experienced biblical scholar, at times confusing. I do not pretend to have a deep understanding.

We will focus here on the simpler relationships, as these will be the ones that are more easily applied in human activities—for example, compositional design in art and architecture. While all of these biblical sources are referred to by architects, such as Palladio and Delorme, the plans of buildings tend to reinforce only those ratios and proportions that correspond to those derived from other sources; for example, from the arithmetical, geometric or musically derived harmonious proportions already discussed.

As well as being able to discern the proportions used in the biblical texts, if an architect is to make use of these, he must understand to what other situations it is appropriate to apply them so that it is *due* proportion. One wonders, in seeing the complexity of these descriptions, just to what degree these were intended by God for architects, as Delorme supposes. Perhaps they are intended more as an aid to interpretation of the text by theologian. So when St. Augustine interprets the dimensions of Noah's Ark in his commentary, he doesn't, to my knowledge, go on to suggest that contemporary boat builders repeat the design.

Here are the examples:

Noah's Ark

The length of the ark shall be 300 cubits, the breadth of it 50 cubits and the height 30 cubits.

St. Augustine linked this to the perfect human form of Christ by the observation that the ratios 1:6, 1:10 and 6:10 govern this structure.

---

23. Genesis 6:15 (Noah's Ark); Exodus 25:10 (Ark of Covenant); Exodus 26, 27 (Moses's tabernacle); 1 Kings 6 (Solomon's temple); Ezekiel 40–44.
24. Rev 21:16–17.

The Ark of the Covenant

Two cubits and a half shall be the length thereof, one cubit and a half in breadth thereof and one cubit and a half in height thereof.

This, therefore, contains the ratios of 6:10 and 1:1 and participates in both the instrumental-musical and human-musical proportions.

The Tabernacle of Moses

And thou shall make an altar of shittim wood, five cubits long, and five cubits broad; the altar shall be foursquare and the height thereof shall be three cubits. . . . The length of the court shall be an hundred cubits, and the breadth fifty cubits and the height five cubits.

This gives ratios of 1:1 and 5:3 in the altar. This last corresponds to the musical interval of a sixth, which was used by Villard de Honnecourt in the design of his church for the Cistercians. In addition to this there are detailed descriptions of boards that line the walls and curtains hanging over them that have unusual dimensions, such as 1:20.

Solomon's Temple

And the house which King Solomon built for the Lord, the length thereof was threescore cubits, and the breadth thereof twenty cubits, and the height thereof thirty cubits. And the porch before the temple of the house, twenty cubits was the length thereof, according to the breadth of the house; and ten cubits was the breadth thereof before the house. . . . And against the wall of the house he built chambers round about, both of the temple and of the oracle: and he made chambers round about: the nethermost chamber was five cubits broad, and the middle was six cubits broad and the third was seven cubits broad. . . . And then he built chambers against all the house five cubits high. . . . And he built twenty cubits on the side of the house, both the floor and the walls with boards of cedar. . . . And the house, that is the temple before it, was forty cubits long. . . . And the oracle he prepared in the house within, to set there the ark of the covenant of the Lord. And the oracle in the forepart was twenty cubits in length, and twenty cubits in breadth, and twenty cubits in height thereof.

Although he does not discuss the dimensions, St. Augustine, in his discourse on Psalm 126, sees the temple of Solomon as a prototype for the Lord's body just like Noah's ark, but here as the mystical body of Christ, the Church. The ratios that run through this are 2:3, 1:2, 1:1, and 1:3. The chambers that skirt the wall of the "house" get successively longer in an arithmetic progression: 5, 6, 7.

The Heavenly City in the Book of Revelation

And the city lieth foursquare, and the length is as large as the breadth: and he measured the city with the reed, twelve thousand furlongs. The length, the breadth and the height of it are equal. And he measured the wall thereof, an hundred and forty and four cubits, according to the measure of the man, that is, of the angel.

This passage uses ratios of 1:1 again. It is uncertain exactly what the units referred to constitute. Some translations of units are not precise. So the Greek *stadion* is translated in the King James Bible as a furlong, for example, which is not precisely equivalent. As proportionality is a relative measure, the reliability of proportions taken from the Bible is higher when the unit quoted is the same. For example, here the heavenly city of the Book of Revelation is quoted in the King James Bible as 144,000 furlongs square, so the ratio 1:1 can be inferred here. The walls, on the other hand, are 144 "cubits" high. One can see that there is a numerical link between the height of the walls and their length, but in order to relate them directly one would need a deeper knowledge than I possess about the units used in the original text.

This concludes the survey of harmonious proportion. In the next chapter we will focus on one proportion that is commonly assumed to be part of the tradition and has not yet been discussed at all, the Golden Section.

Table 1. The 10 Proportional Relationships of Boethius

Boethian name		Mathematical expression	Example
Arithmetic	Major	$a = b$	1 : 2 : 3 : etc... *ad infinitum*
Geometric	Major	$\frac{y}{x} = \frac{z}{y} = \frac{b}{a}$	1 : 2 : 4 :...
Harmonic	Major	$\frac{z}{x} = \frac{b}{a}$	3 : 4 : 6 :...
Fourth or Contrary to Harmonic	Minor	$\frac{z}{x} = \frac{a}{b}$	3 : 5 : 6 :...
Fifth or Contrary to Geometric	Minor	$\frac{y}{x} = \frac{a}{b}$	2 : 4 : 5 :...
Sixth or Contrary to Geometric	Minor	$\frac{z}{y} = \frac{a}{b}$	1 : 4 : 6 :...
First of Four	Major	$\frac{z}{x} = \frac{a+b}{a}$	6 : 8 : 9 :...
Second of Four	Minor	$\frac{z}{x} = \frac{a+b}{b}$	6 : 7 : 9 :...
Third of Four	Major	$\frac{y}{x} = \frac{a+b}{a}$	4 : 6 : 7 :...
Fourth of Four	Minor	$\frac{y}{x} = \frac{a+b}{b}$	3 : 5 : 8 (or 6 : 10 : 16)

Table 2: The Main Musical Harmonies Expressed as Ratios

Name from Boethius	Modern name	Ratio
Double	Octave	1:2 (or 6:12)
Sequitertian	Perfect fourth	3:4 (or 9:12)
Sesquialter	Perfect fifth	2:3 (or 8:12)
Triple	Octave plus fifth	1:3
Quadruple	Double Octave	1:4
(Not in Boethius)	Third	4:5
Sesquioctave	Tone	8:9
(Not in Boethius)	Sixth	3:5

Architectural Examples

There follow several pictures of buildings that follow traditional proportion. In most, the architect uses changing window size to transmit to us a sense of proportionality in which the first relates to the second as the second relates to the third and so on. At the end of the series of architectural photographs, for contrast I will show a couple of modern buildings that clearly lack traditional proportion.

Above: State buildings in Annapolis Maryland, early 19th century; next page: a 17th-century house in the village of Willaston in Cheshire, England. The windows have the ratio, from top to bottom, of 4:6:7, which corresponds to the Third of Four proportion.

Consider now Attingham House in Shropshire. For copyright reasons, we can't show its picture here, but it can be found online at: http://en.wikipedia.org/wiki/Attingham_Park#mediaviewer/File:The_Mansion_at_Attingham_Park.jpg

The design shows a 1, 2, 3 arithmetic progression in the layering of the stories. This example was chosen because each window pane is the same size. This allows us therefore to count the number of panes in each window and then compare directly the size of the window (actually 6 on the bottom, 4 in the middle and two on top, which reduces to the proportion 1:2:3). Visually, this is a striking example, but it is not always so obvious. The design is Palladian and except for the classical portico with the four columns on the front, is very simple. It is a simple square box, and all it has to lend beauty to it is the fact that it is divided up into three uneven stories, which the architect has made visually clear by the changing window size and by adding two lines traced out by horizontal sills that accentuate the division between the stories. Nevertheless, this is considered beautiful enough that is owned by the British National Trust and visited by thousands every year.

The next four photographs below are all scenes from one street (St. Giles) in the city of Oxford in England. On this street once can see a variety of buildings dating from the 16th century, with St. John's College at the bottom, through the 17th, 18th, and 19th centuries (and perhaps very early 20th century) for the other three. Each was built to visibly traditional proportions, sometimes through variation in window size as in the earlier examples, but also through selective painting that accentu-ates the different stories, or other architectural features such as extended sills. The pub, just visible in the background in the photograph immedi-ately below, is the Eagle and Child, the pub in which Lewis, Tolkien, and the rest of the Inklings used to sit and discuss their work. I like to think that the combination of beer (in moderation, of course) and harmoni-ous proportion contributed to their creative thinking in equal measure.

What strikes me is the great variety of styles, shapes and sizes of the buildings. In their desire to use the space to best advantage, the archi-tects were quite happy to create buildings that suited their purpose, had a different architectural style, and were of different heights and number of stories. Rather than creating conflict visually, however, the variety gives the street enhanced beauty and charm. What unites them is their adherence to traditional proportion. The individual style of each points not so much to the others alongside, but rather to the invisible standard of heavenly beauty in which it participates. As each is in harmony with this invisible standard, each is through this connection in harmony with the others.

Here are two more photos (next page) of the same street, placed next to the first. The hotel on the right is the Randolph Hotel, the most famous in Oxford, which was completed in the mid-19th century. It is noticeable how the windows of each of the five stories get steadily smaller. We intuitively pick up a rhythmical pattern in which the first relates to the second as the second relates to the third and so on.

St. John's College, below, was completed in 1550 and exhibits the late English Gothic style. The proportion is made visible by horizontal sills running across it rather than by variation in window size.

Below we have a photograph and illustrating diagram (after Von Simson) of the Galleries of Angels, Abbey of St. Michael, Hidesheim, Germany

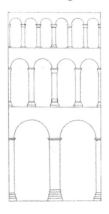

Photograph by Jong-Soung Kimm, taken from the Via Lucis blog, vialucis.word-press.com. We can see the 1:2:3 proportion design in the number of arches (2:4:6), made apparent by the number of arches and columns in each layer. It was built in the 10th and 11th centuries and is in the Ottonian, early Romanesque style.

Incorporating Proportion into Figurative Art

Here is an example of my work, an icon of the Sacred Heart, in which I have consciously tried to link pairs, or ideally triplets, of lines in rhythmical ratios and proportions. A single line might participate in two different proportional groups. Using this device, it is possible to aim for the ideal of avoiding isolated triplets of lines while creating an image in which each line is proportionate within itself, and related to all others. I tried my best! Bernini was a master of this.

You are looking for lines that related to each other such that the turn and length and change of angle seems to suggest a progression, as we can see in the isolated example shown here, to the right.

Next, we consider an icon by the Russian master Andre Rublev, painted in the 15th century. It is of (traditionally) bald St. Paul. If we look at the pattern of lines in his left sleeve (right from our perspective), we can see this pattern. Occasionally, he subtly departs from strict proportionality, sometimes turning a line at its end, for example, in the opposite direction in order to avoid a sense of strict adherence to formula. The general rule when using any principle of design is to follow it broadly but include a few dislocations or deliberate mistakes, so to speak, within. Provided the variations do not dominate one's overall impression of the picture, they always give the design vitality.

Here is an example of an early Renaissance painting that stills owes much to the Gothic. It is the *Raising of Lazarus* by Giotto (13th–14th century). We can see again the proportionate rhythm in the drapery.

Moving now to naturalistic styles, on the next page is a portrait of Louis XIV of France by the Italian sculptor Bernini, dated 1665.[25]

You can see the swirls in his hair follow this rhythmic pattern. The folds in the cloth (especially his upper right arm) are also cut to do so. Bernini has not sculpted precisely what he sees in doing this; he is modifying nature to impose this pattern onto the sculpture and then cutting more deeply into the stone so that the shadow lines are strong. He controls the passage of the eye over the piece by drawing it to the strong contrast between light and dark. He wrote about this, explaining that he did it because he couldn't use color as the painter could. It also explains why Bernini very often controlled the windows and, consequently, the direction of the light source for his work—he wanted to make sure that these shadows would be created.

25. Photo: Coyau / Wikimedia Commons/CC-BY-SA-3.0

As we get into more naturalistic painting, we see that the imposition of proportional lines must be handled carefully. The baroque era relied on an intuitive application of proportional relationships (often called baroque rhythm). The great genius of Bernini and baroque painters such as Rubens or Van Dyke is that they did so in such a way that it does not look unnaturally mechanical or mathematical, yet while retaining a sense of pattern. They deliberately incorporated offset or jarring lines (perhaps a concave relating to convex) as well so as to avoid this. In fact, this contrast of the non-conforming line with the conforming actually accentuates the harmony in a pleasing way and gives the painting greater natural vitality and life.

Here is a sculpture by Bernini of Blessed Ludovica Albertoni.

7

Golden or Fallen? A Note on Phi

My brothers, I implore you by God's mercy to offer your very selves to him;
a living sacrifice dedicated and fit for his acceptance, the worship offered
by mind and heart. Adapt yourselves no longer to the pattern of this
present world, but let your minds be remade and your whole nature thus
transformed. Then you will be able to discern the will of God, and to
know what is good, acceptable and perfect.

Rom 12:1–2

WHENEVER ONE MENTIONS the idea of "sacred proportion," many people, if they are aware of nothing else, will think of the Golden Section (also known as the Golden Mean, or Golden Ratio) and assume that this is what I am talking about. This reflects the fact that many today assume that it was a principle of design in traditional art and architecture. However, my sense is that its importance in the Western tradition has been overemphasized by modern writers.

The Golden Mean is calculated from the ratio of the lengths between adjacent and alternate tips of a five-pointed star to the length of the side of the regular pentagon that contains it: $1: \frac{1}{2}(1+\sqrt{5})$ or, less precisely, 1:1.618. Euclid defined it in his *Elements* as the "extreme and mean" ratio—a line divided in such a way that the smaller is to the greater as the greater is to the whole. It has been represented in the modern era by the symbol φ.

It is this appearance in Euclid's work that has contributed as much as anything to the idea that it was known and used by past artists and architects. Although we can be certain that it was known to the Greeks and thereafter to anyone who was aware of Euclid's geometry, I am not aware of any manuscript written by any architects and artists working prior to the Renaissance describing its use. It does not, for example, appear as one of the proportions recommended by the Roman architect Vitruvius in his famous textbook. Neither am I aware of any Christian interpretation of the symbolism of φ, although we have many interpretations of number and proportion from figures such as Augustine, Boethius, Aquinas, and Bonaventure. The manuscripts of the Gothic masons do not, to my knowledge, refer to it. It does not appear in Boethius's list of 10 fundamental beautiful proportions, and St. Augustine does not mention it in *De Musica* or any other source that I have read. The Pythagorean philosophy, which is the major source of traditional sacred number in the West, had a dislike of any proportions that could not be expressed using whole numbers, and did not give any great consideration to Euclid's ratio; nor have I found a scriptural basis for its use.

Wherever a pentagonal geometry is used in the design of a building—for example, the Gothic cathedral at Amiens—φ is going be found somewhere within it, because it is embedded within the fundamental dimensions of a pentagonal star. But this is as likely to be incidental to the choice of five-fold symmetry as it is a deliberate desire to manifest φ.

It was not until the 16th century that it was first called "Golden" or "Divine," by Luca Pacioli in a work published in 1509.[1] But Pacioli himself does not seem to have attached as much importance to it as many modern commentators assume. He did not propose its use in art or architecture, advocating instead the Vitruvian system based upon the Pythagorean philosophy.

Since then, we can be certain that some artists were aware of it because they refer to it in writing (e.g. Durer, Leonardo, Piero della Francesca), and although they did make use of number and proportion, very often the use of other systems is more apparent than that of φ. There is no written evidence from Leonardo himself, for example, that he used φ in his paintings (aside from his illustrations for Pacioli's book!). And although art historians Hugh Honour and John Fleming remark in their book that Piero discussed the Golden Section in his mathematical works, it does not appear in their analysis of any painting of his. For example, in their discussion of his *Baptism of Christ*, they state that the proportions correspond more the traditional Pythagorean musical harmony system: "the *Baptism* seems to have been geometrically based on a grid of three equidistant horizontals and four verticals, against which the slightest movements vibrate like the gently struck strings of a musical instrument."[2]

1. It has been suggested that Paciolo plagiarized his work from Piero della Francesca. See Mario Livio, *The Golden Ratio: The Story of Phi, the World's Most Astonishing Number* (New York: Broadway Books, 2003), p. 128.

2. Hugh Honour and John Fleming, *A World History of Art*, 7th edition (London: Lawrence King Publishing, 2005), p. 440.

The greatest interest in φ seems to have been from the late 19th and
20th centuries through to the present day. For example, the Swiss French
architect Le Corbusier, the pioneer of modern architecture, used it. As
one of the great pioneers of a modern architecture distinct from what
preceded it, this is hardly an argument in favor of φ being part of the
tradition.

Most of the evidence produced to support the idea that the Golden
Ratio was used prior to the modern era consists of modern geometric
analysis of buildings, often done on photographs of the building in
question. The reliability of conclusions drawn from such measurements, without other supportive evidence, is, in my opinion, low. Any
human process introduces random error, and this includes the design
and construction of building, as well as error in the geometric analysis
done after the fact. The construction lines placed over the photograph,
from which the supporting measurements are taken, are very often
placed on the photograph in such a way that one could use a similar
method to deduce whatever one wanted. The width of the drawn grid
lines placed on the photograph of the building, for example, would
introduce the risk, if one is not careful of a large margin of error. This
does not invalidate the analysis altogether, however; but one would be
more inclined to accept it if it was supported by further evidence indicating that the artist knew about and attached importance to the ratio.

The standard way of reducing random error when considering proportions in the natural world—for example, the ratio of lengths of
human finger-segments—is to take a large sample; in this case, that
would mean taking a large number of readings of many fingers. However, as there can only ever be one Chartres Cathedral, we are dealing
with a sample of one when studying it. This fact should cause us to be
careful when analyzing measurements taken from it.

The likelihood of the readings taken indicating that the builder
intended to build with the Golden Mean is reduced still further when
one considers that the ratio of 1:1.6 is numerically only 1% smaller than
the Golden Mean (if taken to be 1.168). 1:1.6 *is* mentioned by a number
of sources, but this is not the Golden Mean. Rather, it is a proportion
derived from the idealized proportions of the human figure. In this
form Vitruvius refers to it, taking it as 10:16; it is one of the 10 fundamental proportionalities of Boethius; and St. Augustine, who gives it an
explicitly Christian interpretation, referred to it as the ideal proportion
of Christ, matched by the dimensions of Noah's Ark.[3] No such interpretation has come down to us from the Church Fathers for φ.

3. St. Augustine, *City of God*, Bk. XV, Ch. 26.

In the absence of any corroborative evidence, to be certain that a measurement taken to correspond to φ and not the ideal human proportion of Augustine and Vitruvius, it would require us to accept that the error was better than ±0.6%. This is not credible to me. This final error would have contributions from the design made by a Gothic mason in his original drawing, further error introduced by the Gothic builder in translating the architect's proportions in the design to the final building; and the error incurred in making the measurements taken on the buildings, several centuries of erosion later.

There is an argument that says that the Golden Section is so natural to man that even if its presence is not intended, an architect or artist with a well-developed sense of beauty will naturally and unconsciously employ it because it will be pleasing to him. However, according to Mario Livio, even modern psychological research seems to indicate that the human mind has a greater attraction to the traditional Pythagorean ratios, such as 2:1, than to φ.[4]

Why is there such a strong interest in the Golden Mean today? First, φ appears to be the dominant proportionality of the natural world (at one point it was almost universally accepted, but even this is now being disputed). Awareness of this has increased steadily over the last 500 years due to scientific research. Many cite the Fibonacci series, which, it has since been discovered, does describe proportional changes in dimensions in living material undergoing natural growth processes in which the amount of new material depends upon the amount already there. The Fibonacci series is named after the Italian who published it in a math textbook in the 13th century. It is a numerical series in which each term is calculated by adding together the two previous terms: for example, 0, 1, 2, 3, 5, 8, 13, 21... This series will produce a ratio between successive terms that tends to φ as the series progresses to infinity (although its connection with φ was not made by Fibonacci himself and was not observed until much later). Even then, this series was not as new as commonly supposed. It was already known under another name in the West. It is the same as the tenth proportional relationship listed by Boethius in his *De Arithmetica*, called the "Fourth of Four." Like the Fibonacci, the Fourth of Four is a series of numbers that can be extended indefinitely. The first three terms after 1 and 2 are 3, 5, and 8, which is the same proportion as that commonly associated with human proportionality (6, 10, and 16) referred to by Vitruvius, the Roman

4. Mario Livio, *The Golden Ratio: The Story of Phi, the World's Most Astonishing Number* (New York: Broadway Books, 2003), p. 128.

architect, in his textbook published in the first century AD. St. Augustine's commentary about the proportions of Noah's ark compares it to
those of the ideal man, and these dimensions are consistent with those
of Vitruvius. For Augustine that ideal man is Christ himself.

If the series is extended, it corresponds to that of Fibonacci, i.e., 1, 2,
3, 5, 8, 13, 21... As stated, the ratio between any two numbers in this
series is always close to φ and tends towards it, as the number of terms
in the series tends to infinity. In contrast to Boethius, who drew importance to his series from consideration of the beauty of the abstract world
of mathematics, Fibonacci derived his series by consideration of natural
processes (the increase in numbers by reproduction of rabbits!). Perhaps it is this that caused a greater interest in it on the part of modern
man, who finds it more difficult to move from the natural to supernatural.

Some might argue that the ancients recognized the importance of φ
and employed the terms 3, 5, 8 in the Fourth of Four series to generate a
numerical approximation to it. This does not seem plausible to me, as
the same series very quickly generates precise ratios that are much closer
approximations of φ and which would have been just as easy to use if
that was the intention. Also, as mentioned before, they never tell us that
this is what they intended—that is a modern inference—giving instead
the proportions of ideal man as the justification.

The second reason, I suggest, is a consequence of the fact that the
beauty of nature has been exaggerated by the form of paganism that has
steadily taken hold in the West since the Enlightenment. Generally, if
moderns acknowledge any standard of beauty it will be that of the natural world apart from man. The Christian sees the beauty of the world
every bit as much as the neo-pagan, and agrees with him that it is good,
but knows also that it is fallen and there is an even greater beauty that is
consistent with the divine order and which leads ultimately to the idea
of pure Beauty—God. From the point of view of the Christian, mankind should not look to nature for the perfect standard of beauty, but
instead look beyond it to God. Only once we accept that the natural
world is imperfect can we believe that it is possible for the work of man,
with God's grace, to raise it up to something greater so that its beauty is
closer to this heavenly beauty. The farm and the garden are potentially
more beautiful forms of nature than the untouched wilderness from
which they came. Using a slightly different though not unrelated sense
of the word, we say that something is in accordance with its *nature* when
it is what it ought to be. By this definition, then, cultivated land is in fact
more natural that uncultivated. It is just as possible, of course, for the
work of man to lessen the beauty of nature, and this is very often what

we see today in our culture of ugliness. If nature is to become more beautiful, the farm and garden must be farmed and cultivated well.

In regard to the numerical description of the perfect beauty of man, it is interesting that in the ancient world the interest in Boethius's Fourth of Four proportionality focused on the early numbers in the series, which were equated with the ideal human form. The moderns, in contrast, search for an ideal at its end of its more widely known and more recent equivalent, the Fibonacci series, by consideration of what it tends to as the number of terms in the series tends to infinity.

The moderns, it seems, cannot see beyond the proportions of the fallen world, while the ancients followed the advice of St. Paul, who urges us to seek to adapt ourselves "*no longer to the pattern of this present world, but let your minds be remade and your whole nature thus transformed.*" Perhaps the Fourth of Four series traces a mathematical path that leads us from perfection at its beginning to the Fall at its end.

To give just one example of how a recent commentator describes its use without properly establishing it to be so, take a book written by Matila Ghyka, published first in 1947, called *The Geometry of Art and Life*.[5] In this he makes a case for φ as a basis for Egyptian art, the Greek canon of human proportionality of Polyclitus (which has been lost and for which there is no contemporary description in existence) and the Gothic church builders. He cites no single contemporary source, architect, artist, or otherwise, who refers to it as a basis for design. Rather, he relies on modern "harmonic" analyses of paintings and buildings by two people in particular, the 19th-century German Adolph Zeysing and the American Jay Hambidge, writing in 1919. He says:

> The Golden Section also plays a dominating part in the proportions of the human body, a fact that was probably [*sic*] recognized by Greek sculptors, who liked to put into evidence a parallelism between the proportions of the ideal temple and of the human body (cf. Vitruvius) or even to trace a harmonious correspondence between the terms Universe-Temple-Man. The correlation Universe-Man as macrocosmos-microcosmos was studied later by the Kabbala as well as the Christian mystics of the Middle Ages, and by later dabblers in black and white magic.[6]

So Ghyka is connecting the proportion of man, the temple (referring to Vitruvius), and the cosmos. Firstly, as we have said, Vitruvius does not attribute the Golden Section to man. Secondly, the idea of harmonious

---

5. Matila Ghyka, *The Geometry of Art and Life* (Mineola: Dover Press, 1977).
6. Ibid.

proportion was not some secret hidden knowledge of medieval Gnosticism, as he seems to imply, but was well known in Christian tradition. The important part of the correlation that is missing in his analysis, I suggest, is God, so it should be Universe-Man-Temple pointing together to the Creator. The Christian, who acknowledges a fallen world, will seek the idealized perfection of the Universe (or cosmos) and Man rather than the directly observed fallen versions.

A Modern Christian Interpretation of φ

Does this mean that the Christian should reject the use of φ? Even if I am right and there is no reference to it in Christian tradition, this does not rule out its use now. In fact, I would say that there is a strong argument for the fact that a genuinely Christian interpretation of φ could be developed.?

The representation of the fallen world does have its place in Christian tradition of figurative art, and if it is true that φ is a proportion that really does govern elements of a fallen universe, then I suggest that there is a case for its use in a way that reflects this.

As a suggestion, we might consider it in this way: symbolically, it is analogous to shadow in figurative art. The Baroque tradition of the 17th century used light/darkness symbolism. The dark shadow represents the presence of evil and suffering in a fallen world. However, in the Baroque system, the truth that God only permits evil to allow a greater good is communicated through the bright light. It is deliberately painted with light and dark placed next to each other, but in such a way that the overall impression is one of the light—representing the Light of Christ—which "overcomes the darkness." That is to say that hope in Christ overcomes all suffering and unhappiness.

In the context of this discussion, φ is a symbolic geometric representation of the fallen world. This means that, if we are to learn a lesson from the Baroque masters, its use should not be in isolation, but applied in a context that ultimately resolves it into the proportions of perfection. The use of a detail of a composition which is less than perfect to highlight by contrast what has a greater perfection is a traditional device, employed long before the 17th century for enhancing the overall beauty of a work of art. It is described, for example, in the *Summa halsiana* of Alexander of Hales:

> Evil, as such, is misshapen.... Nevertheless since from evil comes good, it is therefore well said that it contributes to good and hence it is said to be beautiful within the order of things. Thus it is not called

beautiful in an absolute sense, but beautiful within the order; in fact it would be preferable to say: "The order itself is beautiful."[7]

To make a musical analogy, there is room for chromaticism and dissonance provided that it doesn't dominate the overall sense and ultimately is resolved.

But If We Are Going to Use It, Please, Change the Name!

Regardless of whether or not there is a place for φ in Christian harmonics, one thing I would wish to change is the common name for φ. "Golden" and "divine" are traditional attributes of the redeemed world and so seem inappropriate names for φ. I would be more inclined to use a name that attaches it to the imperfection of this world: perhaps "Fallen" or "Dark" Section might be better.

---

7. Cf. Alexander of Hales, *Summa halesiana*, II, quoted by Umberto Eco, *A History of Beauty* (New York: Rizzoli, 2004), p. 148.

PART THREE

The Forms of Figurative Christian
Liturgical Art: A Guide for Artists and
Those Establishing a Canon of Images for
Study in an Education of Beauty

8

What are the Figurative Liturgical Traditions of the Catholic Church?

Which Traditions?

THIS SECTION is an overview of the authentic liturgical traditions of Christian figurative art, as identified by Benedict XVI: the iconographic, the Gothic, and the Baroque at "its best." In his book *The Spirit of the Liturgy* he explains persuasively why he chooses these traditions, citing reasons that indicate a deep knowledge of Christian culture.[1] Although he cannot be taken as speaking infallibly on such matters, I take him to be an authority and do not question his judgment.

From this starting point, the intention in what follows is to give the reader sufficient familiarity with the essentials of each tradition to be able to choose examples for a canon of imagery for teaching purposes; and also to be able see how the style of sacred art became the model for non-sacred art, so illustrating the general point that all cultural forms begin with what we hold sacred.

Only These?

In asserting that these three styles are the authentic Catholic liturgical traditions that have been developed in the past, I *am* saying that there are no other mainstream artistic traditions yet developed that can be considered appropriate for the liturgy.

However, I *am not* saying that there are no individual works of art from other times and other traditions that for various particular reasons might be appropriate for the liturgy.

The advantage of staying with the established traditions when choosing art for the liturgy is the greater certainty that it is good simply because over a long period of time many people—patrons of artists and those who pray—have judged these to be good. While this is not abso-

1. Benedict XVI, *The Spirit of the Liturgy* (San Francisco: Ignatius Press, 2000), p. 129.

lute proof of goodness, it is a reasonable indication. This is why it pays to be conservative in regard to the liturgy. To get this wrong is to play with people's souls.

Also, I do not rule out the possibility of the development of more liturgical traditions in the future. As all traditions began at some point with one artist, perhaps even one painting, it might happen again in the future when some new style meets the need of the time that the existing traditions do not. One wonders, for example, if at some point in the future, the Beuron School of the 19th century, which was a Catholic reaction to the exaggerated realism of academic art of the day and looked to ancient Egyptian art for inspiration, might be one of these. Regardless of how good any individual artist might be, there can be great change before an ethos of tradition is re-established. If nearly every artist is seeking to be original, as is commonly the case today, then no work of art, no matter how brilliant, can set the pattern; for all other artists will aim to differ from, not conform to, that which has gone before. One of the hopes of this book is that it might in some small way contribute to the re-establishment of the principle of tradition in contemporary culture.

Furthermore, in promoting the iconographic, the Gothic, and the Baroque as the norm for liturgical art, I am not saying either that other traditions or individual styles have no merit in other contexts, even as private devotional sacred art. Devotional works of sacred art are different from liturgical art and much more a matter of personal choice. If I judge that a particular artist's work helps my prayer at home in an individual way, then it probably does. That is very different, however, from asserting that it will have the same effect on all people. Art that is universal, on the other hand, will appeal to most people, for it manifests something that is good for them all (though some may fail to see it). The liturgical traditions of the Church have demonstrated that they possess this universality.

In *The Spirit of the Liturgy*, Benedict explains why the style of art is as important as its content when considering its merits. He acknowledges that one purpose of sacred art is didactic and pedagogical—that is, its content must instruct the faithful through the representation of the events of history of God in relation to man. However, it must do more. The whole point of sacred art "is to lead us beyond what can be apprehended at the merely material level, to awaken new senses in us, and to teach us a new kind of seeing which perceives the Invisible in the visible."[2] Art reveals invisible truths by deviating partially and in a controlled way from an absolutely literal portrayal of visual appearance.

2. Benedict XVI, *The Spirit of the Liturgy*, p. 133.

Quite how this reveals invisible truths (or for that matter misrepresents them, in the case of bad art) will be discussed in more detail in this section. But it is the way that the artist tries to do so that gives the work of an artist, or a tradition, its characteristic style.

Although sometimes we might wish that it would, the Church has never dictated at the level of canon law exactly what sacred art should look like. This is because it wishes to give full freedom to man's creative impulse to the greater glory of God. So it is always open to innovations and new styles, provided that they have a balanced abstraction in accord with revealing truth; and provided that the innovation is a response to a particular need of the Church (as the Baroque was, for example, being initiated by the requests of the Council of Trent in the mid-16th century.) Pius XII put it as follows in 1947:

> Modern artists should be given free scope in the due and reverent service of the church and the sacred rites, provided that they preserve a correct balance between styles tending neither to extreme realism nor to excessive "symbolism," and that the needs of the Christian community are taken into consideration rather than the particular taste or talent of the individual artist.[3]

The great traditions of figurative art in the Church are models of how this can be done, as well as the platforms from which we must begin if ever there is a need for innovation. Each was developed from the aggregated and accumulated work of many artists over a period of time. Each seeks to reveal the whole person, but at different stages of realization of our human destiny, which is ultimately to be united with God in heaven.

Benedict explains further how the style of the whole liturgical tradition is set by the way in which one person, Christ, is portrayed. Every image of Christ must stylistically represent certain aspects of the *mystery* of Christ, and in this sense must be an image of Easter: "The center of the icon of Christ is the Paschal Mystery; Christ is presented as Crucified, the risen Lord, the One who will come again and who here and now hiddenly reigns over all."[4] Different traditions of liturgical art may emphasize one aspect more than the other, giving "prominence to the Cross, the Passion, and in the Passion the anguish of our own life today, or it may bring the Resurrection and the Second Coming to the fore. But whatever happens, one aspect cannot be completely isolated from another and in the different emphases, the Paschal Mystery as a whole must be plainly evident."[5]

---

3. Pius XII, *Mediator Dei*, 195.
4. Benedict XVI, *The Spirit of the Liturgy*, p. 128.
5. Ibid.

In general, those styles that focus more on the suffering of our temporal existence, such as the Gothic and, especially, the Baroque, will emphasize more strongly also that "human suffering belongs to the mystery and so bring forth also Christian joy derived from the hope that transcends suffering."[6] In the Baroque, the art of the 17th century in which the anguish is sometimes portrayed with great emotional realism, the joy that it reveals is correspondingly intense, described by Benedict as a "unique kind of *fortissimo* of joy, an Alleluia in visual form."[7]

Why Not the High Renaissance?

Before we explain in more detail the features that characterize the three traditions, it is worth making mention, I think, of the High Renaissance. Some may be surprised at the absence of works from the age that produced artists such as Leonardo, Raphael, Michelangelo, and Titian, perhaps some of the most famous artists of all time. I took my guidance here, again, from Benedict XVI, who judged that the art of this period was not truly sacred:

> The Renaissance did something quite new ... its art speaks of the grandeur of man almost as if it were surprised by it; it needs no other beauty to seek. ... The tragic burden of antiquity is forgotten; only its divine beauty is seen. A nostalgia for the gods emerges, for myth, for a world without the fear of sin. ... True, Christian subjects are still being depicted, but "religious art" is no longer sacred in the proper sense. It does not enter into the humility of the other sacraments and their time-transcending dynamism.[8]

This is not a condemnation of all that happened during this period; there were some artists who produced some work that was worthy of the Church (most especially those mentioned above). However, as a general picture of the time it is, I think, a fair reflection. When the Council of Trent asked for a renewed focus on art in the service of the Faith, it was in part in reaction to the period of the High Renaissance that had preceded it. As result, in the middle of the 16th century, artists set themselves to the task, and what emerged eventually in the beginning of the 17th century, starting with Caravaggio, was a synthesis of the best of the previous century. The result was a full integration of the theology and form of high naturalism that had not existed before.

6. Ibid.
7. Ibid., p. 130.
8. Ibid., p. 129.

9

The Theology and Form of
the Artistic Traditions of the Church

EVERY TIME I paint, I have to ask myself two questions: *what* will I paint, and *how* will I paint it? The answers to these questions govern the *content* and the *form*, respectively, of my finished painting and in turn their conformity to what is good, true, and beautiful.

Most discussions of Christian art that I have read focus on the significance of the content. This is good, of course; but in focusing on content one must not forget that form is a vital component, too. As an artist I must seek to ensure that the form of my painting conforms to the transcendentals as much as everything else. This is not only the responsibility of the artist. Patrons must also be aware of this. When as I am selecting works of other artists, no matter what the purpose, I must have some criteria to guide me, so that what I pick is good and appropriate to the purpose.

My approach is first to disregard personal taste. Rather than ask, do I like it?, I ask first, is this true? If the content and form in combination seem to be conveying a message that is in contravention of truth, then I will reject it. I must acknowledge the possibility that my judgment as to what is beautiful is flawed, so regardless of how attractive I might find the painting, I try to judge it first based upon truth. I know that beauty and truth cannot be in opposition, so if reason tells me that something does not conform to truth, then I will disregard my sense of its beauty, which is more intuitive and less easy to rationalize. However, personal taste should not be ignored altogether. Once I have done my best to make a judgment in regard to truth and have decided that it is true, *then* I ask myself the question, do I like it? (Or, if it is to be seen by others, will it be liked by them?)

How does one judge truth? It is easier to see how one can relate truth to content. If what is shown is contrary to the message of the Gospels, for example, then it is false. But what of truth in relation to form? This is a more difficult question to answer. But perhaps the most important factor that governs my ability to do so is an understanding of the nature of the human person and his relationship with God and the rest of creation.

All of creation is made by God so that we might know Him through it. Therefore an image of any aspect of creation must do this also—a landscape, for example, must portray the beauty of the scenery depicted in such a way that the image draws the person who sees it to God, its Creator. Mankind has a privileged place in the hierarchy of Creation, and so, when painting the human figure, the artist has a special responsibility to reflect the truth and beauty of the human person. Because the human figure consists of a profound unity of body and soul, the artist must reveal both. So the figure must both have a body that is recognizably human, and be portrayed so that those looking at the image see a thinking, feeling person.

When we meet someone in the flesh, we know the spiritual aspects of a person most obviously through observation of their actions and words over a period of time. The artist who paints (or sculpts) is forced to create a snapshot, frozen in time. Nevertheless, he must somehow reveal the spiritual through the material. To this end, the good Christian artist will introduce controlled deviations from a strict photographic representation. This partial abstraction, when done well, reveals more, not less, of the reality of what is portrayed.

To abstract means literally to draw out, and so in this context the artist is drawing out the truth. It is this process of partial abstraction that gives an artist's work its characteristic style. When that style reveals truth, the product is a beautiful idealization. When it hides truth, as much modern art does, the result is an ugly distortion. The work of the Christian artist, in the context of figurative art, must always contain this balance of naturalism and idealization. To do so in accordance with the teachings of the Church requires the artist to be theologian, philosopher, liturgist, and craftsman all rolled into one. This is a tall order indeed, but, fortunately, the Church offers us great guidance here in the form of tradition.

The identifiable traditions of authentically Catholic art are distinguishable from one another stylistically because they seek to reveal different aspects of humanity in relation to God and creation. Those who have read John Paul II's *Theology of the Body* will be aware that there are different stages of human existence. First, there is man before the Fall, called Original Man, when Adam and Eve were "naked without shame" and enjoyed innocence that comes from dependence upon God. Second, there is Historical Man, mankind after the Fall, experiencing the fear and resentment that results from a dislocation in the relationships with each other and with God. Though not as good as man ought to be, Historical Man is still good and has the potential for sanctity. As historical men and women, we are all too familiar with this aspect of the human condition. Third, there is Eschatological Man: in this stage we fulfill our human purpose, partaking of the divine nature in heaven in communion with the Trinity in a perfect exchange of love and in perfect and perpetual bliss.

The iconographic tradition reveals Eschatological Man (the example shown on the previous page is a 13th-century Greek icon of St. Michael the Archangel). Drawing on biblical episodes such as the Transfiguration, the style shows, for example, the divine light shining from the saints and eliminates the illusion of space to show that the heavenly dimension is outside time and space.

The Baroque reveals Historical Man. The painting of Abraham and Isaac by Sir Anthony van Dyck is an example of the Baroque style. In contrast with the iconographic style, the baroque sets out to create an illusion of space, using devices such as perspective, and shows deep-cast shadow from external light sources. Shadow represents the presence of

evil and suffering, which is contrasted with brightly lit areas representing the Light that overcomes the darkness.

The Gothic is the third Catholic figurative tradition that Benedict cites as an authentically Catholic liturgical tradition. This appears to oscillate between the styles of Eschatological and Historical Man. Like the spires of the Gothic churches, it reaches up to heaven but is firmly planted on earth. It might be argued that this reflects the fact that although we can never fully make that transformation to Eschatological Man in this world, there is nevertheless a continuum between the two states along which we can make progress through the transforming process of participation in the sacramental life of the Church. The late-Gothic artist Fra Angelico, for example, used elements of both the visual vocabulary of the increased naturalism that was developing around him, such as perspective and shadow and the iconographic prototype of light and "flatness." He did so in a sophisticated and self-consistent way, and his selection of device on each occasion depended upon the theological point he wanted to communicate.

I am not aware of a tradition with a distinctive form that has emerged from a focus on the theology of Original Man. This is not the place for an extended discussion about what the art of Original Man might look like, except to say that the writings of the Church Fathers, such as St. Ephraim the Syrian, and John Paul II himself suggest that he shines with glory in a way that seems to me to suggest the form of a slightly more naturalistic Eschatological Man, clothed in splendor. This would suggest something like the iconographic or the Gothic. If I were given the task of painting Original Man, it is the art of Fra Angelico that I would choose as my starting-point. The example shown above is Fra Angelico's *Resurrection*.[1]

When I paint, I aim to let tradition guide me in my work as far as possible. If I want to paint the human figure, the first question I should ask myself is, "What form of man?" If I decide to portray Eschatological Man, then, rather than trying to develop my own individual style, the sensible thing is to go to the iconographic tradition and let the principles of that tradition guide my hand. This will not lead to pastiche—an unthinking copying of the past—for every truly living tradition is defined by principles, rather than strict rules, which are reapplied in every age. So, for example, someone who knows icons can see from the style alone what geographical region a given icon came from and when it was painted to within, perhaps, 50 years. Only if I am seeking to communicate something previously uncommunicated should I look to create something that is original in style; and then I would go about it as artists did in the past and seek out the guidance of the theologians, philosophers, and liturgists of the Church.

Is there a place for new forms? Hasn't it all been done already? As mentioned before, I think not, and there is a need for thought on how to create the image of Original Man. Certainly, in his *Letter to Artists*, John Paul II called on artists to find new ways to represent human sexuality as gift. Maybe this will be the art of the next age? If so, it will be a dialogue between the artists and the theologians, philosophers and liturgists of the Church that will shape the new form, just as similar dialogues shaped the established ones; and what will drive the development of new forms will be that articulated need of the Church for something new—not the whim of an artist who wants to stand out from the crowd.

The principles of being open to new forms, with the impetus for change coming from the Church rather than the artist, and the need for

1. Those who are interested in a longer discussion about the place of the nude in art, especially in the light of John Paul II's focus on Original Man in his Theology of the Body, should read my essay "The Place of the Nude in Sacred Art" from the collection, Francesca Murphy, ed., *The Beauty of God's House* (Eugene: Cascade Books, 2014).

a balance of naturalism and idealism were expressed with great clarity by Pope Pius XII in *Mediator Dei*:

> Recent works of art which lend themselves to the materials of modern composition, should not be universally despised and rejected through prejudice. Modern art should be given free scope in the due and reverent service of the church and the sacred rites, provided that they preserve the correct balance between styles tending neither to extreme realism or to excessive "symbolism," and that the needs of the Christian community are taken into consideration rather than the particular taste or talent of the individual artist.[2]

So far I have only discussed liturgical form, which pertains to art placed inside the church; but what I say applies just as much to art that is not intended to be seen in a church, or to devotional art. This is because *all* good art should be rooted in the liturgy. It is the cult that is the foundation of Catholic culture. So even if the content is not obviously religious, such as with a landscape, the form can be liturgical, and so the art then becomes a profane signpost, as it were, to the sacred liturgy.[3] The Baroque of the 17th century, for example, began as a liturgical art form intended for church, but it came to dominate the whole culture of the period so that all art, architecture, and music was in conformity with it. Pius XII put it as follows in *Mediator Dei*: "The fine arts are really in conformity with religion when 'as noblest handmaids they are at the service of divine worship.'"[4]

And non-figurative art? Much abstract art produced since the turn of the 20th century is based upon a secular understanding of the human person that is in opposition to the Catholic teaching. So, for example, some abstract expressionists sought to portray human emotion without any reference to the body of the human person. This is, in effect, an abstraction that goes beyond the bounds of truth. It seeks to remove the soul from the body altogether, reflecting the error of dualism. For the Christian, emotion, though an aspect of the soul, is revealed through the body. So we cannot portray human emotion fully in art without portrayal of the body that expresses it.

That is not to say that there is no legitimate Catholic form of non-figurative, "abstract" art. As we know, the traditional *quadrivium*, which is the "four ways" that formed the higher part of the seven liberal arts,

---

2. Pope Pius XII, *Mediator Dei*, 195.

3. It should be noted that this does not rule out the possibility of the portrayal of the imagination, provided that it directs the imagination of the viewer to something that is true, as in good children's stories (and their illustrations), for example.

4. Pius XII, *Mediator Dei*, 196, quoting Pius XI, *Divini cultus*.

sought to represent the divine order mathematically. The fact that mathematics can be conceived in the abstract and represented visually allows for a patterned, geometric art form that is in conformity with truth. The cosmati pavements of the 13ᵗʰ century are examples of this art form. Shown below is the Basilica of San Clemente in Rome.

The mathematical description of the divine order also allows for the structuring and organization of time and space, and the design of just about anything—that is, the culture in the fullest sense of the word: the family, society, business, education—to be ordered liturgically by conformity to the cosmic order that points to the mind of the Creator.

10

The Development of
the Iconographic Style

T HE DEVELOPMENT OF a unique style of Christian art began after
Christianity became the official religion of the Roman Empire
under the Emperor Constantine in the 4ᵗʰ century AD. For the
first time, artists were able to paint works for public viewing on a large
scale. At first, they used the styles that were used for all art in the Roman
Empire. Mosaics in Ravenna, in Italy, dating from 428, such as that of
the Good Shepherd, are indistinguishable in style from the Late Antique
art that existed in the Roman world at that time.

The figures are highly naturalistic: there is a landscape setting for the
figure that creates an illusion of depth and a sense of space using a basic
perspective. There are other mosaics in Ravenna that date from only 120
years later yet are quite different in style. If we look at the mosaic of the
Emperor Justinian and his retinue (see next page), we can see that

though it is clearly derived from the earlier form, the figures are much more stiff and formal. All are portrayed full-face, none in profile. The negative "space" around the figures is not devoted to the depiction of the illusion of depth. The figures almost give the appearance of cut-outs pasted onto a flat surface. All this, and other features we shall discuss later, contribute to a deliberate stylization and can be accounted for in terms of the Christian understanding of the human person and our place in Creation. For example, the flat negative space is a visual representation of heaven or the fullness of God, the eternal sphere where there is no time and no space.

All mankind is made by God to be united with Him in heaven in perfect bliss. To the degree that we choose to cooperate with God's grace, every single one of us will have the chance of seeing Him face-to-face and partaking in the Divine nature. The stylistic features of the iconographic tradition were developed to reveal to us this heavenly ideal of mankind. Through the medium of a painting they portray the idea of what saints look like, so to speak, in heaven, in a way that we fallen people can grasp. Once the new style of iconography had been developed, it spread throughout the whole Christian world. There are icons, such as the Christ Pantocrator (below, next page), painted around the same period in Mount Sinai in modern-day Egypt.

This prototype, which we might refer to as the "Byzantine" and the one we recognize today most commonly as the liturgical art of the Eastern Church, was in fact the prototype for all Christian art, East and

West, Latin and Greek, up to the end of the Romanesque period (about 1200).

While conforming to the iconographic prototype, there have always been identifiable local variations in style, usually achieved through a fusion with other traditional forms. Even when various parts of the West became relatively isolated due to the subsequent disintegration of the Western Roman Empire, contact with other Christian communities never stopped altogether. There was a continuous line of contact through warfare, trade, and monastic religious communities throughout the Christian world. The monasteries especially preserved culture and learning in the West, and even those on the Celtic fringe, in Ireland, were in touch with their Eastern monastic brethren. This is known because of the discovery of Byzantine artifacts in the West. We see Celtic art, Carolingian art (named after Charlemagne), and Ottonian art (named after Otto I, the Holy Roman Emperor crowned in 962) all conforming to the iconographic prototype. These Western art forms incorporated the swirls and flowing lines of their abstract decorative art into a highly stylized figurative art form, but nevertheless they are true to the iconographic ideal. To the right is Christ Enthroned from the 8th/9th-century Irish Book of Kells.

After 1000 there was an increase in communication between East and West, much of it through warfare (including the Crusades), and this affected Western art. What we now recognize as Romanesque art used the greater degree of naturalism (as compared with Ottonian or Celtic art) of the Eastern icons. This period is called Romanesque from a description coined in the 19th century, meaning "debased Roman," that referred to architecture retaining columns and rounded arches. Below is an English illumination from the 13th-century Westminster Psalter that is consistent with the iconographic tradition.

The Development of a New
Non-Iconographic Prototype in the West

The same forces that led to renewed contact with the Christian East also established contact with the Islamic East and West (in Spain). This contact sowed the seeds for the adoption of a different artistic prototype in the West. It is ironic that the society whose art was epitomized by patterned abstraction due to its rejection of figurative art, namely Islam, should, through allowing the "rediscovery" of the philosophy of Aristotle, provide a strong impetus for a greater naturalism in Western art.

Through the incorporation of Aristotle into Western Christian thought by theologians such as St. Thomas Aquinas, people started to look at the world in a new way. The force that turned this change in outlook of the scholarly circles into a more widespread phenomenon was spiritual. St. Francis of Assisi, who loved the beauty of nature, was a hugely popular and influential saint. Franciscan spirituality created an enthusiasm and love for the natural world that had not existed before to the same degree and caused the development of the scientific observation of nature as well as an increased naturalism in art. Gothic art and architecture reflects this, beginning a shift in art towards a greater consideration of man's place in the fallen world, which would culminate in the Baroque.

The art of the Eastern Church was not affected by the development of the Gothic style in the West, but it was affected by the Renaissance. Unlike in the West, however, this did not result so much in new authentic liturgical forms, but in an inferior iconographic form. The degeneration of the iconographic form was accelerated during the Enlightenment, which affected Russia particularly, under Peter the Great and Catherine the Great. The re-establishment of what we think of the "pure" iconographic prototype in the Eastern Church didn't occur until the mid-20th century under figures such as the Greek Photius Kontoglou, and especially by Russian expatriates in France such as Leonid Ouspensky and Gregory Kroug. Catholics especially should remember that much of what we read today about the iconographic tradition was in fact generated by a 20th-century examination of past icons by these Orthodox figures. As a result, it tends to assert Orthodox theology and mysticism very strongly. Generally, this is a good thing, but it tends as well to promote a view that anything exclusively Catholic is invalid. In the context of art, therefore, it encourages the erroneous view that the icon is the only legitimate form of liturgical art, and sometimes also the idea, also erroneous, that icons and their veneration is the exclusive preserve of the Eastern Church.

The Theology of Icons

As we have stated, the "ideal" of man that an icon-painter seeks to portray is mankind in heaven, where all are purified without trace of sin in the state of final unification with God. In trying to ascertain what mankind looks like in heaven, theologians and artists looked primarily to the Bible. Man in heaven is described in the book of Revelation. A glimpse of the divine appearance of the body was also seen in Christ himself at the Transfiguration (Matthew 17:1–8; Luke 9:28–36; 2 Peter 1:16–18). In this passage, Christ and the apostles Peter, James, and John went up "on a high mountain where they were alone." Christ is described in Luke's Gospel: "the fashion of his face was altered, and his garments became white and dazzling." Matthew says that his face was "shining like the sun, and his garments became white as snow." Peter describes a "splendor that dazzles human eyes." In John's vision of heaven, described in Revelation, he says that the saints "will see the Lord face to face, and his name will be written on their foreheads. It will never be night again and they will not need lamplight or sunlight, because the Lord God will be shining on them" (Revelation 22:4–5).

When the apostles saw Christ transfigured, they saw Him for those few moments as those who are pure see Him when they are in heaven. The ascent of the mountain is often interpreted as a metaphor for the ascent of their souls towards heaven. There appeared also with Christ two prophets known to be in heaven, Elijah and Moses. The light that was seen is referred to as "uncreated" in the sense that it is the divine light that exists throughout all time. This is to be contrasted with the "created" light that we normally see in the material universe, such as that from the sun or electric light bulbs.

We know saints in heaven partake of the divine nature in heaven. There are also recorded cases of the saints revealing aspects of heaven while still on earth as they became purer or holier. In the book of Exodus, we read that the skin of Moses's face shone with an unearthly radiance after he had conversed with God on Mount Sinai; for a time he had to wear a veil because the Israelites could not bear to look to look on this brightness (Exodus, 34:29–35). St. Paul refers to this in the second letter to the Corinthians and says explicitly that this transfiguration is open to all of us: "It is given to us, all alike, to catch the glory of the Lord as in a mirror, with faces unveiled; and so we become transfigured into the same likeness, borrowing glory from that glory, as the Spirit of the Lord enables us" (2 Corinthians 3:18).

As a result of the Fall, a level of disorder exists in the world. There is a tension in mankind's relationship with visible creation, which has become alien and hostile and, like man, is now subject to decay. The icon provides a contrast with the fallen world we see around us and portrays creation as redeemed. As the purpose of icons is to give us a glimpse of how things will seem when we are in heaven, and man in heaven appears different from man on earth, there is no interest in portraying man naturalistically. This is not to say that man in heaven bears no relation to man on earth. The final resurrection at the end of time will be a resurrection of the body, and in the age to come we will be complete in our nature, with both body and soul. We will have bodies with arms and legs and so on that are recognizable as such.

When painting icons, individual style is never sought as an end in itself. Quite the contrary, the artist seeks to conform to the accepted standards. This does not prevent individual styles from emerging quite naturally, however. The work of well-known iconographers is instantly recognizable, and we have already noted that given a previously unseen icon, anyone who knows icons well will be able to identify at least the geographical region that it came from and the time that it was painted, perhaps to within 50 years. The appearance of characteristic styles occurs in a different way from that of modern art, in which individualism is deliberately sought. The distinctive style of an icon is never sought directly, but occurs through the humble desire of the individual to conform to the will of God. It is a true "self-expression," a reflection of the person God intends us to be; and a realization of the maxim that in self-forgetfulness we find our true selves.

The Stylistic Elements of Icons

The style of the icon reflects our knowledge of the ideal it is portraying. First, some features of the saints are exaggerated. The organs that receive information are slightly enlarged: the eyes, the ears, and the nose are lengthened. Those parts of the body that are expressive are slightly reduced in size: the mouth, the hands (the fingers on the hand, however, are given a gracefulness by being made slightly tapered and lengthened). This is to emphasize the saintly qualities of temperance and humility: the saint always listens and considers information received before acting with wisdom. They are not shown displaying great emotion, but with a controlled and calm demeanor.

Because the saint is a source of light, there is no deep shadow as in Western naturalistic art. A shadow is only cast when there is a light source that is distinct from the object that is casting it. For the same reason, the eyes never have the glint of reflected light on them. If you go into any art gallery that has traditional Western portraits, the chances are that every single one will have a reflective glint painted on the eyes. Furthermore, egg tempera, the medium used in iconography, has a higher visual register than, for example, oil paint. (Egg tempera is made by making a paste of the pigment with egg yolk and then diluting with water.) One might characterize it as looking like morning light, while oil looks like evening light (and acrylic looks as though it is illuminated by fluorescent strip lighting!). Gold is often used to represent the glow of uncreated light around the saint. The disc of gold around the head is the halo. (The icon on the previous page is a modern icon of the Archangel Gabriel, and in this the golden background, indicating the presence of God, is differentiated from the light emanating from the angel's head by a red circular line.) It is interesting to note, therefore, that the halo is not a symbol, as such, of sainthood. Rather, it is a direct representation of uncreated light that emanates from saints. When the halo is depicted as a yellow hoop floating above the crown of the saint, as in some Western art, the halo is reduced to an arbitrary symbol unrelated in appearance to the reality it portrays.

Saints, such as the Archangel Gabriel, shown above, are depicted full-face-to-three-quarters turned towards us, never in profile, so that we have a sense of seeing them "face-to-face." This gives them a characteristic look that interacts with those looking at the icon and pulls their attention towards it. Usually the sense in icons is that there is no foreground portrayed; figures always appear to occupy the far or, at closest, middle ground. There is always a sense of distance between them and us. So, as fast as their gaze pulls us in, they keep receding into the middle ground. This effect is achieved by controlling the angle of vision; that is, the size of the figures portrayed relative to the distance from which they will commonly be seen. This should be contrasted with Western naturalistic tradition of the Baroque, which (for different but nevertheless sound theological reasons) generally places the protagonists in the foreground. In Caravaggio's *Supper at Emmaus*, for example, shown below (painted at the beginning of the 17th century and now housed in the National Gallery in London), the viewer is almost made to feel as though he is sitting at the empty space of the table with Christ and the apostles. He brings the saints right to us.

In iconography, everything is deliberately painted to be two-dimensional; there is very little sense of depth behind the plane of the panel (we will explain why this is undesirable in a moment in the section entitled "Windows to Heaven"). This is achieved by the lack of deep shadow, as mentioned before, and by the use of the medium of egg tempera, which always appears flat. Oil paint was rejected as a medium because it creates imagery that is too three-dimensional. When oil paint is used in dark glazes, the painting sinks into the depths beyond the plane of the painting. In contrast, when tempera uses black, for instance, it just sits like soot on the surface. Also, because egg tempera dries in just a few minutes (if it is the first application to the gesso surface, it dries even quicker, in a matter of seconds), blending of tones and colors is difficult and there is little scope for expressive brushwork. Oil, in contrast, takes days to dry and so can be blended easily and seamlessly, and is a good medium for subtle modeling. These properties mean that oil paint helps the artist to enhance the sense of naturalism, while tempera inhibits the naturalism of the painting and heightens the sense of symbolism in the image, which is desirable in an icon.

There is very little landscape detail shown in icons, and few buildings; only what is necessary to the events being depicted is shown. These are shown idealized as well, as seen through the eyes of purity. The expulsion from Eden is not a geographical displacement, but a radical change in the human relationship to God and to creation. Once matter is redeemed, as it will be at the final end of all time, it enters into the heavenly realm that is outside time. Although it is a future event when considering things in the temporal sense, those things outside time are in a state of perpetual being, so one could almost say that if it will happen, it already has happened. Just as the liturgy of the Church is a temporal participation in the eternal heavenly liturgy, the uncreated light painted emanating from saints portrayed as still alive is revealing a temporal participation in their eternal redeemed state. The icon is the eternal momentarily bursting through into the temporal. When the icon shows redeemed matter other than people, e.g., plants and so forth, they are shown as redeemed and without decay. Also, nature is portrayed so as to emphasize its place in the natural hierarchy and order, with man at the pinnacle, and Christ foremost among mankind, followed by Mary, the Mother of God. Therefore, trees and rocks might be depicted as bowing or bending towards a saint.

Where landscape details or buildings are depicted, it is usual to avoid conventional Western perspective. In fact, there are many types of perspective used in icons to help us emerge from our egocentric worldview and see as God sees, with the eyes of purity. One example is the *multi-view perspective*, where the front and back of an object are portrayed at once, encouraging us to see the world immersed in the omnipresent God. It suggests that when we look at something with purity we are not restricted in our knowledge of it by our position in relation to it; we can in a sense know it fully. Once, when I was teaching a 12-year-old about icons, we were painting an icon of St. Luke (facing) in which both the front and the back were simultaneously portrayed. I described the idea of this to her by saying that in heaven, which is outside time and space, we can be everywhere at once and so it as though we can walk around the back, have a look, and come back to the front again, and yet no time has elapsed. *Inverse perspective* makes us rather than a fictitious place within the image the vanishing point. By moving through the real space between the icon and ourselves, the lines of this perspective convey grace to the area before us. Inverse perspective also gives the sense that the saints are looking at us, that we are the object of the icon's contemplation. *Isometric perspective*, where planes and lines remain parallel and undistorted by distance, affirms the integrity of each thing in itself, regardless of how it appears to the physical senses. The general *flatness* of icons helps us to pass through the image to meet the holy person who is its subject. The related *tipped perspective*, where, for example, a horizontal surface is portrayed at an angle tipped toward us, so that all things on it are clearly visible, allows things to be arranged more freely on the vertical plane than with conventional single-point perspective designed to create a sense of depth. This permits greater use of traditional, "sacred" geometry as an abstract system of order so as to lend harmony to the image. It also allows the iconographer to use *hieratical perspective*, where things are arranged according to their spiritual importance—the more important figures are made more prominent in the composition through variation in size and placement.

In addition, in design terms the lines of the inverse perspective bring  the eye towards the saint from all parts of the icon as they radiate out from it. Furthermore, it enhances the sense that everything is taking place in the plane of the painting. If a building is depicted, for example, reason tells us that it should occupy a large space beyond the icon plane, and our minds will tend to create that space for it to occupy. In the icon, however, every time our minds try to take our attention to occupy a space beyond the icon plane, these perspective systems ensure that we are pushed back; it deliberately works to destroy the illusion of space.

As mentioned above, I was taught to order the composition of icons in accordance with principles of sacred geometry. In common with all figurative art, in order for the artist to be able to arrange the figures without destroying the sense of unity, relatively simple geometry is employed. I was taught to use simple ratios such as the musically derived harmonies of 1:2, 2:3 and 3:4. These would be applied to the outer proportions of the icon; and within, the important events of the compositional theme were placed at positions of approximately a half, a third and a quarter-way across the image. However, these were never seen as an end in themselves, but simply as guidelines that can lead us to a well-balanced composition. At the end of the process, I was taught always to look at the painting as a whole and modify according to intuition so that it looks unified and well-balanced.

Windows to Heaven: How Icons Affect Prayer

All the elements described combine to create a dynamic process that first pulls the viewer into the icon and then sends the attention beyond the icon itself to heaven. The full-faced gaze of the saint arrests our attention, pulls us in, and holds us on itself. Icons encourage us to see them close at hand: the abundance of detail in the painting encourages us to scrutinize and contemplate what is revealed as we get closer. As our eyes scan the painting, the design of it allows us to contemplate each detail, but then pushes us back to the central figures: the two-dimensionality of the icon ensures that our attention is kept firmly in the plane of the painting, which is occupied by these central figures. Within this plane, the other elements described, such as the radial inverse-perspective lines, guide our eyes towards the intended focal points.

Just as there are forces at work that push our gaze back to the central figure or figures, our thoughts and attention are deliberately given one escape route, so to speak—that is, up to heaven. While our gaze is always happiest when towards the icon itself, there are devices that build in a dissatisfaction and desire to get closer still. First, because the icon is generally painted in the middle ground, it always appears physically distant. No matter how close we get to the icon, the figure depicted will always recede into the middle ground. Second, the sober and calm expression of the icon (called the "bright sadness") gives an emotional distance. We don't feel emotionally involved with the figures depicted in the way that we do with Baroque art. The divide between us, the viewers, and the figures in the icon is one that we want to overcome but can't. Even if our noses are pressed up against the icon, the figure always seems distant. Also, the lack of naturalism always jars to a degree: we can never rest content knowing that we are with the saint depicted; the inbuilt symbolic qualities always remind us that this is an image.

The only way for us to get closer is to turn our attention to the real saint who is at that very moment in heaven. So while our gazes our fixed on the icon of the Mother of God, our thoughts go beyond the image to the real Mother of God who is looking at us from heaven.

There is no hidden mystery to praying with icons; therefore, one simply prays as one would otherwise—chanting, reciting, singing, or praying silently—but allows his gaze to rest upon the icon and be open to the dynamic that the icon involves us in. The well-painted icon does the work for us. I have watched many Eastern Christian families praying at home, for example, before a meal or when retiring at night, and they turn to the icon or icon-corner and chant their prayers out loud while looking at it.

Further Resources:

Aidan Hart, *The Techniques of Icon and Wall Painting* (Leominster: Gracewing, 2011). This is the best art instruction for painters that I have ever seen, and I recommend it to all artists regardless of the style they eventually wish to focus on. Throughout, and particularly in the introductory chapter, there is an excellent description of the theology of icons and coverage of the traditional Western variants. Catholics should beware, though, that Hart is Orthodox and so maintains the Orthodox view, not held by Catholics, that the iconographic form is the only legitimate tradition for the liturgy.

Fr. John Baggley, *Icons, Reading Sacred Images*; (London, Catholic Truth Society, 2007). This is a short booklet on the subject, written by a Catholic priest. A great, reasonably priced, and accessible summary.

Icons on pages 191–198 painted by David Clayton: Archangel Gabriel, St. Luke, Mandylion (Face of Christ), and Mother of God and Our Lord.

MP ΘΥ
HAIL MARY, FULL OF GRACE
THE LORD IS WITH THEE

Icon Case Study

The Icon of New Martyr Elizabeth

As an example that we can look at in detail in order to illustrate a little more of the theology of icons, here is an account by my teacher, Aidan Hart,[1] of how he created an icon of New Martyr Elizabeth, a member of the Russian royal family who was martyred after the Bolshevik revolution. He writes:

1. Aidan Hart is based in Shropshire in England; his website is http://www.aidanharticons.com/.

Icons depict people who are full of he Holy Spirit. These saints are radiant with the same divine glory seen by Peter, James and John when Christ was transfigured. Icons therefore depict a world seen not only with the eyes of the body, but with the eye of the spirit. They show us not just a bush, but a burning bush. This presents a challenge for iconographers called upon to paint a contemporary saint of whom photographs exist. On the one hand these saints are unique human persons, and their icons need to include at least some of their unique attributes. On the other hand, icon painters are not called to paint naturalistic portraits. They are concerned not only with what the physical eyes see but also with what the spirit sees—the indwelling presence of Christ.

How, then, does an iconographer create an icon of a contemporary saint? They cannot ignore the saint's physical likeness as revealed in their photographs, nor can they simply reproduce it. They need somehow to affirm both visible and invisible realities.

What I briefly describe below is my own approach to this challenge, illustrated by a particular icon of New Martyr Elizabeth that I was commissioned to design and paint. St. Elizabeth was martyred in 1918, and many photographs of her were readily available.

1. First I prayed. Saints are alive and well in Christ, and can help the iconographer to represent them worthily.

2. I then re-read Elizabeth's life, making notes about salient features of her character. Of these I selected what seemed to be the chief three: compassion, suffering, and deep inner composure. These were what I had to express more than anything else. While writing can expand on details, an image must distill the essence.

3. Beside these characteristics, I jotted down possible ways of their being expressed in the icon. I find that this is best done by brainstorming—some ideas will be kept, many discarded.

4. I then sought out photographs and chose one or two that best expressed the saint's life.

5. The design work then began. The small panel size of the commission suggested a half-length work, a bust. In the final design Elizabeth's right hand is raised in a gesture of both prayer and witness (the word *martyr* means witness). The other hand holds a cross, symbol of martyrdom. Elizabeth founded a hospital, and for cleanliness' sake devised a white monastic habit for her nuns who served in the hospital. I therefore combined elements of this white habit with the more traditional black of the Orthodox nun. I included Elizabeth's abbatial cross, keeping the chain the same design but making the cross a little smaller.

6. Using iconographic techniques, I adapted the folds of her garments to suggest a more spiritual quality. Curves were made more angular, and highlighting was created by layering three distinct tones rather than using naturalistic modelling and blending. The face is the highest revelation of personhood, so the icon tradition simplifies garments to prevent them drawing attention away from the face.

7. Photographs revealed that important features of St. Elizabeth's face were a somewhat angular outline, deep eyes, and sorrowful eyebrows. I tried to incorporate these into the final design of the face, especially the angular outline, which is emphasized by the close-fitting veil.

8. While accommodating her likeness, I did, however, change some facial proportions to emphasize her inner spiritual state. Such abstractions are a feature of the icon tradition. The organs of expression—lips and gestures, for example—tend to be made smaller or refined. Why? Saints are full of divine power, so their words and deeds are very potent: they need not say or do a lot for a lot to happen. I therefore made Elizabeth's lips less wide and less full than in nature, and kept her gestures and facial expressions calm, without exaggeration.

9. By contrast, the organs of reception—eyes, ears, nose—are enlarged or elongated in icons. This is to show that a saint is one who contemplates divine mysteries, hears the word of God and does it, and smells the fragrance of paradise. I therefore emphasized St. Elizabeth's eyes and made her nose a bit narrower than life, which gives the effect of elongating it.

10. Our eyes give light—"the eye is the lamp of the soul"—said Christ. But our eyes are also a window into our soul, the mouth of a cave with mysterious depths. Consequently the white of the eye is rarely white in icons. Its base is a dark shadow tone, which is then partially

overlaid with a brown-grey made of raw umber and a little white. These deep tones evoke the mysterious depths of the human person, made in God's image. On top of these dark tones are painted two small crescents of nearly pure white. This white is the light of grace which shines out of the saint.

The icon is completed with the halo—a symbol of the indwelling Holy Spirit common to all saints—and the saint's name, a sacrament of the saint's uniqueness.

11

What Catholics Believe About Icons and What Makes an Image Holy

The Seventh Ecumenical Council and the Theology of St. Theodore the Studite

WHENEVER I WRITE ABOUT ICONS it always provokes a flurry of responses from people who have strongly held views about the subject. Most comments relate to the following three issues, and so it is these that I thought I would address here:

First, how is the image related to the saint depicted in the image? Is the icon, for example, a grace-filled vessel in which there is a personal presence of the saint in question?

Second, how does the status of icons relate to sacramentals such as crosses or rosaries?

Third, what is the status of what we recognize today as the iconographic form? How does it compare to other styles in Christian art (for example, those styles referred to by Pope Benedict XVI as also authentically liturgical—the Baroque "at its best" and the Gothic)? Is the icon a higher art form than any other?

What I hope to offer is the traditional Catholic understanding of these things.[1]

Consideration of these points is not new. The debate that eventually sorted them out took place over centuries, as part of the debate about the legitimacy of the veneration of sacred images. This was established dogmatically by the Seventh Ecumenical Council at Nicaea of 787. Although this closed one period of iconoclasm—when those who opposed the use of sacred imagery destroyed it—its decision was not universally accepted. Another iconoclastic period arose shortly afterwards. After further theological clarification (and power struggles

---

1. I would like to acknowledge the help of Dr. Caroline Farey at the School of the Annunciation in writing this.

within the Byzantine Empire), this second iconoclastic period ended in 843 with the Synod of Constantinople, celebrated in the Eastern Church as the Feast of the Triumph of Orthodoxy.

The theological struggle over the legitimacy of imagery was essentially was one of Christology. It rests on the understanding of the Incarnation and the relationship between Christ's divinity and his humanity. The main protagonists here are figures such as St. Cyril of Alexandria, St. Maximus the Confessor, and George Cyprius. The three great defenders of icons during the later, iconoclastic period were St. John of Damascus, St. Nicephorus of Constantinople, and, finally, St. Theodore the Studite.

For the purposes of this article, we shall consider for the most part the relevant conclusions rather than the detail of the deliberations, focusing firstly on the judgment of the Council, and then primarily on the theology of St. Theodore the Studite whose interpretation of the Council corresponds to what I understand to be the view traditionally held by the Catholic Church. In support of what I say, I shall include extended quotation from Theodore in a separate section at the end. The stance of the Church has not, to my knowledge, changed since in regard to these matters; and subsequent councils, such as the Council of Trent and the Second Vatican Council, have served to reinforce what had already been stated.

The Seventh Ecumenical Council stated as follows:

> We, therefore, following the royal pathway and the divinely inspired authority of our Holy Fathers and the traditions of the Catholic Church (for, as we all know, the Holy Spirit indwells her), define with all certitude and accuracy that just as the figure of the precious and life-giving Cross, so also the venerable and holy images, as well in painting and mosaic as of other fit materials, should be set forth in the holy churches of God, and on the sacred vessels and on the vestments and on hangings and in pictures both in houses and by the wayside, to wit, the figure of our Lord God and Savior Jesus Christ, of our spotless Lady, the Mother of God, of the honorable Angels, of all Saints and of all pious people. For by so much more frequently as they are seen in artistic representation, by so much more readily are men lifted up to the memory of their prototypes, and to a longing after them; and to these should be given due salutation and honorable reverence, not indeed that true worship of faith which pertains alone to the divine nature; but to these, as to the figure of the precious and life-giving Cross and to the Book of the Gospels and to the other holy objects, incense and lights may be offered according to ancient pious custom. For the honor which is paid to the image passes on to that which the image represents, and he who reveres the image reveres in it the subject

represented. For thus the teaching of our holy Fathers, that is the tradition of the Catholic Church, which from one end of the earth to the other hath received the Gospel, is strengthened. Thus we follow Paul, who spake in Christ, and the whole divine Apostolic company and the holy Fathers, holding fast the traditions which we have received. So we sing prophetically the triumphal hymns of the Church, "Rejoice greatly, O daughter of Sion; Shout, O daughter of Jerusalem. Rejoice and be glad with all thy heart. The Lord hath taken away from thee the oppression of thy adversaries; thou art redeemed from the hand of thine enemies. The Lord is a King in the midst of thee; thou shalt not see evil any more, and peace be unto thee forever."

So this is clear: the veneration of icons is legitimate. The image is distinct from the person it portrays and the honor paid to the image passes on to that which is portrayed. The Council does not answer directly, however, the questions that we are asking here. In order to do that we must look to Theodore the Studite, the abbot of a monastery in Constantinople.

The resolution of the question of the legitimacy of sacred images was only possible once the question of how the person of Christ could be at once both divine and human was resolved. This was established at the Fifth Ecumenical Council, which took place in 553 in Constantinople. The Catechism states it as follows:

Jesus Christ is true God and true man, in the unity of his divine person. For this reason he is the one and only mediator between God and men. Jesus Christ possesses two natures, one divine and the other human, not confused but united in the one person of God's Son. The Incarnation, therefore, is the mystery of the wonderful union of the divine and human natures in the one person of the Word.[2]

So the critical thing is just this: Jesus Christ is one divine person, but two natures, divine and human.

Why is this important? How is this applied to consideration of the production of images? The answer, the Church Fathers say, relates to what a human artist is capable of representing in a work of art. Theodore is clear that His divine *nature* cannot be "captured" in an image (the translation I read used the word "circumscribed") and one should not try to do so.

However, Theodore states, the divine *person* of Christ *as man* can be circumscribed. This allows for the possibility of the creation of an image. Any individual man is characterized by his individual features, those that distinguish him from all others. So, if we see a likeness to an

2. *Catechism of the Catholic Church*, nn. 480, 481, 483.

individual represented in an image, we behold the person. In the case of the divine person, therefore, we see the face of Christ, both God and man in nature, when we see his likeness in the icon.

Theodore says, however, that the icon does not participate in the nature of the individual. That is, it does not contain any aspects of human nature or divine nature; it is just an image. Therefore, the relationship between the image in the icon and the saint in heaven is established by our perception and apprehension of the likeness. That relationship cannot exist in a way that involves the icon when we are not apprehending the likeness portrayed in the image; then, the icon is just wood, paint, gold, gesso, etc. A crucial role in establishing this relationship between icon and saint is played by the imagination, which takes our thoughts from image to saint. It is clear from this that we pray "with" icons only in the sense that we use them when we pray. But when we do so, we pray along with the saint, just as the saint is praying along with us. Icons, because they are inanimate objects, do not pray.

Theodore's description is consistent with the Church's teaching on sacramentals. That is, once blessed by a prayer (and also, by tradition, in the case of icons, by writing the name of the saint on the painting and capturing the characteristics of the person), the icon is a sacramental.

As with all sacramentals (and distinct from a sacrament), the icon predisposes us, by our perception of it, to cooperation with grace. The Catechism puts it thus: "Sacramentals do not confer the grace of the Holy Spirit the way that sacraments do, but by the Church's prayer, they prepare us to receive grace and dispose us to cooperate with it":

> For well-disposed members of the faithful, the liturgy of the sacraments and sacramentals sanctifies almost every event of their lives with the divine grace which flows from the Paschal mystery of the Passion, Death and Resurrection of the Christ. From this source all sacraments and sacramentals draw their power. There is scarcely any proper use of material things which cannot be thus directed toward the sanctification of men and the praise of God.[3]

Prior to the clarification by Theodore, there was confusion in this respect. It persists even in the earlier writing of the great proponent of icons at the time of the Council in Nicaea, John of Damascus. In his desire to affirm the value of matter, he does not sufficiently differentiate between sacrament and sacramental. This is because he establishes the relationship between the icon and the saint entirely from the perspective of participation in the essence (i.e., the nature) of the person. So

3. Ibid., 1670.

even though he modifies it by degrees, he *is*, it seems, always describing a grace-filled vessel in a way that is beyond the mode of the icon as wood, gold, paint, etc. He then appears to elevate the status of all matter to that of sacrament, by describing icons, crosses, relics, and the Body and Blood of Our Lord as operating in the same way. This was corrected by Nicephorus and finally and most forcefully by Theodore. Make no mistake: Theodore is still describing a profound and direct relationship between image and person, but this relationship exists by virtue of the icon circumscribing the human *person* of a saint, or the divine person as man. The mind is the means by which the relationship is made real. It jumps from image to person when the icon is observed.

The holy image is made worthy of veneration by bearing these essential elements described by Theodore: that is that it has the characteristics of the person depicted and that it has the name of the person depicted inscribed. A blessing is necessary in order for it to become a sacramental. A holy image that has not been blessed is not a sacramental, but it is still worthy of veneration. (However, many would say that it is desirable to bless holy images.)

The theology of Theodore the Studite in regard to sacred images applies as much to the Gothic, the Baroque, or any other style. To the degree that these forms bear the likeness or characteristics of Our Lord, Our Lady and so on, and the name, they are legitimate. In the case of Our Lord and Our Lady, the characteristics are handed down to us by tradition. What is striking when one looks at the portrayal of, for example, Christ, across all of these traditions is the large degree of conformity to the traditional understanding of what they looked like. We can say also, therefore, that the tradition, as articulated by Pope Benedict XVI, that recognizes the iconographic, the Gothic, and the Baroque as authentic liturgical art forms is consistent with the Council and the theology of St. Theodore. This is not to diminish the status of iconographic style to something lower than the esteem with which the Eastern churches holds it; rather, it raises the status of the Gothic and Baroque to the same level.

The Words of St. Theodore and St. John Damascene[4]

"*The icon of someone does not depict his nature but his person,*" Theodore states, and he is the first to offer a theologically balanced explanation for

---

4. Quotations from Theodore the Studite are taken from J. P. Migne, ed., *Patrologiae cursus, series graeca* (Paris, 1857ff.) unless otherwise stated. The translations are as they appear in Cardinal Schönborn's book, *God's Human Face*, and the page numbers given relate to the page in this book that the translations are taken from. The italics are quotations from Theodore; otherwise, the words are Schönborn's.

this simple observation that had been made time and time again during the icon controversy. Theodore gives this clarification:

> *For how could a nature be depicted, unless it is concretely seen in a person? Peter, for example, is not portrayed in an icon insofar as he is a being endowed with reason, mortal, and having a mind and intelligence. For all this characterizes not only Peter but also Paul and John and everyone else belonging to the same species. Peter rather is portrayed according to those specific qualities he possesses in addition to the common definition as a human being, such as the curved nose, the curly hair, the pleasing complexion, the kindly eyes, and anything else in terms of specific properties of his appearance, by which he is distinguished from the other individuals of the species.* (219–220)

Theodore holds in the full Aristotelian sense that the general concept subsists only in the concrete individuals. Contrary to Platonism, he considers as really existing only the concrete individuals, while general concepts exist only in abstract and mental form: "*What is general we grasp only with our reason and our mind; what is particular we grasp with our eyes, as they see the things of the senses.*" The icon portrays only what is visible in a man, only what is particular to him, what distinguishes this man from all other men (221):

> *The original model is not present in the icon according to its essence, otherwise we could call the icon "original" and the original we could call "icon." This would not make any sense, as both natures [that of original and of icon] each have their own definition. Rather, the original is present in the icon based on the likeness in relation to the person.*

The original is truly present in the icon, but this presence is entirely based on a relationship to a person. This alone constitutes the icon's dignity. With this, St. Theodore corrects a certain questionable tendency (which we found, in rudiments, in John Damascene) to consider the icon itself and as such, in its material, to be some kind of grace-filled vessel, "*as if it contained a divine nature or power that would require our veneration*" (the way the Council of Trent describes this tendency). Theodore the Studite does not hesitate to present this correction forcefully by pointing out that God is neither more nor less present in the icon than in any other piece of wood:

> *The depicted body is present in the icon, not as to its nature, but only as regards a relation [schesis]. Much less is the Divinity, which cannot be "circumscribed" at all, present in the icon . . . : not more than he is present in the shadow cast by Christ's body. Where in any rational or brute creature, where in any animated or lifeless creation would the Divinity not be present? Of course, he is present to a greater or lesser*

degree, according to the analogy of the receiving nature. Should someone say that God is present in this manner also in the icon, it would not be false. The same, then, certainly applies to the symbol of the cross and the other sacred objects. (225–226)

Theodore quotes a custom already mentioned by Leontius of Neapolis and by Patriarch Germanus: once an icon is worn and has lost its "imprint" (*charakter*), it will without hesitation be thrown into the fire "*like any useless piece of wood.*" If the icon as such were a grace-filled object, nobody would dare burn it. It would in itself be some kind of sacred relic. Unlike John Damascene, who places icons and relics on the same level, Theodore the Studite sees the sacredness of the icon entirely in its *character*, its portraying depiction (226).

All this does not mean, though, that material things are somehow worthless. Theodore emphasizes their proper value. But he refuses to assign some kind of sacred character to material things, by which the icon would be raised to the level of a sacrament. Material things as such receive in the sacramental mysteries a certain healing and sanctifying power. The bread, changed into the Eucharist, is really the Body of Christ; it is not his image. The baptismal water obtains its sanctifying power through the Holy Spirit. The wood of the icon, in contrast, does not turn in such a way into a vehicle of grace. True, an icon also sanctifies; but not in the manner of a sacrament: rather, through nourishing a spiritual relationship to the person depicted. This difference is once again clearly presented when Theodore explains in what sense one can say that the icon of Christ is Christ himself:

If we consider both as to their nature, then Christ and his icon are essentially different from one another. And yet, as to their name, both are the same. Based on the icon's nature, we call its visible reality not "Christ," not even "image of Christ," but wood, paint, gold, silver, or some other material employed. Yet based upon the image of the person depicted, the icon is called "Christ" or "image of Christ"; Christ because of the identity in name, "image of Christ" because of the relationship [of the image to Christ]. (227)

St. Theodore says that the act of inscribing the name on the icon, as it was understood then, constitutes the consecration as such of the icon. Consequently, St. Theodore insists that "image of Christ" not be written on the icon, but "Christ," since we really behold Christ himself, his person, in the icon; this does not imply some kind of hypostatic union between Christ and his image, but is only based on the relationship of intention and similarity between the icon and the person of Christ, even in the case of a rather remote similarity, for example, when the artist's skill is wanting (227–228).

The image is not a concession to the weak. It is rooted in man's nature, which the Eternal Word has taken on forever by becoming man himself. Consequently, contemplation does not exclude visual beholding. Indeed, the saintly abbot of the Studion does not hesitate to instruct his monks not to neglect the power of the imagination:

> *Imagination is one of the five powers of the soul. It is a kind of image, as both are depictions. The image, therefore, that resembles imagination cannot be useless. . . . If imagination were useless, it would be an utterly futile part of human nature! But then the other powers of the soul would also be useless: the senses, recollection, intellect, and reason. Thus a reasoned and sober consideration of the human nature shows how nonsensical it is to despise the image and the imagination.*

Imagination is not something negative; it is a natural potential. On the way to contemplation there is no need to eliminate it (as the Evagrian tradition teaches); it only ought to be purified, just like all the other powers of the soul. But, of course, the imagination is not purified by never engaging it, but by focusing it more and more on pure and sacred matters. Here we should recall the monastic tradition and experience of constantly having one's mind on God as a way of purification. Theodore, in his instructions, reserved an important place for the mind's dwelling on God. And the icon plays an important part in this. The frequent gazing upon sacred images purifies the imagination in the same way as the frequent listening to the word of God (231–232).

Theodore repeats almost word-for-word the profound reflections of Maximus the Confessor on the relationship between the person and nature: "*Christ therefore is truly one of us, though he is also God; for he is one of the three Divine Persons. As such he is distinct from the Father and the Holy Spirit by his property of being Son. He then, as man, is distinct from all other men by his personal [hypostatic] qualities.*"

This is the decisive point. The iconoclasts say that Christ is a Divine Person; he cannot be depicted. Any such attempt would mean to assign to Christ a second person, entirely human and portrayable. Theodore replies by briefly recalling the Church's doctrine of the "composite person" as developed in the wake of the Fifth Ecumenical Council (553):

> *Were we to assert that the flesh taken on by the Word possesses its own hypostasis, the argument [of the iconoclasts] would be valid. But we follow the Faith of the Church and profess that the Person of the Eternal Word became the person common to both natures, and that this same person provided the intrinsic existence to the particular human nature with all its properties by which it is distinct from all other human beings. Thus we are justified in proclaiming that the one and the same Person of*

the Eternal Word, as to its divine nature, cannot be "circumscribed," yet as to its human nature, can certainly be "circumscribed." The human nature of Christ does not exist beside the person of the Logos, in an individual, independent person; it rather obtains its existence in the person of the Logos (for there is no nature that would not subsist in a specific hypostasis), and in the person of the Logos can—as specific individual—be seen and circumscribed.

Regarding St. John Damascene (John of Damascus)

"Do not despise matter!" John touches here the critical spot of those iconoclastic tendencies for which the materiality of the icon becomes an insult to the divine original. "Through matter my salvation is accomplished." Matter does not lie in the farthest and lowest regions of relationship to God, as Neoplatonism holds; it is not farthest away from the spiritual realm and therefore utterly without salvific value. On the contrary: the entire economy of salvation has always employed material things as well as spiritual. Thus matter is not at all an obstacle on the way to God, but becomes by its participation in Christ's mystery the medium through which salvation is accomplished (196).

In this positive view of matter, however, John does not sufficiently elaborate that not every material thing is by itself already an instrument of salvation. John does not distinguish clearly enough between, for example, the Body of Christ and other material realities (such as the cross, icons, etc.). The body of Christ seems to stand at the same level as the icon (196).

All other matter however I simply honor and venerate, insofar as it was instrumental in my salvation and for this reason was endowed with divine power and grace. The wood of the cross, full of gladness and blessedness, is it not indeed matter? The venerable sacred mountain [Calvary], the Skull Place [Golgotha]—are they not matter? The life-giving, life-bringing rock—are they not matter? The gold and silver used to make crosses, patens and chalices—are they not matter? And is not before everything else, the Lord's Body and Blood not matter? You ought to ban the cult and veneration surrounding these things, or else leave in force the tradition of venerating also images that are sanctified by the name of God and his friends and thus are overshadowed the grace of the divine Spirit. Do not despise matter! It is not without honor. For nothing that comes from God is without honor (195).[5]

5. Referenced as "Damascene, I, 16 (1245AC); translation, slightly adapted, taken from H. Hunger, *Byzaninische Geisteswelt* (Baden-Baden, 1958), 121f."

12

Aristotle, Aquinas, and St. Francis:

How the New Naturalism of Gothic Art Developed[1]

LTHOUGH THERE ARE discernible stylistic differences in Christian art that depend upon the time and location from which they emerge, pretty much all Christian figurative art from the time of its appearance until the end of the Romanesque (about 1200 AD) conformed to the iconographic prototype.

The departure from the iconographic prototype occurred due to a different sense of the reliability of human experience and the value of information received through the senses as a potential source of the grasping of truth. Tied in with this is the belief that the world we live in, although fallen and imperfect, is nevertheless good, ordered, and beautiful. So there may be evil and suffering in the world, and it may not be as good and beautiful as it ought to be; but it is nevertheless God's creation and still good and beautiful. This ultimately caused the rise of naturalism in art and the development of science.

A number of factors combined to cause this. Around 1000 AD, the Latin West came into increased contact with the Greek East and Islam through trade and warfare (for example, the Crusades). These were forces that reinvigorated Western art quickly through a new Byzantine influence that became what we now call the Romanesque style. Byzantine art at this time conformed to the iconographic prototype, just as the Western figurative art did; but, relative to its Western counterpart, there was a greater degree of naturalism. The Romanesque reflected this greater naturalism, but did not depart from the iconographic principles. Nevertheless, it helped to initiate the move to naturalism as the dominant approach.

1. Much of the following discussion of the development of ideas is based on a lecture given by Stratford Caldecott in Oxford, England.

The *Reconquista*, or re-conquest of Spain south of Santiago from the Moors—Toledo fell in 1085—gave Western Europe access for the first time to many of the treasures of ancient philosophy, particularly in the form of Arabic transcriptions of Aristotle. For the next hundred years Christian, Jewish, and Moslem scholars would collaborate on the translation and interpretation of these texts. It was the friars, the new mendicant orders, both Franciscan and Dominican (who, thanks to the support of the Papacy, which had given them the task of combating heresy, were now dominating the new Universities in Paris and later Oxford), who managed to achieve this synthesis of the new learning with the tradition coming from St. Augustine and the Church Fathers.

These syntheses were not always accepted. In Paris, for example, the work of St. Albert the Great (1206–1280) and St. Thomas Aquinas (1225–1274) was brilliant, but found itself quickly condemned by the Bishop of Paris, not to be accepted until the canonization of St. Thomas in 1323. Franciscans in Oxford University, such as Duns Scotus, William of Ockham, and Roger Bacon, had a greater impact. Roger Bacon (1214–1294) particularly attacked both the superstitions of the masses and the hostility towards the science of the Paris schoolmen common at that time. He called for the empirical investigation of nature and urged men to experiment, although he himself was unable to achieve very much in this field. (However, he is reputed to be the inventor of spectacles!) Bacon had his own vision, so to speak, of the technical world of the future: ships without oarsmen, submarines, automobiles, airplanes, small magical gadgets for releasing oneself from prison, magical fetters (for use on other people), and devices for walking on water.

The influence of these Franciscans was not always positive. William of Ockham proposed a "nominalism" in which good and evil were not objective qualities in themselves, but evaluations arbitrarily assigned by God. Nominalism is often seen as opening the door that Descartes and the modern philosophers who followed were to walk through.

The development of science and naturalistic art was not only as a result of a new intellectual outlook. It was driven also by a newly fired curiosity in the natural world. This intense curiosity came from the man who inspired the order to which Roger Bacon (and leading figures of the Renaissance) belonged: St. Francis of Assisi (1182–1226). St. Francis loved the natural world as God's creation. This love and curiosity was a powerful driving force that affected Western society profoundly. In fact, an interesting case could be made for tracing the Renaissance and the civilization that followed it to the inspiration provided by St. Francis. He inspired an energetic Christian curiosity about the natural world, an attitude that was subsequently reflected by his followers and became a driving force for change in art and for the development of what we now think of as scientific investigation.

The new curiosity and sense of wonder in the fallen, natural world that grew in this Christian society should be distinguished from paganism. St. Francis's life was a paradox. His spirituality was not just one of love of nature, but also a conscious spirituality of human and divine suffering. He was an ascetic who loved the world of nature, and by his asceticism—his life of voluntary penance—he somehow managed to purge the ancient paganism, and made possible a new and innocent interest in the order of creation.

Francis loved nature, but put it also in its proper place in relation to God. For the pagan, the natural world is the ideal of beauty to which all else must strive to conform. If nature is the highest standard to which man can conform, then man's work must necessarily fall short of this ideal. For the Christian, nature is not the highest form of beauty but one that points to something greater, the divine order. Once man sees nature as an imperfect, though still good, form of what it is meant to be, he can speculate as to what nature ought to be and to the form of the highest order, that is, the divine order to which it points. Therefore man's work can form nature in accordance with his vision of what it ought to be and, through the grace of God, create a culture that surpasses the beauty of the wilderness, untouched by man.

The New Naturalism

The greater emphasis on direct observation in art was reflected first in the artistic style that we now call the Gothic. The substrate with which this naturalism was fused was the iconographic. So, what began in the Romanesque as a more naturalist iconographic style (compared with earlier Western iconographic forms) became so naturalistic that it broke the boundaries of what constituted an icon (for example, through the introduction of cast shadow and the depiction of people in profile). Nevertheless, the Gothic owes something stylistically to the iconographic. It retains, for example, that emotional distance that is maintained in the portrayal of figures. As a result, the observer always feels slightly detached from the scene described. If one looks even at late Gothic styles, such as that of the Flemish artist Hieronymous Bosch, we can see in this regard how much the Gothic owes to the iconographic style.

13

Gothic Art: Case Studies

A s DISCUSSED, the increased naturalism of the Gothic was fused with the iconographic style that had existed before in the West, what we now call Romanesque art. The early masters of the Gothic style would be Duccio or Simone Martini, and then artists up to and including the period of the 15th century, such as the Flemish masters Jan Van Eyck and Rogier Van der Weyden.

At some point in its development, the Gothic became so naturalistic that it broke the boundaries of what constituted iconography. For example, icons always have saints in either full face or at least three-quarter profile (so that you can see both eyes), because this symbolizes the truth that in heaven we know each other fully: we hide nothing of ourselves, and when we look upon others, no aspect of them is hidden from us. Only those who are not saints, such as the devil, would be in profile. Or, to use another example, in an icon no saint would be hidden, even in part by being placed behind someone else or something else. This is partly for the same reason as with the previous example—we want to show that the full person is revealed in heaven—and partly also because by putting one object behind another, you necessarily create the illusion of depth, and part of the image looks as though it is in a region behind the plane of the panel it is painted on.

If we look at the early Gothic Masters such as Duccio or Simone Martini, we see art that in many ways is just very naturalistic iconography. However, they do break these two conventions of iconography. This is a greater reflection of naturalism which takes into account not just the physical appearances of the objects painted, but also how in the realm outside heaven, they interrelate with each other in space. We discuss this in the case study below.

Because of this property of being partly in heaven (by virtue of the iconographic influence) and partly on earth (by virtue of the increased naturalism), we might characterize the Gothic as the art of holy pilgrimage. Like a Gothic spire soaring upwards, stylistically the Gothic spans the divide between the art of heaven and the art of fallen man here on earth.

Gothic Case Study 1

Duccio di Buoninsegna, Italian, 13th century: *Transfiguration*
This painting of the Transfiguration by Duccio shows our Lord on

Mount Tabor flanked by the two prophets Moses and Elijah and observed by apostles Peter, James, and John. This displays many of the characteristics of iconographic art: for example, Christ, the most important figure, is the largest, and the mountain, which in nature would have been bigger than any of the people present, is reduced significantly in size. Through these differing relative sizes, the hierarchy of being is communicated to us—Christ is the highest and inanimate mountains are the lowest. Furthermore, there is no scenery other than what is necessary to the narrative. We are not given the full landscape in which this is taking place. The desire is to communicate the spiritual message above all. All the figures have halos, and Christ has gold leaf (real gold) lines on his garment, indicating that even his clothes are shining with the heavenly "uncreated" light. All this is very iconographic.

However—and here is the difference—the figure of John, in the center, is in profile. Duccio has done this in order to give some connection with the figure of Christ. He wants to show John looking at Christ. John is closer to us than Jesus in this scene, and so in order to be looking at him in real life, he would have to turn around and face him; if that were shown literally in this painting, we would have to see only the back of his head. Duccio uses a visual illusion to enable us to see the face of John while he looks at Christ—he has shown John looking directly upwards, as though Christ is physically above him. What Duccio is doing here is playing tricks with perspective. We note that Peter and James, to the left and right, are looking at Christ too, but Duccio can show these two in three-quarter profile and still create the illusion that they are looking at Jesus because each is off to one side and so need to rotate their heads partially to look to us as though they see him.

Compare this with a standard iconographic image of the Transfiguration, such as this 16th-century Russian icon (facing page).

In this icon only Peter on the left is shown looking at Jesus, and the artist achieved this just as Duccio did, by showing him in three-quarter profile. In this portrayal, the other figures look away from Our Lord. He could have portrayed James on the right in a pose which mirrored Peter's, rather as Duccio did, so that he looked at Our Lord. However, he could not have done that with John, given his central placement in the composition, without resorting to Duccio's visual device and showing him in profile; and this would break the iconographic convention of not showing figures in profile, so he does not do it.

Gothic Case Studies 2 and 3

Fra Angelico's *Resurrection* and *Annunciation*

Fra Angelico, the 15th-century Florentine artist, is normally considered late Gothic in style. The evidence is anecdotal, but my experience from talking to others is that his work appeals very much to people today. It seems that he has just the balance of naturalism and symbolism that

nourishes the prayer of modern man. John Paul II gave him a special mention in his *Letter to Artists*.

Working late in the period, Fra Angelico is very interesting to study for his selective use of the features of well-observed naturalism such as perspective and shadow; and his retention at other times of features of iconographic art. If we look at his *Resurrection*, a fresco from one of the cells in the monastery of San Marco in Florence, we see Christ rising in an almond-shaped mandorla, the traditional symbol of His glory, carrying the red-and-white Resurrection pennant. His painting has the figures in the middle distance, as would occur in an icon. However, unlike an icon, the background is shadowy and dark, and we see the tomb drawn with naturalistic perspective. The angel is in profile, which would never be seen in an iconographic painting, though he is shining with uncreated light, which one would expect in iconographic art.

There is one stylistic feature that Fra Angelico uses that interests me greatly. This is his habit of putting the face of Christ in such dark shadow. On first sight this is strange, since he shows the rest of the person of Christ shining with light, and the face of the angel, a great but nevertheless lesser being, is totally in light. When I first noticed this I wondered why. A Dominican friar in England told me his interpretation of this: Fra Angelico is showing a light that is brighter still. In fact, it is so bright that it blinds us—it is too much for us to bear. We are fallen human beings and so cannot see as the pure see. Like the man emerging from Plato's cave, we are dazzled by the light of truth. I find this explanation convincing, especially because we see that other paintings by Fra Angelico, such as the *Transfiguration* and the *Sermon on the Mount*, have the same feature.

Consider now another fresco by Fra Angelico, of the *Annunciation*, on the walls of a cell at San Marco in Florence.

He consciously employs some of the developments of the new naturalism: there is cast shadow and single-point perspective creating a sense of depth in the covered cloister; the archangel is in profile. But there are also stylistic aspects that we are accustomed to seeing in iconography: the figures are painted in the middle distance, the edges of each shape are all sharply defined, and the color is evenly applied (unlike in the Baroque, which has selectively blurred or sharp edges and selective use of color or monochrome, usually sepia, rendering).

Examining further, if we look at the eaves we can see that the light source that is casting shadow is from the left. If cast light were the only source, the face of the Archangel would be dark, and the figure would cast a shadow on the right as we look at it; yet the face is bright, and there is no shadow. Fra Angelico is showing the face of the Archangel glowing with the uncreated light of holiness, which is what we are used to seeing in the iconographic form. This blend of shadow and uncreated light means that this painting is at once looking back at the iconographic style and anticipating the deep shadow of the Baroque.

I was giving a lecture once about this painting when a student asked me about the shadow. He pointed out that Our Lady is a saint; he could see that her face wasn't in shadow and that there was strong halo representing the uncreated light coming from her; but there was a strong cast shadow on the floor beneath her. Wouldn't you expect her radiance to obliterate that, he asked? I agreed with him, and was at a loss to explain why Fra Angelico had painted it like this. I speculated that perhaps it was due to the fact that there were two light sources from the left—the natural light and the uncreated light from the angel—and that the combined intensity of light would cause the shadow against the wall. I had to admit even as I said it that my answer sounded contrived.

Later, someone in another class, a priest, gave a convincing explanation. Luke 1 tells us that the words of the angel Gabriel were: "The Holy Spirit *will come upon you*, and the power of the Most High will *overshadow* you."

14

Baroque Art: Case Studies

THE BAROQUE, the artistic and cultural movement of the 17th century, produced the most naturalistic of the traditional authentic styles of painting appropriate for the liturgy. While a degree of abstraction is certainly present, it is far more subtle than in the other two liturgical traditions. It developed as part of the Catholic Counter-Reformation, and its great exponents include Velazquez, Rembrandt, Van Dyke, Ribera, Guido Reni, Sassoferrato, Zurbarán, and Rubens, to name just a few. Only a century or so after its appearance, the tradition started to decline due to the influence of the Enlightenment, with the Venetian school lasting longest and going on well into the late 18th century, even as others declined around it. It closed when Napoleon invaded Venice and opened a new academy which mirrored the attitudes of the post-Revolutionary French Academy. The last Baroque master of sacred art was, in my opinion, Tiepolo, who was from this Venetian school.

Although sacred art in the period that followed this was sub-standard, mundane art flourished in the 19th century. The portrait-painting and landscape-painting of this period surpassed that of earlier times (in my opinion), incorporating new influences before declining, too, under the influence of post-Impressionist modernism in the early 20th century. The last great artist in this field was the American John Singer Sargent. Sargent trained in Paris in a small *atelier* run by Carolus-Duran. Duran, whose interest was mundane art, consciously taught students to paint in the style of the 17th century masters, especially Velazquez.

In contrast to the iconographic style, Baroque art deliberately makes strong use of cast shadow and external light sources. Each was employed in a dramatic interplay that was not just an aesthetic device. Shadow represented, as it had for the Church Fathers right back to Augustine, the presence of evil and suffering in a fallen world. The light with which it was contrasted represented the hope that lay in *the* Light, Christ. Always, the masters of the Baroque wanted to reinforce the message of

Christian hope in which the Light of the World overcomes darkness. The Christian message is not one of despair: hope due to the Christ the Redeemer is always with us, even in the darkest periods.

In contrast with the iconographic style, the Baroque deliberately sets out to create an illusion of space, using devices such as perspective, and shows deep-cast shadow from external light sources.

How the Style of Baroque Art
Creates a Unique Dynamic of Prayer

Have you ever had the experience of walking into an art gallery and being struck by a wonderful painting on the far side of the room? You are so captivated by it that you want to get closer. As you approach it, something strange happens. The image goes out of focus and dissolves into a mass of broad brushstrokes and its unity is lost. In order to get a unified picture of the whole you have to recede again. The painting is likely to be the work of an Old Master in the style of the 17th-century baroque, perhaps a Velazquez, a Ribera, or a later artist who retained this stylistic effect, such as John Singer Sargent. My class at Thomas More College recently made a trip to the art museum in Worcester, Massachusetts, where there was a portrait by Sargent that was about 12 feet high and forced us back perhaps 35 feet so that the angle of vision was small enough that we could view the whole in a single glance.

This is a deliberately contrived effect of Baroque painting. These paintings are created to have optimum impact at a distance. The stylistic elements of the Baroque relate to its role firstly as a liturgical art form in the Counter-Reformation. It should be of no surprise that this has an impact upon prayer.

The best analysis of the stylistic features of the Baroque of the 17th century that I have seen is in a book about Velazquez, published in 1906 and written by R.A.M. Stevenson (the brother of Robert Louis). In this he says: "A canvas should express a human outlook on the world and so it should represent an area possible to the attention; that is, it should subtend an angle of vision confined to certain natural limits of expansion."[1] In other words, we need to stand far enough away from the painting so that the eye can take it in as a single impression. Traditionally (following on from Leonardo), this is taken to be a point three times longer than the greatest dimension of the painting. This ratio of 3:1 is in fact an angle of 18°, slightly larger than the natural angle of focused vision of the eye, which is about 15°. When you stand this far away, the whole painting can be taken in comfortably, without forcing

---

1. R.A.M. Stevenson, *Velazquez* (Whitefish: Kessinger Publishing, 2006), p. 30.

the eye to move backwards and forwards over it to any extent that is uncomfortable.

If the intention is to appear sharp and in-focus at a distance of three times the length of the canvas, it must be much painted as much softer and blurred on the canvas itself. In practice this means that when one approaches a canvas, the brush stroke is often broader than one first expected. So if we do examine a painting up close, it is often hard to discern anything; it almost looks like a collection of random brush strokes. The whole thing only comes together and knits into an image once we retreat again far enough to be able to see it as a unified image. This property makes Baroque art particularly suitable for paintings that are intended to have an impact at a distance. The scene jumps out at us.

There is an additional optical device that contributes to this. The composition of the painting is such that the figures are painted in the foreground. Two things affect the sense of whether the image is in the foreground, middle ground, or background in relation to the observer: the placement of the horizon and the relationship between the angle of vision of the perimeter of the canvas and that angle which spans each figure within. Baroque art tends to portray the key figures in the fore-

ground. When these two effects are combined, the effect is powerful. If we consider the very famous painting of Christ on the Cross by Velazquez, for example, its appearance at a distance is of a perfectly modeled figure.

As we approach we see that much of the detail is painted with a very loose, broad brush. I have picked out the loin cloth and face as detailed examples. The artist achieves this effect by retreating from the canvas, viewing the subject at a distance, and then walking forward to paint the canvas from memory. Then, after making the brushstroke, the artist returns to review the work from the position from which he intends the viewer to see it, several feet back. I learned this technique when I studied portrait-painting in Florence. I was on my feet, walking backwards and forwards for two three-hour sessions a day (punctuated by cappuccino breaks, of course). Over the course of an academic year, I lost several pounds! I was told, though I haven't been able to confirm the truth of it, that Velazquez did not feel inclined

to do all that walking, so he had a set of brushes with 10-foot handles made especially for him.

This dynamic between the viewer and the painting is consistent with the idea of Baroque art, which is to make God and his saints present to us here, in this fallen world. There may be evil and suffering, but God is here for us. Hope in Christ transcends all human suffering. The image says, so to speak, "You stay where you are—I am coming to you. I am with you, supporting you in your suffering, here and now." The stylistic language of light and dark in Baroque painting supports this also. The deep-cast shadow represents evil and suffering, but it is always contrasted with strong light, representing the Light that "overcomes the darkness."

This is different from the effect of the two other Catholic liturgical traditions identified by Pope Benedict XVI, the Gothic and the iconographic. These place the figures compositionally always in the middle ground or distance, and so they always pull you in towards them. As you approach them they reveal more detail. In this respect these traditions are complementary, rather than in opposition to each other.

Baroque Case Study 1

The Scourging of Christ is by Giulio Cesare Procaccini (1574–1625), an Italian, based in Milan.

Light and shade: Most of the painting is shrouded in shadow. But we can see how Procaccini has contrasted this shadow, which represents the presence of evil and suffering in the world, with the lights which represent the Light overcoming the darkness. In this case the light is literally the body of Christ. It runs up and down the full figure of the Redeemer. When we were drawing and painting the figure in Florence, I was told to do the same thing so that the emphasis would be on the whole person, reflecting a Christian humanism (you would not do this in a portrait!). This means that relative to the shining torso, the face is somewhat shadowy. If you look at Velazquez's famous Crucifixion, you see the same effect.

Sacred art and portraits are distinct in style in this respect. In a portrait, the face is everything, for that is what we look at to discern the unique qualities of the person. In religious art, the artist wishes to emphasize as much those general characteristics of a good person that are common to all of us, and so, relative to a portrait, the face is played down slightly. If we were to summarize the difference, we would say that a portrait seeks to portray what differentiates this particular person from all others. In sacred art, the artist must paint a unique individual, too, but do so in such a way that those characteristics that are common to each of us, such as suffering or virtue, are emphasized as well so that we can empathize with the suffering (or even feel that the saint shares it with us), and, so it is hoped, inspire us to emulate the virtue they display.

Focus and color: When we look at anything in the world around us, those areas that are in peripheral vision, as projected onto the retina of the eye, are always depleted of color and out of focus. We don't often see it that way in our mind's eye, so to speak, because the missing information is supplied by the memory or the imagination of the viewer (although we are often not aware that this is happening). The Baroque artist understood this and only put full natural color and sharp detail in those areas that are of primary interest in the painting. If you can find a color image, you would notice how muted the color is, for example in the rendering of the sleeve of the soldier on the left.

The assumption behind this is that the natural world is made by God for us, so that through its beauty we can know its Creator. Then, so the idea goes, if we paint a painting so that it gives visual information in the way that we naturally take it in, we will perceive it as beautiful also and it will raise our souls to contemplation of heavenly things just as nature does.

Another stylistic feature of the Baroque is the control of the sharpness of edges and general focus. When the defining edge of an object is painted so that it is blurred, the effect of blurriness is reduced if you retreat from the canvas to view the picture from farther away, and it will appear to sharpen. This means that even those areas that are intended to seen as detailed and sharp should be painted so that they are soft and blurred to some degree when seen from nearby. In this case, paintings are painted so that the ideal distance to them is three times their greatest dimension. This is a rough guideline (developed by Leonardo) which says that you want to be far enough back so that you can see all of it without have to move your eyes or you head. Therefore, they are painted so that the focus and the color pop into place when viewed at this ideal distance, so it can be seen with a single impression.

The fact that there is an ideal distance from which to view the painting gives rise to the special property of Baroque art to create impact at a distance. The sense is that the scene almost jumps out at us, and the spiritual message of this is to tell us that Christ is with us, supporting us through this life.

Baroque Case Study 2
Gianbattista Tiepolo, Italian, 18th century, the *Immaculate Conception*

It might be said of Venetian painter Giovanni Battista Tiepolo (1696–1770) that he was one of the last great painters of sacred art who painted in the Baroque tradition (as distinct from the cold, sterile, over-polished neo-classicism of the French Academy). Tiepolo was a master who added his own developments to the form of the Baroque of the previous century, but without compromising the principles of the tradition. This makes him worthy of attention today, I feel. If we re-establish the Baroque as a living tradition, it must develop it so that it speaks of today as well. As we now know, the mark of a living tradition is that it able to reapply its principles without compromising on those aspects that define it.

This is different from pastiche, which is a rigid copying of style. (Although, frankly, I think pastiche is underrated—I'd take decent pastiche of the 17th-century baroque over a modernist painting every time.) This style of painting the Immaculate Conception was developed in Spain. Francisco Pacheco (1564–1644), who was the teacher of Spanish baroque masters Alonso Cano and Velazquez (he was also Velazquez's father-in-law), described the iconography of the Immaculate Conception in his influential book, *The Art of Painting* (*Arte de la Pintura*) published posthumously in 1649.

With reference to the *Immaculate Conception*, Pacheco wrote:

> The version that I follow is the one that is closest to the holy revelation of the Evangelist [John writing in Revelation] and approved by the Catholic Church on the authority of the sacred and holy interpreters. . . . In this loveliest of mysteries Our Lady should be painted as a beautiful young girl, 12 or 13 years old, in the flower of her youth. . . . And thus she is praised by the husband: *tota pulchra es amica mea*, a text that is always written in this painting. She should be painted wearing a white tunic and a blue mantle. . . . She is surrounded by the sun, an oval sun of white and ochre, which sweetly blends into the sky. Rays of light emanate from her head, around which is a ring of twelve stars. An imperial crown adorns her head, without, however, hiding the stars. Under her feet is the moon.[1]

He also specified that her hands are to be folded on her bosom or joined in prayer. The sun is to be expressed by a flood of light around her. The moon under her feet is to have the horns pointing downwards, because illuminated from above. Round her are to hover cherubim bearing roses, palms, and lilies; the head of the bruised and vanquished dragon is to be under her feet. She ought to have the cord of St. Francis as a girdle, "because in this guise she appeared to Beatriz de Silva," a

---

1. Robert Enggass, Jonathan Brown, *Italy and Spain 1600–1750* (Englewood Cliffs: Prentice Hall, 1970), p. 165.

noble Franciscan nun who was favored by a celestial vision of the Madonna in her beatitude.

All these accessories are not absolutely and rigidly required, and the 17th century Spanish artist Murillo, who is perhaps the painter most known for the Conception, strayed from Pacheco without being considered the less orthodox for it. His moon, for example, is sometimes full, or when a crescent, with horns pointing upwards instead of downwards (as we see in Tiepolo's).

The rose symbolizes Our Lady, and the white color, as with that of the lily, symbolizes the purity of the Virgin. Palms, deriving from Palm Sunday, symbolize spiritual victory and triumph over death (often used with martyrs). In this case it is emphasizing Mary's crucial role in the victory achieved by her Son. The dove, of course, symbolizes the Holy Ghost.

In this example, Tiepolo varies the focus, and where he mutes the color he uses tonal variation to describe form, in characteristic Baroque mode. Find a color image on the internet and look, for example, at the mantle. This is intended to be seen in our mind's eye as uniformly blue in accordance with Pacheco's specifications. However, only part of what is painted is actually blue. Much is rendered tonally in brown ochre and sepia.

Tiepolo is noted for giving his paintings a lightness and airiness that did not exist in those works by artists who worked in the previous century. He achieved this by using colors in a higher register than many of his 17th-century counterparts would have done—more pale blue, bright yellow and orange for example. He also deftly varied the color that he used for the purely tonal description. As mentioned in connection with the mantle, he uses sepia and brown ochre. Elsewhere he uses yellow ochre. Contrast this with, for example, Zurbarán's St. Francis in prayer.

In Zurbarán's painting, all the areas other than the figure are in brown, and this gives it a somber, penitential feel. This can be good (as it is in this painting), but it can be restricting if it is the only visual device available to you. Tiepolo's use of lighter ochres and paler grays offers the possibility of a visual vocabulary that can communicate Christian joy.

15

Why We Need Different Artistic Traditions

Here is a passage taken from the Office of Readings, Saturday, 6th week of Eastertide. It is part of St. Augustine's Commentary on the Gospel of John:

> There are two ways of life that God has commended to the Church. One is through faith, the other is through vision. One is in pilgrimage through a foreign land, the other is in our eternal home; one in labor, the other in repose; one in a journey to our homeland, the other in that land itself; one in action, the other in the fruits of contemplation.
>
> The first life, the life of action, is personified by the Apostle Peter; the contemplative life, by John. The first life is passed here on earth until the end of time, when it reaches its completion; the second is not fulfilled until the end of the world, but in the world to come it lasts for ever. . . ."

The painting below is the release of St. Peter by Strozzi, the Italian Baroque painter of the 17th century.

St. John, 15th-century icon
by Andrei Rublev, Russian

This passage seems to me to describe very well why the Church has different liturgical artistic traditions and how each is complementary to the others. The form of the iconographic tradition is governed by the theology of the "world to come that lasts forever," symbolized by St. John—the art of heaven.

Gothic is art of the "pilgrimage through a foreign land," as Augustine puts it. Stylistically the Gothic is a modified form of iconography that has a greater correspondence to natural appearances. It is almost as if the art form gradually appears from heaven, descending to earth to join the pilgrims. In its early forms—the work of Duccio, for example (see facing page), who lived in the late 13th and early 14th centuries—it has a style that is very closely related to the iconographic. In its later forms, such as with the great Dominican Fra Angelico in the 15th century, it uses both the iconographic visual vocabulary as well as naturalistic ones that were being developed in Italy at this time (such as perspective and shadow) in a theologically coherent way.

The baroque of the 17th century is the most naturalistic of the three. In this context, the Baroque is ground zero. The Baroque is the starting point of our pilgrimage; the Gothic describes the partial and gradual ascent to that heavenly state that we make in this life before reaching the final repose; and the iconographic represents that ultimate destiny.

Here is the closing section of the same passage from St. Augustine:

> We should not separate these great apostles. They were both part of the present life symbolized by Peter and they were both part of the future life symbolized by John. Considered as symbols, Peter followed Christ and John remained; but in their living faith both endured the evils of

the present life and both looked forward to the future blessings of the coming life of joy.... Individually, Peter and John represent these two lives, the present and the future; but both journeyed in faith through this temporal life and both will enjoy the second life by vision, eternally.... It is not Peter alone who binds and looses sins, but the whole Church. It is not John alone who has drunk at the fountain of the Lord's breast and pours forth what he had drunk in his teaching of the Word being God in the beginning, God with God, of the Trinity and Unity of God—of all those things which we shall see face to face in his kingdom but now, before the Lord comes, we see only in images and reflections—not John alone, for the Lord himself spreads John's gospel throughout the world, giving everyone to drink as much as he is capable of absorbing.[1]

Christ is with us as we begin our journey. He is with us as we take the holy pilgrimage in this life and He is with us at the end. Until we reach that glorious end, we see, as Augustine puts it, "only images and reflections." Images and reflections! This may be all we have, but images and reflections can be powerful. They can potentially distract us, attract us, or attract and direct us. A truly Christian culture both attracts and re-directs.

---

1. St. Augustine: *Commentary on the Gospel of John*, taken from the Office of Readings, Saturday, 6th week of Eastertide.

Our culture must be a culture of beauty that inspires man and calls him into motion right at the start of our journey; it must help to reinforce the faith and help us to maintain momentum while on the journey; and it must give us a firm picture of our happy destiny so that we always know where we are heading. It must help us always, as St. Paul puts it, to "keep our sights on heavenly things," wherever we happen to be.

Each of us is called to take that journey. But to be a traveler is not enough. We are also bound also to help our fellow travelers. We must all contribute to the creation and maintenance of a culture of beauty, by cooperating with God's grace so that it permeates all that we do. We must strive to make our lives joyful and replete with images and reflections that call and direct others to their home. Our work must bear the beauty that pierces the hearts of those who see it.

St. Augustine, St. Peter, and St. John, pray for us!

PART FOUR
Afterword and Appendices

The Way of Beauty: Afterword
A Model for Art Schools for Today[1]

I N 1999, POPE ST. JOHN PAUL II wrote a *Letter to Artists*. In this he called for a *"new epiphany of beauty"* and for a *"renewed relationship between Church and culture"* in the spirit of the Second Vatican Council.

A "new epiphany" will not just happen by itself. We need art schools that will give artists, including Catholic artists, the training to create beautiful sacred art. (For the time being let us define "sacred" art simply as art with a specifically religious purpose. It might be intended for private devotion in the home, for example, or for incorporation within a liturgical celebration or building).

The pope also called for good "secular" artwork. There is in fact a strong connection between the two. Historically, one might even argue, as I have heard it said, that *the fine arts were born on the altar*—that religious inspiration and patronage lay behind all the great cultural movements of the past. If this was true once, it can be so again. Once standards of beauty have been set, once a vision of human existence and its ultimate meaning have been established for all to see, the culture at large will tend to measure itself against these standards, and to draw inspiration from this vision. Beauty is its own argument.

I am hoping for the eventual appearance of a new, post-Vatican II style of art, as distinctive as the Gothic or the Baroque which characterized earlier Christian eras. But this is unlikely to happen unless the training of artists instills within them the virtues and skills necessary to create prayerful, beautiful art that is capable of drawing us closer to God.

The method suggested here is based on the way artists have always been trained in traditional societies the world over: that is, through disciplined imitation. This makes artists adept at conforming their skills to the creation of art with an external purpose. The need for *beauty in the making* is important for the fulfillment of this purpose. It is proposed here that beauty is not simply "in the eye of the beholder"—a matter of

---

1. This first appeared in *Second Spring: A Journal for Faith and Culture* in 2003.

personal taste. We may disagree about what we find attractive, but there is an element of objectivity that has to be acknowledged. And this implies that the artist can be educated to discern and to love beauty. It cannot be sought directly, in the "abstract" as it were, and the artist need not even be very interested in a "theory of aesthetics." Nevertheless, some consideration of the nature of beauty is necessary for those devising the training of artists.

What is Beauty?

In his *Letter to Artists*, Pope St. John Paul II cites the famous and mysterious phrase of Dostoyevsky: *Beauty will save the world*. Does this mean that the beauty that is in the world will save it? Or must we look for a beauty from beyond the world? The answer is a bit of both. The beauty that is in the world comes from beyond it. It directs us to where it comes from. The Christian religion, especially, is all about this saving beauty.

Hans Urs von Balthasar writes (in the first pages of the first volume of his series *The Glory of the Lord*):

> We no longer dare to believe in beauty and we make of it a mere appearance in order the more easily to dispose of it. Our situation today shows that beauty demands for itself at least as much courage and decision as do truth and goodness, and she will not allow herself to be separated and banned from her two sisters without taking them along with herself in an act of mysterious vengeance. We can be sure that whoever sneers at her name as if she were the ornament of a bourgeois past—whether he admits it or not—can no longer pray and soon will no longer be able to love.[2]

So what is beauty? I see it, like its sisters, truth and goodness, as an objective quality. It is a quality in a thing that directs us to God. It calls us to first to itself and then beyond, with an invitation to go to Him. If we heed that call we respond with love to that beauty and open ourselves up to it and to its ultimate source, the inspiration of the artist, God. When we do this it elevates the spirit and provides consolation to the soul. Beauty is the quality in a painting through which the artist can "bear witness to the Light."

Beauty is not the only thing in art that directs us to God. Sometimes, the subject matter, even if poorly represented, can do this also. It is possible, therefore, to have ugly art that fulfills its liturgical function in a mechanical sense. For example, an image of the Blessed Virgin Mary,

---

2. H.U. von Balthasar, *The Glory of the Lord: A Theological Aesthetics, Volume 1: Seeing the Form* (Edinburgh, T&T Clark, 1982), p. 18.

though poorly painted, may still be recognizable as such, and so in some way will direct our thoughts to Our Lady in heaven. But this ugly sacred art would do the job so much better if it were beautiful as well. (And just as it is possible to have an ugly image of a beautiful object, it is possible to have a beautiful image of an ugly object!)

Beauty's call can manifest itself in different ways. It could be as a shout or trumpet-blast, revealing God's glory, splendor and might—I feel that Turner's dramatic seascapes do this. It can be a beacon, iridescent with reflected light, the source of which is beyond the world—I would choose Monet as an example. Aidan Hart, the Orthodox iconographer, refers to this as "burning-bush art"—because it "burns" with the fire of God's glory.

But, in contrast, the call of beauty can be as the "still, small voice" that punctuates the silence. These might be the shadowy, numinous paintings, perhaps with a melancholy edge, that suggest a presence of something that is beyond what is portrayed, and seem to reveal the hope and solace that lie there. The portraits of Rembrandt and the still-life paintings of Giorgio Morandi come to mind.

Beauty can also call to us like the "cry of one in the wilderness." It acknowledges the despair and pain of human suffering, but it does not leave us in desolation, for at the same time it seems to reassure us of the hope that is in the world to come, which transcends suffering. This hope is present even in death. Grünewald's crucifixion, is perhaps, an example of this. When paintings of this type show human suffering, they allow the viewer to grow in compassion and love through empathizing with the suffering, and to sense the hope that lies at the root of all suffering, through God. In contrast, the distorted figures of Francis Bacon, though brilliantly executed, mock those who suffer and diminish our love for mankind and God. So for me, although Bacon's art is powerful, that power is misdirected and is not beautiful; therefore, it is not good art.

Just as beauty can manifest itself in a variety of ways, so our reactions to it can be varied. We may respond fully, with love for God. This love is fueled by grace. When this happens we experience a powerful call to God, and recognize it as such. In its fullest sense, it is similar to the response to Christ from some of those who saw and heard him in his ministry. (In his *Letter to Artists*, Pope John Paul II describes beauty as "the Good made visible." Christ, the Word made flesh, is the purest example of this, making Christ the Form of beauty.) When St. John describes the effect of Christ on those who saw and heard his ministry, he says that some reacted positively to the Light, "grace answering to grace" (John 1:16).

Others, when confronted with the same example of beauty, will respond, knowing that it is good, but will not know the full meaning of the call. When Samuel was a boy he heard the "still, small voice" (1 Samuel 3:3–19). He responded three times, and responded obediently. But he did not know that it was a call to God, for he was "a stranger to the divine voice," and ran to Eli each time. Finally, Eli had to tell him to whom he should go. To draw a parallel, many will recognize beauty and be attracted to it, but never move beyond that, unless something acts as Eli did for Samuel, so that they may know the full truth. These people are the aesthetes who see beauty as an end in itself. It is as though they savor the smell of cooking, but never eat the meal. The passage in Samuel, where Eli taught Samuel to know the voice for what it was, suggests that our ability to apprehend beauty can be taught and can develop.

Some, of course, will see what is beautiful and be unmoved, or even respond negatively. They may lack the grace to make any sort of loving response. Some hate what is good. We are all free to ignore or reject God's love. However, when this happens, we are unlikely to say: "I see an object of beauty, which I know to be a call to God. I do not love God; therefore, I choose not to respond lovingly." Beauty provokes first a response that takes place deep in our hearts. For complex emotional or moral reasons to do with our own upbringing or personal history, that response may involve a feeling of displeasure. Equating feeling with judgment, we may see what is beautiful and call it ugly. Or we may do the reverse, opening ourselves to the ugly and mistakenly calling it beautiful. Some even claim to have a preference for what perturbs the soul, what shocks or depresses, claiming that this alone can be "real" or "true."

No one is purely loving or, indeed, purely self-centered, and so no one is ever likely to be completely consistent in his or her reaction to beauty. Without a pure visible standard available to us, which we could use to measure beauty objectively, it is difficult to know who is right and who is wrong. This difficulty is what gives rise to the currently fashionable, though false, idea that beauty is a subjective quality. Certainly, to know something as beautiful is a fragile kind of knowing, for it requires heart and mind, will and intellect, to be in harmony. But just as in the case of truth and goodness, we can be educated to improve our perception of beauty.

Educating for Self-Expression

The Church needs beautiful and inspiring sacred art. Perhaps we could simply equip artists with the necessary drawing and painting skills, and then give them their commission, together with some guidelines or patterns for modern iconography, and suggest that they pray to God for inspiration and paint the best they can?

The problem that faces us is that the ethos of individuality and self-expression is so ingrained in our society that many will be unable to recognize and co-operate with divine inspiration when it comes. Art is nowadays often regarded merely as a form of self-expression. Therefore, the danger exists that having acquired the ability to draw and paint, the artist will fall in love with his own skill. If this were to happen, the temptation to draw attention to himself (perhaps through a flamboyant use of that skill) would be great, whatever the subject matter or the purpose of the art he is creating. Humility is traditionally inculcated through the practice of obedience to a master. Because of our difficulties in obtaining a consensus on masters of modern styles, it must be taught through an *apprenticeship in time*, in which the greatest artists from the past are imitated.

Our apprentices would also learn something of the ethos of the great artists and their cultural milieu, partly through historical study. This process will not be an uncritical one. We cannot know precisely what was in the mind of any artist when he painted, even those who worked within a clearly defined tradition. So part of this process will be one of discovery, for pupils and teachers alike. The important point is to learn to associate the art of the past with its purpose: a purpose external to the self.

It is my conviction that it is only when this habit of the subjugation to the patterns of tradition is ingrained in the soul that there can be confidence that the artist can achieve an expression of the true self: that authentic individualism in which God is able to work through the person to achieve something genuinely original. This process of *discipline before freedom* will allow the originality of each artist to shine through without being forced. As the prayer of St. Francis of Assisi puts it: "In self-forgetfulness we find our true selves."

I would hope that in this way, the authentic individuality of the artist would emerge quite naturally, without being forced for its own sake. For some this will mean the creation of new and previously unimagined styles, and for others it will mean working within existing traditions, including the sacred, in their own unique way. Whatever form their work takes, artists cannot help but reflect the age they live in. This is as true for the most devout cloistered monk as it is for those who are fully integrated with society. As a consequence a distinctive look, one that characterizes our time, will eventually emerge.

As far as sacred art is concerned, special attention would be paid in our school to the authentic liturgical traditions of the Roman Church, as articulated by Pope Emeritus Benedict XVI in his book *The Spirit of the Liturgy*: the iconographic, the Gothic and the Baroque styles of art. Each has a particular value in terms of the evident integration it achieves between form, content, and function. The school's repertoire could also include secular art, however (the portraits of Rembrandt, the landscapes and seascapes of Turner, etc.), and art from other cultures (Chinese or Japanese watercolors, Mughal and Russian miniatures, etc.).

It should go without saying that Christian art is not the only kind that is beautiful or good. Any art is beautiful to the degree that it incorporates the timeless principles that comprise beauty. Various attempts have been made to isolate and list these principles, but the academic study of these would not necessarily greatly help an artist in his painting. It is more important, in the end, that the artist should gain through experience an intuitive sense of those common principles. The careful study of natural forms would facilitate this—landscape, still life, and especially the human figure and portraiture, and their expression with the acquired skills appropriate to a given medium. These are an essential part of the education of an artist, even one intending to work in the field of sacred art.

The study of traditional proportion described numerically would also be important. This is an ancient tradition based upon the observation of the rhythms and patterns that underlie the order of the cosmos. The most commonly seen are those mathematical relationships that are derived from a common perception of musical harmony. They are a broad framework for the set of design principles that in the past were used for architectural design, from the Romans through to the early 20th century; and in compositional design in paintings.

Spiritual Formation

The modern world has seen a development of "art for art's sake." This phrase is usually applied to art that is intended for display in galleries and so is seen by some as having no purpose beyond its own creation. However, whether such art is intended for decoration or education, or merely for entertainment, it still has a purpose and so is not created as an end in itself in the mind of the artist. The question is not whether the work is intended to fulfill an aim, but whether that aim is a worthy or noble one.

Now the artist is a man or woman like any other. Morality and spirituality must be taken into account. But it is important also to remember that moral rectitude or piety is no guarantee of artistic quality. Furthermore, God can inspire whomsoever he pleases: there is no accounting for inspiration or those who will respond to it. (This was the message of *Amadeus.*) How do we balance these considerations? It seems clear that a person will be more inclined to submit his creative skills to the will of God if he is habitually turning to God in the other areas of his life. For this reason there should be time spent in the school on the study of religion, philosophy and theology, all of which, in combination with spiritual guidance, can contribute to the growth of the individual. Another way of putting this is that an art school of the kind I am envisaging should aim to support its students in their spiritual journey, and guide them sensitively towards sources of wisdom.

Catholics in particular should receive an education in the iconographic content of sacred Catholic art as well as a full liturgical education—the context into which their art would be placed. This might include an account of the meaning of the different parts of the Mass and other rites; an exploration of ideas of sacred space and time and the meaning of the sacraments; an explanation of how the Church year is linked to the principal mysteries of the life of Christ and the lives of the saints; an introduction to the history of the liturgy and its development.

Criteria of Admission

It is not assumed, however, that only practicing Catholics will be admitted to a school that provides such an education. Provided that the principle of objective truth is not compromised, people of any background, even avowed atheists, could be admitted without necessarily undermining the ethos necessary for the study of art—if not sacred art. Only relativism is excluded, for relativism is incompatible with the search for truth. Relativism is driven instead by an intolerance of disagreement. Rather than saying, "Let's agree to disagree," it says, "Disagreement is agreement." This is a contradiction that cannot be reconciled with truth, and cannot be accommodated in the ethos of the proposed school.

There is a practical point to consider also. In the United States there is a large Catholic population that could provide pupils, teachers, and patrons; and an established tradition of universities and colleges that have a religious affiliation. In Britain, where I come from originally, none of these conditions exist. What I can foresee happening in Britain, however, is the establishment of a school of sacred art in which, after their foundational training, students will be free to specialize in or take their inspiration from any artistic tradition or religion.

This would be no bad thing if, again, the principle of devotion to objective truth is retained along with a spirit of tolerance. It would create an environment in which there would be disagreement, but at the same time respect for the fact that others can be genuinely involved a search for truth even if they reach different conclusions. Such a school would attract many people who would not otherwise wish to come to a "Catholic School of Art"—perhaps, initially, simply by the chance to get a decent training in currently neglected skills such as drawing and painting. Once admitted, these students would receive an exposure to

Christian sacred art in the foundational years of study that they might not otherwise have had. Provided that such a school does not compromise in offering the Catholics who do attend exactly what they need, we stand to lose nothing, and to gain much. (I would, of course, value the comments of readers on this point.)

In the light of this I suggest the following principles as a list that could define the teaching ethos for what for the moment I will call the Academy of Visual Arts:

1. Artists should aspire to be good artists. Good artists create good works of art. Good works of art possess or reflect both objective truth and beauty.

2. Artists can be educated to grow in their love of goodness, beauty, and truth. Such an education will enhance their ability to manifest these transcendental, objective qualities in their work.

3. Artists have a responsibility to provide a social and spiritual service to mankind. Good art, whether sacred or secular in subject or context, uplifts, enlarges, and inspires the hearts of those who see it to a deeper love for the Creator and his Creation. This is manifested in a deeper love for mankind and increasing compassion for human suffering.

4. Artists need to acquire a deep understanding of their craft, and a sufficiently high level of skill to enable them to work effectively to commission with an almost unconscious fluency.

5. Artists are called to creativity, in the likeness of their own Creator. Authentic originality in a work of art is not absolute: it derives from the artist's submission to objective values beyond the individual self.

6. Artists belong to a tradition, which is the handing-on of the knowledge and positive experience of the past. Respect for tradition is concretely expressed by apprenticeship to the great artists of the past ("masters"), in order, through humility and training, to achieve mastery in turn. For some this will mean continuing to work in their own unique way within established and prescribed sacred forms; for others it will lead to the creation of new and previously unimagined styles.

7. Provided they share a belief in the objectivity of truth, goodness and beauty, and are well disposed to the above principles, our Academy will admit students of any religious faith or none. Since we hold that the good artist must look beyond the individual self for inspiration, we will encourage them to develop a living relationship with the Source of life. We will support our students in their religious search as well as their artistic training.

Appendix 1
Liturgical Science

How the Quadrivium Can
Stimulate the Creativity of the Modern Scientist

I N THE CANTICLE OF DANIEL, chanted on Lauds Sunday Week One and all feast days in the Divine Office, all of creation is called to give praise to God. The frosts, hail and snow, wind and rain, and all the other inanimate aspects of creation listed in this canticle do not give praise to God literally, but through their beauty they direct our praise to God. The cosmos is made for us. Through it, we perceive the Creator. In this sense the whole of Creation is ordered liturgically, in that it directs us to God, and we give Him thanks, praise and glory. That thanks and praise of man is expressed most perfectly in the liturgy.

As our understanding of the order of the cosmos increases through modern science, this wonder increases, and this connection between its beauty and the liturgy is reinforced further, it seems.

In his excellent book *Modern Physics and Ancient Faith*, Stephen M. Barr describes the scientific investigation of a grouping of sub-atomic particles which he refers to as a "multiplet" of "hadronic particles." He describes how when different properties, called "flavors" of "SU(3) symmetry," of nine of these particles were plotted mathematically, the result was a patterned arrangement that looked like a triangle with the tip missing.

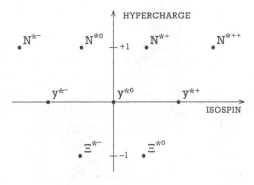

He tells us:

> Without knowing anything about SU(3) symmetry, one could guess
> just from the shape of the multiplet diagram that there should be a
> tenth kind of particle with properties that allow it to be placed down at
> the bottom to complete the triangle pattern. This is not just a matter of
> aesthetics, the SU(3) symmetries require it. It can be shown from the
> SU(3) that the multiplets can only come in certain sizes. . . . On the
> basis of SU(3) symmetry Murray Gell-Mann predicted in 1962 that
> there must exist a particle with the right properties to fill out this
> decuplet. Shortly thereafter, the new particle, called the Ω was indeed
> discovered.[1]

This result would have been of no surprise to anyone who had under-
gone an education in beauty based upon the *quadrivium*. The shape
that Murray Gell-Mann's work completed was the triangular arrangement of 10 points, known as the tectractys. This is the triangular
arrangement of the number 10 in a series of 1:2:3:4. 1, 2, 3, and 4 are the
first four numbers, which symbolize the creation of the cosmos in three
dimensions generated from the unity of God; and from notes produced
by plucking strings of these relative lengths, we can construct the three
fundamental harmonies of the musical scale.

The idea that the tectractys might be governing the arrangements of
properties of these sub-atomic particles does not prove that it is a cor-
rect theorem (although I do find it intriguing!). Nor, even, is knowledge
of the tectractys necessary to see the missing dot in this case. As Barr
points out, it is obvious once you look at the incomplete graph. But it is
obvious only once one works on the assumption that nature is ordered
symmetrically. Once Gell-Mann did this, his intuition gave him the
missing point. This intuitive leap is the first step in any creative process.
We come up first with an idea of what we think it might be, and then
test it with reason.

I do not have a deep knowledge of particle physics, but I doubt that
the traditional *quadrivium* contains the full range of symmetries that
one is likely to see and would need to use as a research particle physicist.
Nevertheless, I would maintain that the traditional education in the
quadrivium would enable the research scientist to be more creative in
his work. A traditional education in beauty trains the mind to work in
conformity to the divine order to which, in turn, the natural order conforms. Such a mind is open to inspiration from the Creator, and is more

---

1. Stephen M. Barr, *Modern Physics and Ancient Faith* (Notre Dame: University of
Notre Dame Press, 2006), p. 99.

likely to make the necessary intuitive leap when given an array of data. The mind that habitually looks to the divine symmetry is more likely to see the natural symmetry.

Physicist A. Zee put it thus:

> Symmetries have played an increasingly central role in our understanding of the physical world. From rotational symmetry physicists went on to formulate ever more abstruse symmetries . . . fundamental physicists are sustained by the faith that the ultimate design is suffused with symmetries. Contemporary physics would not have been possible without symmetries to guide us. . . . Learning from Einstein, physicists impose symmetry and see that a unified conception of the physical world may be possible. They hear symmetries whispered in their ears. As physics moves further away from everyday experience and closer to the mind of the Ultimate Designer, our minds are trained away from their familiar moorings. . . . The point to appreciate is that contemporary theories, such as grand unification or superstring, have such rich and intricate mathematical structures that physicists must martial the full force of symmetry to construct them. They cannot be dreamed up out of the blue, nor can they be constructed by laboriously fitting one experimental fact after another. These theories are dictated by Symmetry.[2]

And what has this to do with the liturgy? The traditional *quadrivium* is essentially the study of pattern, harmony, symmetry, and order in nature and mathematics, viewed as a reflection of the Divine Order. When we perceive something that reflects this order, we call it beautiful. For the Christian this is the source, along with Tradition, that provides the model upon which the rhythms and cycles of the liturgy are based. Christian culture, like classical culture before it, was also patterned after this cosmic order; this order which provides the unifying principle that runs through every traditional discipline. Literature, art, music, architecture, philosophy—all of creation and potentially all human activity—are bound together by this common harmony and receive their fullest meaning in the liturgy.

When we apprehend beauty we do so intuitively. So an education that improves our ability to apprehend beauty develops also our intuition. All creativity is at source an intuitive process. This means that professionals in *any* field, including business and science, would benefit from an education in beauty, because it would develop their creativity. Furthermore, the creativity that an education in beauty stimulates will gen-

---

2. A. Zee, *Fearful Symmetry: The Search for Beauty in Modern Physics* (London: Macmillan, 1986), p. 281. Quoted by Stephen M. Barr, *A Student's Guide to Natural Science* (Wilmington: ISI Books, 1986), p. 71.

erate not just more ideas, but *better* ideas—better because they are more in harmony with the natural order. The recognition of beauty moves us to love what we see. So such an education would tend to develop also, therefore, our capacity to love, and leave us more inclined to the serve God and our fellow-man. The end result for the individual who follows this path is joy.

When the person is habitually ordering his life liturgically, he will tap into this creative force, for he will be inspired by the Creator. Meanwhile along with the frost and the snow, all those multiplets of hadronic particles in the cosmos will be giving praise to the Lord.

Appendix 2

Trinity and trinity:
The Beauty of Three

The Ancient Greeks

A S FAR BACK AS ANCIENT GREECE, the number three, it seems, has been seen as fundamental to the organizational principle of all beauty. Beginning with awe and wonder and the self-evident truth that the cosmos is beautiful and, connected with it, the fact that certain combinations of musical tone sound good together, the classical philosophers concluded that properly ordered relationships come in threes.

Harmonious proportion, which is intrinsic to beauty, is the network of relationships between three different things. In arithmetic it is three different numbers. In music theory, right up to the present day, a chord is incomplete unless it has three notes. When I ask musicians why this is, they tell me it is because if you only have two you can't tell precisely what the chord is: it could be a minor or a major chord. It is not until that third note is added that it takes on the full characteristic. Up until that point, with just two notes, it is ambiguous. So when we hear two notes in harmony, we are imagining one of two possibilities for the third that will complete the chord. Therefore, the composer crystallizes that third, previously imagined note for us as a real sound so that we know which it is.

In architecture (before traditional proportion began to be rejected at the turn of the last century), the idea for a house was to have three or more stories of different magnitudes, as this gave it its full beauty. However, when people could not afford to pay for three stories, two would be built. This still allows for a pleasing combination if not the full effect, just as with music. And, again just as with music, if we only have two objects in relation we feel as though a third ought to be there; the builder, therefore, would add features to suggest its presence. For example, a window smaller than the others might be inserted to the gable end of a loft window in order to indicate a loft that is smaller than the stories below; or a window might be inserted at ground level suggesting a basement that is larger than the stories above (see next page).

Above: Three windows in proportion, Annapolis, Maryland

Below Left: a two story house, Groton, MA, with a third placed as a light for the loft. Below Right: a two-story house, with the basement window inserted at ground level. Although the window is smaller, we get a sense that it is part of a much larger one which is partially buried because the single pane of glass is longer than the rest.

Superabundance

This "Threeness" is so bound up in harmony that in fact it is present even when we initially have only two objects in harmonious relationship with each other. Consider a chord created by playing two notes simultaneously, say a perfect fifth. We can hear both notes in the scale distinctly even when they are played together. But in addition something new is created. We perceive a chord as something distinct from its two parts. Combination does not destroy the integrity of each. It is as though we can not only hear the notes with our ears, but in our minds we hear also the relationship between them as a distinct entity.

This effect always strikes me most strongly when I hear a very good choir gel. Once when I was attending Mass at the London Oratory, the choir, unusually, came down from the loft to take communion first and then stayed down by the altar-rail very close to where people were receiving Communion. I watched them from only a few yards away, closer than I had been before. I could hear the separate notes and each mouth moving as each member sang; but I was struck by the fact that I heard a single harmonious voice that was somehow separate from the body of people who were contributing to it. One expected a blended sound when they were some distance away up in the choir loft, but to hear their voices bound together so tightly while being able see the separate components that contributed to it so clearly made the effect all the more striking. It was like being able to enjoy a piece of cake while still being aware of the eggs, flour, milk, and sugar as separate ingredients.

With this expert choir, I had a real sense of something distinct created that was different from a mere sum of its parts. An entity had been created out of nothing. In fact, I was perceiving the *relationships* that existed between the separate notes, created by their proximity in time and space.

In the light of Revelation, Christians can add to the understanding of this, especially in consideration of the love of God and love in personal relationships. The word for the creation of something out of nothing is "superabundance." It is used most commonly not of musical relationships, but rather in the context of loving personal relationships. One might consider a loving personal relationship as a harmony of a sort, a harmony of wills in which each simultaneously acts for the good of the other and accepts gracefully the good offered by the other.

In his encyclical *Deus Caritas Est*, Pope Benedict XVI describes how a loving relationship contains this dynamic—people simultaneously offering the gift of themselves, and accepting that gift from the other. He identifies these two components of love as agape (giving) and eros (ordered acceptance). Each person in the relationship is simultaneously giving and receiving. If agape and eros are the components, the harmonized "voice" that is created through this relationship and which is created out of nothing is love, which is the combination of the two. In any loving relationship, there are always three things present: the Lover, the Beloved, and the Love. The Love is comprised in this description of the intermingling of agape from the lover and eros from the beloved. Each gives to the other in a dynamic of mutual self-gift and ordered acceptance.

In a subsequent encyclical, *Caritas in Veritas*, Pope Benedict tells us that superabundance is always the product of this love, for such love invites (so to speak) God, who is love, into the scenario, and He becomes supernaturally present as a third person in the relationship: "Charity is love received and given. It is 'grace' (*charis*). Its source is the wellspring of the Father's love for the Son, in the Holy Spirit. Love comes down to us from the Son. It is creative love, through which we have our being; it is redemptive love, through which we are recreated. Love is revealed and made present by Christ and 'poured into our hearts through the Holy Spirit' (Rom 5:5). As objects of God's love, men and women become subjects of charity, they are called to make themselves instruments of grace, so as to pour forth God's charity and to weave networks of charity.... Charity always manifests God's love in human relationships."[1] Then, relating this love of mutual self-gift to superabundance, he says: "Gift by its nature goes beyond merit, its rule is that of superabundance. It takes place first in our souls as a sign of God's presence in us, a sign of what he expects from us."[2]

Where love is present, there is present also a divine creativity that creates something out of nothing—God is the source of all superabundance. There is a pop-song cliché that describes two people in love as "two hearts beating as one." In fact, because of this principle of superabundance it might be more accurate to say that when love is present, two hearts beat not as one, but as three!

In human relationships this love is most strikingly superabundant in a family, when the result is the creation of human life. That love is crystallized, so to speak, as a new baby. The baby is the third note that completes the chord, a materialization of the relationship that exists between the two others.

The materialization of the third simultaneously multiplies the number of relationships that exist. There are now three relationships between people. Each of these is founded in love and is superabundant (the fruitfulness of that superabundance is always properly ordered to the nature of the relationship, so the product is not always a baby!).

This is why population-growth can never be a problem. The superabundant love made present by the addition of one more person will always be more productive than the need created by one more mouth to feed. It also indicates why anyone without a sense of the supernatural

1. Benedict XVI, *Caritas in Veritate*, nn. 5, 6.
2. Ibid., 34.

would always argue for depopulation. The atheist does not factor in superabundant love when he considers the ramifications of new life.

Love, this harmonious giving and acceptance, can arise potentially in any relationship, not just those that are particularly deep. This can be true potentially for just about any interaction, however casual. Even a cheery hello to a bus driver and smile in response can reflect love properly ordered to the nature of a relationship between driver and passenger. This is primarily a business relationship, but it need not be devoid of this personal aspect. In *Caritas in Veritate*,[3] Pope Benedict XVI describes the importance of the presence of this dynamic exchange of love in economic transactions. He uses the word "gratuitousness" to describe it, and is clear that the personal element in business relationships is more than a desirable add-on to the main purpose of creating wealth. I would say that in fact this gratuitousness is the fundamental basis for the creative principle by which all wealth is created. Contracts and the rule of law that enforces them are necessary for economic flourishing, but they alone cannot drive prosperity (considered even in the narrowest, monetary sense)—genuine consideration for the other must be present if wealth is to be generated, rather than simply transferred. This is the case even in an exchange between two self-interested parties. Assuming they enter into it freely,[4] each must have some consideration for the needs (or desires, at least) of the other if the transaction is to take place. Wherever the interest of the parties goes beyond this narrowest of forms into a genuine concern for the well-being of the other (the pope uses the word "gratuitousness" for this), as it invariably does, the principle of superabundance is invoked, wealth is created, and both parties will flourish as human beings as a result.

Another Aspect of Three in the Beauty of Creation

There is a paradox built into Creation. Each detail, each object seems complete in itself, yet everything is created to be in harmonious relationship with something else. It seems that being "relational"—the capacity for harmonious relationship—is an essential aspect of being for all God's creatures.

Take the example of a rose. Each petal within the bloom is in harmonious placement in relation to the next in a way that is just right for a rose. It has "due proportion," as those who study aesthetics would say. It also give us a sense of being complete—it is fully a rose. This unity is demonstrated by the fact that if I give my love a red rose as a symbolic

---

3. Benedict XVI, *Caritas in Veritate*, nn. 34–40.
4. By this I mean freedom as defined in the *Catechism of the Catholic Church*, 1731.

gesture of love, but that rose has half the petals removed, she is more likely to be insulted than gratified. For it is plain that this is incomplete. Conversely, if I present her with a full bloom, she may be pleased or embarrassed (depending upon how she feels about me), but regardless of how she takes the gesture, the rose says it all.

But there is a slight tension here. In some ways a single rose demands to be with others in a rose bush (or a bunch of roses). And when we look at the rose bush in bloom, just like the rose, it too has a unity to it and is beautiful: each flower, stem and leaf is placed in harmonious relation to the other (especially when tended well by a gardener). Going further and broadening our horizon again, this time considering the garden from which it came, let us note that if that garden is well-designed and well-tended, then each bush has its place within it.

This paradoxical property of being runs right through nature. Starting at the human scale, we can focus our attention onto successively smaller detail, right through to the microscopic; or we can move in the other direction and steadily broaden our horizon until we consider galaxies in the sky. Whether the scope of our vision is narrow or broad, we see at each stage an object that is beautiful in itself by virtue of the patterned arrangement of the details within it, and we see that this object is simultaneously a detail in a broader scene, placed beautifully in its proper setting. The relational property of being always directs our attention. It says, "Look at me"; and at the same time it says, "Look at these things I am in relationship with." This is why Creation is beautiful regardless of the level of scrutiny we apply. To use the terminology of proportion, every detail is beautiful because it is a mean between two extremes, and each extreme, both the larger and the smaller, is, if considered beautiful, the mean between two further extremes successively larger or smaller, and so on.

To What Does the Universe Relate?

In my description of this chain of consideration of nature to successively narrower focus or broader horizon, one might ask what happens once we reach on the one hand the broadest horizon possible, or on the other the narrowest focus possible.

First, consider the broadest view we can see or could conceivably see, that is, the whole of the created cosmos. Does the cosmos contain within it a capacity for relationship with something else? If capacity for relationship is intrinsic to being along with beauty, the answer must be yes. But if that is so, to what can it possibly relate if no broader horizon is possible? There is no material object in existence beyond the cosmos.

Similarly, if we go down to the narrowest focus possible and consider the smallest object that is resolvable by the eye, or even the smallest object that we can resolve when seen through a powerful microscope, is this really the end of the chain? If each aspect of creation is beautiful through its very being, then this must apply to the tiniest detail that we can see, for which we can resolve no smaller part. It must apply to those that we cannot view directly, but know to exist—sub-atomic particles. Let us say that the smallest of these is a quark: then quarks must be beautiful too, as beauty is a property of being. What smaller detail can the quark relate to if it is to be beautiful, if it is itself the smallest part that exists?

If the quark and the universe are the smallest and largest material objects that exist, respectively, and both are beautiful and relational by virtue of their existence, then both must relate to something else that is smaller and something that is bigger, respectively. Each is simultaneously the mean and the extreme in a proportion. As nothing bigger, or smaller, exists in the universe, for this statement to be true there must be something to which they relate that is in another sort of existence, i.e., that is not part of the material universe. The must be something beyond the physical realm of existence which makes them beautiful.

For Christians, the answer as to what is smaller than the smallest thing and larger than the largest is the same in each case. What they point to is God. All of Creation points to Him by virtue of the beautiful relationship it has with Him. God as Creator is present to His creatures as a cause is present to its effect.

Even though we have taken a step into the metaphysical (literally, from the Greek, "beyond the physical"), we have still not quite reached the first point (or the last) in this line of thinking. God is that standard to which all that exists points to, but He is different from all else that exists because He does not depend on anything else for His existence. At first sight, therefore, there is an anomaly here. We assert that God is the standard of beauty, Beauty itself. But if beauty is the product of harmonious relationships, it suggests that God needs something that is not God to relate to in order to be beautiful. But if this is so, it would contradict either the idea that He does not depend on anything for his existence, or the idea that He is Beauty itself.

The Trinity

The answer is that God, unlike the created world, contains within Himself the fullness of being: that is, he is simultaneously relational *and* self-sufficient. And being the essence of what it is to be in relation, it seems reasonable to suggest it is likely to consist of the simplest, fundamental aspects of relationship as we have described them so far. This constitutes three subjects in relation to each other, a trinity. Through the "three-ness" of its beauty, the world points us to the beauty of a trinity—a divine Trinity.

But we do not know by this anything about the nature of the three individual aspects that are in relation in God. For that we need to consider love.

Love, the Human Person, and the Trinity

Everything we have said so far applies to man, as one of God's creatures, as much as it does to a rose or anything else in Creation. Even if our consideration is limited to man's physical being, he is beautiful. However, in the case of man, an additional dimension comes into play. Mankind possesses free will and can choose to enter into relationships with other free-thinking individuals based upon a principle of mutual self-sacrifice. The name that we give the special beauty of this harmony in human relationships is *love*. This special, loving relational nature of humanity is what makes a human being a *person*, a special sort of being. Personal relationships are loving relationships between persons who have the same nature.

If God is the fullness of love, then one would expect this personal aspect to be present within him. The trinity is a Trinity that is Beauty and Love between three *persons*. Within God there are three divine *persons*.

Christian Revelation

We know from Revelation that the three Persons of the Trinity are the Father, the Son, and the Holy Spirit. In the Nicene Creed, which stems from two ecumenical councils of the Church (in 325 and 381), we are told that the Holy Spirit: "proceeds from the Father and the Son." If God is Love, then one would consider the exchange of love that takes place within the Godhead to be superabundant too. Take the love between any two, in a dynamic of the exchange of agape and eros that proceeds between them, and the third is a crystallization of that love.

This is explained by St. Augustine as follows:

> Now love is of someone who loves and something is loved with love. So then there are three: the lover, the beloved, and the love (*De Trinitate*, Bk. 8, Ch. 10). If then, any one of these three is to be specially called love, what more fitting than that this should be the Holy Spirit? In the sense, that is, that in that simple and highest nature, substance is not one thing and love another thing, but that substance itself is love and that love itself is substance whether in the Father or the Son or the

Holy Spirit, yet that the Holy Spirit is especially to be called love (Bk. 15, Ch. 17).

This love that is crystallized, as it were, is now in relationship with the other two, and there are three loving relationships where first we considered only two. Each of these is superabundant and fruitful. Each time it bears fruit, a new matrix of relationships between it and all else is created and there is exponential growth of self-generating Love that overflows into all that is.

We who are created out of that love can enter into the mystery of its source at our final end when we see God and partake of the divine nature. When we "see" God, we know Him deeply in the deepest form of knowing, which is love. The action of love that draws us into in this mystery now is worship of God in the liturgy. The Holy Spirit is the Love that draws us into the Son. Through personal relationship with the Son, we participate in His personal relationship with the Father. We are part of the mystical body of Christ, the Church. This is what liturgy is: the worship of the Father, through the Son, in the Spirit.

Appendix 3
Liturgy and Intuition

I N A GREAT SERIES of recorded lectures entitled *The Art of Critical Decision Making*,[1] Michael A. Roberto discusses the importance of intuition in making decisions and the factors that influence the reliability of our intuitive faculty. He illustrates his points with some striking real-life stories of people relying upon or ignoring intuition (sometimes with dire consequences), and backs up what he says with modern psychological research.

He tells, for example, of a number of occasions when nurses in cardiac intensive care units predicted that a patient was going to have a heart attack, despite the fact that the specialist doctors could see no problem and the standard ways of monitoring the patients' condition indicated nothing wrong either. When such nurses were asked *why* they think the situation is bad, they could not answer. As a result their predictions were disregarded. As it turned out, sadly, the nurses were often right. As a consequence, formal research into why the nurses could tell there was a problem was initiated. What was it they were reacting to?

The most dramatic tale he related was of a crack team of firefighters who were specialists in dealing with forest and brush fires. They were ready to be helicoptered into locations anywhere within a large part of the West to deal with fires when they broke out. The leader of the group, a respected firefighter, was a taciturn individual who led by example. He was not a good natural communicator, but usually this did not matter. One day they responded to a call and went to a remote site in California. When they assessed the situation, they discerned the pace of the spread of the fire and the direction it was going and so worked out how to deal with it safely. These judgments were important because if they got it wrong the brush fire could move faster than any man could run and they would be in trouble. Initially, things went as expected, but then suddenly the leader stopped and told everybody to do as he was doing.

1. http://www.thegreatcourses.com/tgc/courses/course_detail.aspx?cid=5932.

He threw a match to the ground and burnt an area in the grass of several square yards and then extinguished the fire. He then lay down on the burnt patch and waited. When asked why, he was unable to answer except to say that he thought they were in danger. He couldn't articulate clearly the nature of the danger or why this would action help. As a result, even though he was respected, his advice was ignored by the team. Suddenly the fire turned and headed straight at them; in the panic, the reaction of even these firefighters was to run. This was the wrong thing to do. The fire caught them and, tragically, they died. The only survivor was the leader. He was lying in the already-burnt patch that was surrounded by brush fire as it swept through the area, but was itself untouched by the advancing blaze as there was no grass to burn within it. He just waited until the surrounding area burnt itself out and then walked away.

In both cases, the practitioners were experienced people who got it right, but weren't believed by others because people were not inclined to listen to their warnings that arose solely from intuition.

Dr. Roberto describes how the research into such events since suggests that it is the level of experience *in situ* that develops an intuitive sense that is accurate enough to be relied upon. What experience teaches is the ability to recognize *patterns* of events. Through repeated observation, one knows that when certain events happen, they are usually related to others, and in a particular way. Even in quite simple situations, the different possible permutations of events would be quite complex to describe numerically and so scientific theorems may have difficulty predicting outcomes based upon them. However, the human mind is good at grasping the underlying pattern of any given situation at an intuitive level, and then can compare it with what usually happens by consulting the storehouse of the memory of past events. In these situations described, of the fire and the cardiac unit, all the indicators usually referred to by the textbooks were within the range of what was considered safe when considered individually. However, what the experienced nurse and firefighter spotted was a particular unusual combination that pointed to danger. This discernment was happening for them at some pre-conscious level and was not deduced step-by-step; hence their difficulties in articulating the detail of why they felt as they did.

As a result of this, it was recognized that good decision-making processes ought to take into account the intuition of experienced people. Professor Roberto described how hospitals and firefighters and others learning from them have incorporated it into their critical decision-making processes. This should be done with discernment—intuition is not infallible, and the less experienced we are in a particular environment, the less reliable our intuition is, so this must be taken into account as well.

It also depends on the person. Some people develop that sense of intuition in particular situations faster than others because the intuitive faculty is more highly developed. This, in my opinion, is where the traditional education in beauty might help. In order to develop our sense of the beautiful, this education teaches us to recognize intuitively the patterns and interrelationships that exist in the natural order of the cosmos. When we do so, we are more highly tuned to its beauty, and if we are artists we can incorporate that into our work. For non-artistic pursuits, we can still apply this principle of how things ought to be to make our activity beautiful and graceful.

Also, we have a greater sense of what is wrong when there is a lack of beauty because either the pattern of relationship between its parts is imperfect; or the relationship of the whole to things around it is distorted. In these situations we can see how to rectify the situation. This is the part that would help the firefighter or nurse, I believe. The education I am describing will not replace the specialist experience that gave those nurses the edge; but by deeply impressing upon our souls the overall architecture of the natural order, it will develop the faculty to learn to spot the patterns in particular situations and allow them to develop their on-the-job intuition faster.

Appendix 4
Modern and Ancient Cosmology in Harmony?

A Reflection on Seeing the Film *The Privileged Planet*[1]

I HAVE MET A NUMBER OF PEOPLE over the years who say that they believe in God and acknowledge the need to conform to a moral code (quite how they discern it is another matter) but reject "organized religion," which they see as an arbitrary creation of mankind. I think that perhaps the beauty of the cosmos provides an argument of sorts for the Church as an organized religion.

There is a book (and a film based on it) called *The Privileged Planet*. The book was written by Jay Richards and Guillermo Gonzalez. The film describes how recent developments in astrophysics impact our sense of the place of the earth in the universe and the chances of life occurring within. It runs through all the conditions necessary for mankind to exist. (For example, we have an atmosphere on Earth that both shields us from the harmful part of the solar spectrum and is transparent to the life-sustaining part of the same spectrum.) Then it details the chances of all these conditions (and there are dozens) occurring in the same place through processes that are governed by the laws of physics and chemistry in the universe. When all these probabilities are taken into account, the mathematics says that the chance of a place existing that can support us is negligible—so low that it is almost certain that there is no other life in the universe at all. The earth is probably the only planet in existence in the universe that can sustain intelligent life like us.

Furthermore, if we compare the extremely low probability of all the conditions for life occurring simultaneously with the amount of time so far available for such an event to occur—that is, the probable age of the universe—we might argue that it is surprising that these conditions

---

1. Jay Richards and Guillermo Gonzalez, *The Privileged Planet: How Our Place in the Cosmos is Designed for Discovery* (La Mirada: Illustra Media, 2010).

occurred simultaneously and in one place even once, as they have here on earth.

Then it goes further: the fact that scientists are able to study such things at all depends on the fact that man is able to observe the universe from here on earth to obtain data about the rest of the universe, which he can then analyze and from which he can draw conclusions. Surprisingly, it is not a given that he would be able to do this. In order for us to be living within the universe and able to observe the rest of it, another string of specific conditions have to be met (for example, a transparent atmosphere through which we can see the stars). It turns out that these conditions coincide with those necessary for the existence of life. That is, the conditions that allow a particular form of intelligent life to exist at all are the same conditions that allow the same form of intelligent life to observe the rest of the universe. The odds of this happening are lower than negligible, such that it is even harder to accept that it could ever happen. Yet it has.

Although this does seem to point to a force or forces other than the laws of physics and chemistry in operation here, one should be careful in drawing such a conclusion. The film neither proves nor disproves that God as Creator exists (or even an intelligent Designer, to use the word from the full title of the film); but nevertheless it is consistent with it—strikingly so.

Similarly, it does not prove it to be the case, but it supports beautifully the idea that the universe is made for man. Read the following from a sermon by the 5th-century Doctor of the Church, St. Peter Chrysologus:

Why then, man, are you so worthless in your own eyes and yet so precious to God? Why render yourself such dishonor when you are honored by him? Why do you ask how you were created and do not seek to know why you were made? Was not this entire visible universe made for your dwelling? It was for you that the light dispelled the overshadowing gloom; for your sake was the night regulated and the day measured, and for you were the heavens embellished with the varying brilliance of the sun, the moon and the stars. The earth was adorned with flowers, groves and fruit; and the constant marvelous variety of lovely living things was created in the air, the fields, and the seas for you, lest sad solitude destroy the joy of God's new creation. And the Creator still works to devise things that can add to your glory. He has made you in his image that you might in your person make the invisible Creator present on earth; he has made you his legate, so that the vast empire of the world might have the Lord's representative. Then in his mercy God assumed what he made in you; he wanted now to be truly manifest in man, just as he had wished to be revealed in man as in an image. Now he would be in reality what he had submitted to be in symbol.[2]

This passage leads us more deeply into the question of man's place in this universe. If God made the universe for us to observe, then one can assume that he wanted man to go ahead and observe it. But why? This is not discussed in *The Privileged Planet*. If God went to such lengths to make man so that he could see and respond to the cosmos, then it suggests that there might be reasons for his doing so. I put forward the following reasons speculatively:

First, the beauty and order of the cosmos point us to its Creator. We are hardwired to see the divine order that permeates all of creation. The cosmos bears the thumbprint of the One who made it, and when we see its beauty we are moved to love Him and to praise Him. The scientific description of this order only increases the wonder and sense of its beauty when that analysis is synthesized and brought together to give us a more complete picture of the whole universe as an single entity.

Second, the beauty and order of the cosmos are models that show us how to direct that praise. The rhythms and patterns of the cosmos and the numerical description of its beauty (for example, the movements of the sun, the moon) are those upon which the patterns of our worship are based. The seasons of the liturgical year, the patterns of worship in each week and each day, are based upon this. This is the organizing principle behind "organized" religion, which is so detested by modern man. If we all worship in harmony with the cosmos, then we worship also in harmony with each other. That is why when we go to church there are others there too. They are following the same principle. God gave us this cosmic sign to order our worship. When we worship in harmony with the cosmos, we are in harmony with all the saints and angels in the heavenly liturgy. This is what makes the liturgy the most "effective and powerful" prayer there is (as the *Catechism* says). Our action of love for God is synchronized perfectly with his gift of himself to us, and his grace. This is our route, therefore, to greatest joy in this life. In his encyclical *Deus Caritas Est*, Benedict XVI describes a dynamic of love between man and God which is realized fully in the Eucharist. In this, God gives himself in love. Benedict uses the traditional Greek phrases for the different kinds of love he refers to. So this self-giving love is termed *agape*. Our loving response, he tells us, is the properly ordered and graceful acceptance of His love, termed *eros*. *Eros* is the fulfillment of that aspect of love that desires the other. It is properly ordered when

---

2. Sermon 148, taken from the Office of Readings on his feast day, July 30.

we are conforming fully, both exteriorly and interiorly, to the form of the liturgy. The cosmological pattern is one crucial part of this.

Third, the beauty and order of the cosmos are the models upon which all other human activity, beyond the church, can be ordered. The culture in the broadest sense of the word can be infused with these values. To the degree that man can order time and space, he can do so in harmony with the cosmos, and therefore with the liturgy. All that he creates and does can be graceful and beautiful. When the culture reflects the cosmic order in this way, then just as with the cosmos itself, it can raise hearts and minds to God and to praise of Him in the liturgy. Everything stems from and points back to the liturgy. God is still the ultimate author of its beauty, but is now working through man and inspiring each person in his work. Historically, all Christian culture was founded on this principle, and it is an important part of what makes the liturgy the basis of culture. Scientific research that increases our understanding of the order of the cosmos can serve to help the ordering of our own activities and the beauty of the culture, *provided* that it is understood in this way and applied discerningly.

Furthermore, the worship of God in the liturgy is the basis of the deepest personal relationship that it is possible to have; it is an earthly but supernatural participation in the heavenly state for which we are made: a perfect and dynamic exchange of love with God the Father, through the Son, in the Spirit, by which we are transformed, by degrees, and partake of the divine nature. Therefore, the consideration of man as a human person is founded first on this relationship. Both modern astrophysics and ancient cosmology point to the same idea: that the "heavens proclaim the glory of the Lord" and that it is intrinsic to man's nature to see this and to respond with praise and worship of God. Any anthropology that ignores the liturgical nature of the human person is incomplete. Benedict XVI makes this point in *The Spirit of the Liturgy*: "The Son could only become incarnate as man because man was already planned in advance in relation to him, as the image of him who is in himself the image of God."[3]

While it is not a formal proof, the beauty of the cosmos is a song that opens our heart to the idea not only of the existence of a Creator but of the liturgy. It sings the song that calls us to church, and to pray the Mass and Liturgy of the Hours. It is appropriate to recall again the following: the Mass is a jewel in its setting, which is the Liturgy of the Hours; and the Liturgy is a jewel in its setting, which is the cosmos.

The heavens, therefore, point to Heaven, and we participate in the

3. Benedict XVI, *The Spirit of the Liturgy* (San Francisco: Ignatius Press, 2000), p. 123.

Heavenly dynamic through the liturgy, which is modeled on the heavens . . . and so the cycle is completed, forever reinforcing and adding to itself. All of this is for man. He is indeed a privileged person.

After I had written this piece, a number of people brought to my attention newspaper reports of recent discoveries of other habitable planets. Does this undermine any of the arguments discussed above, they wondered? I don't think so. The authors of the book upon which the film was based simply presented the statistical basis for such an event occurring. The chances, while negligible, were not zero. This means that for it to happen once is possible, but nevertheless astounding (I would say). For it to happen twice is possible too, but would be even *more* astounding, since such chances are even less. As such, this reinforces the arguments I make.

Furthermore, before we accept that such planets other than our own exist, we should try to find out how certain the information is. If it is merely hypothesis, then it is not yet scientifically proven. Many newspaper articles mistakenly present what are merely scientific hypotheses in tones that portray the information as proven theory.

As Jay Richards, one of the authors of *The Privileged Planet*, put it to me recently:

> We have discovered many hundreds of extra-solar planets, but none that come anywhere near fulfilling the basic conditions for habitability. Often when an extra-solar planet is discovered, though, NASA puts out a press release claiming we've discovered an earthlike planet. The most earthlike planet we know of is . . . Mars.
>
> That said, nothing in our argument requires that Earth be unique. Our argument simply entails that however many habitable planets there are, they will be extremely earthlike, and they will be better platforms for scientific discovery than the alternatives.

The fact that there might turn out to be more such privileged planets does, one might argue, lessen our privilege in a relative sense (there would be another part of the universe that is habitable; then that privilege would be shared between two of us rather than be exclusively our own). However, it does not lessen the privilege in an absolute sense. First, the *a priori* chances of any one planet in the universe possessing such a privilege remain unchanged. In fact, when we believe that it is God's love that is at the foundation of our creation, then the fact that He loves someone else too to the same degree doesn't lessen His love for us; rather, it increases the amount of love bestowed in this way. Accordingly, one might argue that the material evidence of God's love has increased, not decreased.

CPSIA information can be obtained
at www.ICGtesting.com
Printed in the USA
LVHW050241240920
666963LV00005B/1657